Edwin Donnelly

THE BIRTH OF TRAGEDY OR HELLENISM AND PESSIMISM

FRIEDRICH NIETZSCHE

TRANSLATED BY
W. A. HAUSSMANN

REVISED BY
WILLIAM MANN

mannwilliam.org

Designed and Edited by William Mann

ISBN 9798505282304

CONTENTS

DIONYSUS VERSUS APOLLO

H. L. Mencken

In one of the preceding chapters[1] Nietzsche's theory of Greek tragedy was given in outline and its dependence upon the data of Schopenhauer's philosophy was indicated. It is now in order to examine this theory a bit more closely and to trace out its origin and development with greater dwelling upon detail. In itself it is of interest only as a step forward in the art of literary criticism, but in its influence upon Nietzsche's ultimate inquiries it has colored, to a measurable extent, the whole stream of modern thought.

Schopenhauer laid down, as his cardinal principle, it will be recalled, the idea that, in all the complex whirlpool of phenomena we call human life, the mere will to survive is at the bottom of everything, and that intelligence, despite its seeming kingship in civilization, is nothing more, after all, than a secondary manifestation of this primary will. In certain purely artificial situations, it may seem to us that reason stands alone (as when, for example, we essay to solve an abstract problem in mathematics), but in everything growing out of our relations as human beings, one to the other, the old instinct of race-and-self-preservation is plainly discernible. All of our acts, when they are not based obviously and directly upon our yearning to eat and take our ease and beget our kind, are founded upon our desire to appear superior, in some way or other, to our fellow men about us, and this desire for superiority, reduced to its lowest terms, is merely a desire to face the struggle for existence—to eat and beget—under more favorable conditions than those the world accords the average man. "Happiness is the feeling that power increases—that resistance is being overcome."[2]

Nietzsche went to Basel firmly convinced that these fundamental ideas of Schopenhauer were profoundly true, though he soon essayed to make an amendment to them. This amendment consisted in changing Schopenhauer's "will to live" into "will to power." That which does not live, he argued, cannot exercise a will to live, and when a thing is already in existence, how can it strive after existence? Nietzsche voiced the argument many times, but its vacuity is apparent upon brief inspection. He started out, in fact, with an incredibly clumsy misinterpretation of Schopenhauer's phrase. The philosopher of pessimism, when he said "will to live" obviously meant, not will to begin living, but will to continue living. Now, this will to continue living, if we are to accept words at their usual meaning, is plainly identical, in every respect, with Nietzsche's will to power. Therefore, Nietzsche's amendment was nothing more than the coinage of a new phrase to express an old idea. The unity of the two philosophers and the identity of the two phrases are proved a thousand times by Nietzsche's own discourses. Like Schopenhauer he believed that all human ideas were the direct products of the unconscious and unceasing effort of all living creatures to remain alive. Like Schopenhauer he believed that abstract ideas, in man, arose out of concrete ideas, and that the latter arose out of experience, which, in turn, was nothing more or less than an ordered remembrance of the results following an endless series of endeavors to meet the conditions of existence and so survive. Like Schopenhauer, he believed that the criminal laws, the poetry, the cookery and the religion of a race were alike expressions of this unconscious groping for the line of least resistance.

---

[1] This Introduction is Chapter 6 of *The Philosophy of Friedrich Nietzsche.*

[2] *Der Antichrist,* § 2.

As a philologist, Nietzsche's interest, very naturally, was fixed upon the literature of Greece and Rome, and so it was but natural that his first tests of Schopenhauer's doctrines should be made in that field. Some time before this, he had asked himself (as many another man had asked before him) why it was that the ancient Greeks, who were an efficient and vigorous people, living in a green and sunny land, should so delight in gloomy tragedies. One would fancy that a Greek, when he set out to spend a pleasant afternoon, would seek entertainment that was frivolous and gay. But instead, he often preferred to see one of the plays of Thespis, Aeschylus, Phrynichus or Pratinus, in which the heroes fought hopeless battles with fate and died miserably, in wretchedness and despair. Nietzsche concluded that the Greeks had this liking for tragedy because it seemed to them to set forth, truthfully and understandably, the conditions of life as they found it: that it appeared to them as a reasonable and accurate picture of human existence. The gods ordered the drama on the real stage of the world; the dramatist ordered the drama on the mimic stage of the theatre—and the latter attained credibility and verisimilitude in proportion as it approached an exact imitation or reproduction of the former. Nietzsche saw that this quality of realism was the essence of all stage plays. "Only insofar as the dramatist," he said, "coalesces with the primordial dramatist of the world, does he reach the true function of his craft."[3] "Man posits himself as the standard . . . A race cannot do otherwise than thus acquiesce in itself."[4] In other words, man is interested in nothing whatever that has no bearing upon his own fate: he himself is his own hero. Thus the ancient Greeks were fond of tragedy because it reflected their life in miniature. In the mighty warriors who stalked the boards and defied the gods each Greek recognized himself. In the conflicts on the stage he saw replicas of that titanic conflict which seemed to him to be the eternal essence of human existence.

But why did the Greeks regard life as a conflict? In seeking an answer to this Nietzsche studied the growth of their civilization and of their race ideas. These race ideas, as among all other peoples, were visualized and crystallized in the qualities, virtues and opinions attributed to the racial gods. Therefore, Nietzsche undertook an inquiry into the nature of the gods set up by the Greeks, and particularly into the nature of the two gods who controlled the general scheme of Greek life, and, in consequence, of Greek art,—for art, as we have seen, is nothing more or less than a race's view or opinion of itself, i.e. an expression of the things it sees and the conclusions it draws when it observes and considers itself. These gods were Apollo and Dionysus.

Apollo, according to the Greeks, was the inventor of music, poetry and oratory, and as such, became the god of all art. Under his beneficent sway the Greeks became a race of artists and acquired all the refinement and culture that this implies. But the art that he taught them was essentially contemplative and subjective. It depicted, not so much things as they were, as things as they had been. Thus it became a mere record, and as such, exhibited repose as its chief quality. Whether it were expressed as sculpture, architecture, painting or epic poetry, this element of repose, or of action translated into repose, was uppermost. A painting of a man running, no matter how vividly it suggests the vitality and activity of the runner, is itself a thing inert and lifeless. Architecture, no matter how much its curves suggest motion and its hard lines the strength which may be translated into energy, is itself a thing immovable. Poetry, so long as it takes the form of the epic and is thus merely a chronicle of past actions, is as lifeless, at bottom, as a tax list.

The Greeks, during Apollo's reign as god of art, thus turned art into a mere inert fossil or record—a record either of human life itself or of the emotions which the vicissitudes of life arouse in the spectator. This notion of art was reflected in their whole civilization. They became singers of songs and weavers of metaphysical webs rather than doers of deeds, and the man who could carve a flower was more honored among them than the man who could grow one. In brief, they began to degenerate and go stale. Great men and great ideas grew few. They were on the downward road.

What they needed, of course, was the shock of contact with some barbarous, primitive people—an infusion of good red blood from some race that was still fighting for its daily bread and had had no time to grow contemplative and retrospective and fat. This infusion of red blood came in good time, but instead of coming from without (as it did years afterward in Rome, when the Goths swooped down

[3] *Die Geburt der Tragödie*, § 5.

[4] *Götzendämmerung* ix, § 19.

from the North), it came from within. That is to say, there was no actual invasion of barbarian hordes, but merely an auto-reversion to simpler and more primitive ideas, which fanned the dormant energy of the Greeks into flame and so allowed them to accomplish their own salvation. This impulse came in the form of a sudden craze for a new god—Bacchus Dionysus.

Bacchus was a rude, boisterous fellow and the very antithesis of the quiet, contemplative Apollo. We remember him today merely as the god of wine, but in his time he stood, not only for drinking and carousing, but also for a whole system of art and a whole notion of civilization. Apollo represented the life meditative; Bacchus Dionysus represented the life strenuous. The one favored those forms of art by which human existence is halted and embalmed in some lifeless medium—sculpture, architecture, painting or epic poetry. The other was the god of life in process of actual being, and so stood for those forms of art which are not mere records or reflections of past existence, but brief snatches of present existence itself—dancing, singing, music and the drama.

It will be seen that this barbarous invasion of the new god and his minions made a profound change in the whole of Greek culture. Instead of devoting their time to writing epics, praising the laws, splitting philosophical hairs and hewing dead marble, the Greeks began to question all things made and ordained and to indulge in riotous and gorgeous orgies, in which thousands of maidens danced and hundreds of poets chanted songs of love and war, and musicians vied with cooks and vintners to make a grand delirium of joy. The result was that the entire outlook of the Greeks, upon history, upon morality and upon human life, was changed. Once a people of lofty introspection and elegant repose, they became a race of violent activity and strong emotions. They began to devote themselves, not to writing down the praises of existence as they had found it, but to the task of improving life and of widening the scope of present and future human activity and the bounds of possible human happiness.[5]

But in time there came a reaction and Apollo once more triumphed. He reigned for awhile, unsteadily and uncertainly, and then, again, the pendulum swung to the other side. Thus the Greeks swayed from one god to the other. During Apollo's periods of ascendancy they were contemplative and imaginative, and man, to them, seemed to reach his loftiest heights when he was most the historian. But when Dionysus was their best-beloved, they bubbled over with the joy of life, and man seemed, not an historian, but a maker of history—not an artist, but a work of art. In the end, they verged toward a safe middle ground and began to weigh, with cool and calm, the ideas represented by the two gods. When they had done so, they came to the conclusion that it was not well to give themselves unreservedly to either. To attain the highest happiness, they decided, humanity required a dash of both. There was need in the world for dionysians, to give vitality an outlet and life a purpose, and there was need, too, for apollonians, to build life's monuments and read its lessons. They found that true civilization meant constant conflict between the two—between the dreamer and the man of action, between the artist who builds temples and the soldier who burns them down, between the priest and policeman who insist upon the permanence of laws and customs as they are and the criminal and reformer and conqueror who insist that they be changed.

When they had learned this lesson, the Greeks began to soar to heights of culture and civilization that, in the past, had been utterly beyond them, and so long as they maintained the balance between Apollo and Dionysus they continued to advance. But now and again, one god or the other grew stronger, and then there was a halt. When Apollo had the upper hand, Greece became too contemplative and too placid. When Dionysus was the victor, Greece became wild and thoughtless and careless of the desires of others, and so turned a bit toward barbarism. This seesawing continued for a long while, but Apollo was the final victor—if victor he may be called. In the eternal struggle for existence Greece became a mere looker-on. Her highest honors went to Socrates, a man who tried to reduce all life to syllogisms. Her favorite sons were

[5] "This enrichment of consciousness among the Greeks ... showed itself first in the development of lyric poetry, in which the gradual transition from the expression of universal religious and political feeling to that which is personal and individual formed a typical process." Dr. Wilhelm Windelband, *A History of Ancient Philosophy*, tr. by H. E. Cushman.

rhetoricians, dialecticians and philosophical cobweb-spinners. She placed ideas above deeds. And in the end, as all students of history know, the state that once ruled the world descended to senility and decay, and dionysians from without overran it, and it perished in anarchy and carnage. But with this we have nothing to do.

Nietzsche noticed that tragedy was most popular in Greece during the best days of the country's culture, when Apollo and Dionysus were properly balanced, one against the other. This ideal balancing between the two gods was the result, he concluded, not of conscious, but of unconscious impulses. That is to say, the Greeks did not call parliaments and discuss the matter, as they might have discussed a question of taxes, but acted entirely in obedience to their racial instinct. This instinct—this will to live or desire for power—led them to feel, without putting it into words, or even, for awhile, into definite thoughts, that they were happiest and safest and most vigorous, and so best able to preserve their national existence, when they kept to the golden mean. They didn't reason it out; they merely felt it.

But as Schopenhauer shows us, instinct, long exercised, means experience, and the memory of experience, in the end, crystallizes into what we call intelligence or reason. Thus the unconscious Greek feeling that the golden mean best served the race, finally took the form of an idea: *i.e.* that human life was an endless conflict between two forces, or impulses. These, as the Greeks saw them, were the dionysian impulse to destroy, to burn the candle, to "use up" life; and the apollonian impulse to preserve. Seeing life in this light, it was but natural that the Greeks should try to exhibit it in the same light on their stage. And so their tragedies were invariably founded upon some deadly and unending conflict—usually between a human hero and the gods. In a word, they made their stage plays set forth life as they saw it and found it, for, like all other human beings, at all times and everywhere, they were more interested in life as they found it than in anything else on the earth below or in the vasty void above.

When Nietzsche had worked out this theory of Greek tragedy and of Greek life, he set out, at once, to apply it to modern civilization, to see if it could explain certain ideas of the present as satisfactorily as it had explained one great idea of the past. He found that it could: that men were still torn between the apollonian impulse to conform and moralize and the dionysian impulse to exploit and explore. He found that all mankind might be divided into two classes: the apollonians who stood for permanence and the dionysians who stood for change. It was the aim of the former to live in strict obedience to certain invariable rules, which found expression as religion, law and morality. It was the aim of the latter to live under the most favorable conditions possible; to adapt themselves to changing circumstances, and to avoid the snares of artificial, permanent rules.

Nietzsche believed that an ideal human society would be one in which these two classes of men were evenly balanced—in which a vast, inert, religious, moral slave class stood beneath a small, alert, iconoclastic, immoral, progressive master class. He held that this master class—this aristocracy of efficiency—should regard the slave class as all men now regard the tribe of domestic beasts: as an order of servitors to be exploited and turned to account. The aristocracy of Europe, though it sought to do this with respect to the workers of Europe, seemed to him to fail miserably, because it was itself lacking in true efficiency. Instead of practising a magnificent opportunism and so adapting itself to changing conditions, it stood for formalism and permanence. Its fetish was property in land and the worship of this fetish had got it into such a rut that it was becoming less and less fitted to survive, and was, indeed, fast sinking into helpless parasitism. Its whole color and complexion were essentially apollonic.

Therefore Nietzsche preached the gospel of Dionysus, that a new aristocracy of efficiency might take the place of this old aristocracy of memories and inherited glories. He believed that it was only in this way that mankind could hope to forge ahead. He believed that there was need in the world for a class freed from the handicap of law and morality, a class acutely adaptable and immoral; a class bent on achieving, not the equality of all men, but the production, at the top, of the superman.

THE BIRTH OF TRAGEDY

OR

HELLENISM AND PESSIMISM

Die Geburt der Tragödie

oder

Griechentum und Pessimismus

Versuch einer Selbstkritik

1

Was auch diesem fragwürdigen Buche zugrunde liegen mag: es muß eine Frage ersten Ranges und Reizes gewesen sein, noch dazu eine tief persönliche Frage – Zeugnis dafür ist die Zeit, in der es entstand, *trotz* der es entstand, die aufregende Zeit des deutsch-französischen Krieges von 1870/71. Während die Donner der Schlacht von Wörth über Europa weggingen, saß der Grübler und Rätselfreund, dem die Vaterschaft dieses Buches zuteil ward, irgendwo in einem Winkel der Alpen, sehr vergrübelt und verrätselt, folglich sehr bekümmert und unbekümmert zugleich, und schrieb seine Gedanken über die *Griechen* nieder, – den Kern des wunderlichen und schlecht zugänglichen Buches, dem diese späte Vorrede (oder Nachrede) gewidmet sein soll. Einige Wochen darauf: und er befand sich selbst unter den Mauern von Metz, immer noch nicht losgekommen von den Fragezeichen, die er zur vorgeblichen »Heiterkeit« der Griechen und der griechischen Kunst gesetzt hatte; bis er endlich, in jenem Monat tiefster Spannung, als man in Versailles über den Frieden beriet, auch mit sich zum Frieden kam und, langsam von einer aus dem Felde heimgebrachten Krankheit genesend, die »Geburt der Tragödie aus dem Geiste der *Musik*« letztgültig bei sich feststellte. – Aus der Musik? Musik und Tragödie? Griechen und Tragödien-Musik? Griechen und das Kunstwerk des Pessimismus? Die wohlgeratenste, schönste, bestbeneidete, zum Leben verführendste Art der bisherigen Menschen, die Griechen – wie? gerade sie hatten die Tragödie *nötig*? Mehr noch – die Kunst? Wozu – griechische Kunst?...

Man errät, an welche Stelle hiermit das große Fragezeichen vom Werte des Daseins gesetzt war. Ist Pessimismus *notwendig* das Zeichen des Niedergangs, Verfalls, des Mißratenseins, der ermüdeten und geschwächten Instinkte? – wie er es bei den Indern war, wie er es, allem Anschein nach, bei uns, den »modernen« Menschen und Europäern ist? Gibt es einen Pessimismus der *Stärke*? Eine intellektuelle Vorneigung für das Harte, Schauerliche, Böse, Problematische des Daseins aus Wohlsein, aus überströmender Gesundheit, aus *Fülle* des Daseins? Gibt es vielleicht ein Leiden an der Überfülle selbst?

An Attempt at Self-Criticism

Whatever may lie at the bottom of this doubtful book must be a question of the first rank and attractiveness, moreover a deeply personal question—in proof thereof observe the time in which it originated, *in spite* of which it originated, the exciting period of the Franco-German war of 1870-71. While the thunder of the battle of Wörth rolled over Europe, the ruminator and riddle-lover, who had to be the parent of this book, sat somewhere in a nook of the Alps, lost in riddles and ruminations, consequently very much concerned and unconcerned at the same time, and wrote down his meditations on the *Greeks*—the kernel of the curious and almost inaccessible book, to which this belated prologue (or epilogue) is to be devoted. A few weeks later: and he found himself under the walls of Metz, still wrestling with the notes of interrogation he had set down concerning the alleged "cheerfulness" of the Greeks and of Greek art; till at last, in that month of deep suspense, when peace was debated at Versailles, he too attained to peace with himself, and, slowly recovering from a disease brought home from the field, made up his mind definitely regarding the "Birth of Tragedy from the Spirit of *Music.*"—From music? Music and Tragedy? Greeks and tragic music? Greeks and the Art-work of pessimism? A race of men, well-fashioned, beautiful, envied, life-inspiring, like no other race hitherto, the Greeks—indeed? The Greeks were *in need* of tragedy? Yea—of art? Wherefore—Greek art?...

We can thus guess where the great note of interrogation concerning the value of existence had been set. Is pessimism *necessarily* the sign of decline, of decay, of failure, of exhausted and weakened instincts?—as was the case with the Indians, as is, to all appearance, the case with us "modern" men and Europeans? Is there a pessimism of *strength*? An intellectual predilection for what is hard, awful, evil, problematical in existence, owing to well-being, to exuberant health, to *fullness* of existence? Is there perhaps suffering in overfullness itself? A seductive

Eine versucherische Tapferkeit des schärfsten Blicks, die nach dem Furchtbaren *verlangt*, als nach dem Feinde, dem würdigen Feinde, an dem sie ihre Kraft erproben kann? an dem sie lernen will, was »das Fürchten« ist? Was bedeutet, gerade bei den Griechen der besten, stärksten, tapfersten Zeit, der *tragische* Mythus? Und das ungeheure Phänomen des Dionysischen? Was, aus ihm geboren, die Tragödie? – Und wiederum: das, woran die Tragödie starb, der Sokratismus der Moral, die Dialektik, Genügsamkeit und Heiterkeit des theoretischen Menschen – wie? könnte nicht gerade dieser Sokratismus ein Zeichen des Niedergangs, der Ermüdung, Erkrankung, der anarchisch sich lösenden Instinkte sein? Und die »griechische Heiterkeit« des späteren Griechentums nur eine Abendröte? Der epikurische Wille *gegen* den Pessimismus nur eine Vorsicht des Leidenden? Und die Wissenschaft selbst, unsere Wissenschaft – ja, was bedeutet überhaupt, als Symptom des Lebens angesehn, alle Wissenschaft? Wozu, schlimmer noch, *woher* – alle Wissenschaft? Wie? Ist Wissenschaftlichkeit vielleicht nur eine Furcht und Ausflucht vor dem Pessimismus? Eine feine Notwehr gegen – die *Wahrheit*? Und, moralisch geredet, etwas wie Feig- und Falschheit? Unmoralisch geredet, eine Schlauheit? O Socrates, Socrates, war das vielleicht *dein* Geheimnis? O geheimnisvoller Ironiker, war dies vielleicht deine – Ironie? – –

fortitude with the keenest of glances, which *yearns* for the terrible, as for the enemy, the worthy enemy, with whom it may try its strength? from whom it is willing to learn what "fear" is? What means *tragic* myth to the Greeks of the best, strongest, bravest era? And the prodigious phenomenon of the Dionysian? And that which was born thereof, tragedy?—And again: that of which tragedy died, the Socratism of morality, the dialectics, contentedness and cheerfulness of the theoretical man—indeed? might not this very Socratism be a sign of decline, of weariness, of disease, of anarchically disintegrating instincts? And the "Hellenic cheerfulness" of the later Hellenism merely a glowing sunset? The Epicurean will *counter* to pessimism merely a precaution of the sufferer? And science itself, our science—ay, viewed as a symptom of life, what really signifies all science? Whither, worse still, *whence*—all science? Well? Is scientism perhaps only fear and evasion of pessimism? A subtle defence against—*truth!* Morally speaking, something like falsehood and cowardice? And, unmorally speaking, an artifice? O Socrates, Socrates, was this perhaps *your* secret? Oh mysterious ironist, was this perhaps your—irony?...

2

Was ich damals zu fassen bekam, etwas Furchtbares und Gefährliches, ein Problem mit Hörnern, nicht notwendig gerade ein Stier, jedenfalls ein *neues* Problem: heute würde ich sagen, daß es das *Problem der Wissenschaft* selbst war – Wissenschaft zum ersten Male als problematisch, als fragwürdig gefaßt. Aber das Buch, in dem mein jugendlicher Mut und Argwohn sich damals ausließ – was für ein *unmögliches* Buch mußte aus einer so jugendwidrigen Aufgabe erwachsen! Aufgebaut aus lauter vorzeitigen übergrünen Selbsterlebnissen, welche alle hart an der Schwelle des Mitteilbaren lagen, hingestellt auf den Boden der *Kunst* – denn das Problem der Wissenschaft kann nicht auf dem Boden der Wissenschaft erkannt werden –, ein Buch vielleicht für Künstler mit dem Nebenhange analytischer und retrospektiver Fähigkeiten (das heißt für eine Ausnahme-Art von Künstlern, nach denen man suchen muß und nicht einmal suchen möchte...), voller psychologischer Neuerungen und Artisten-Heimlichkeiten, mit einer Artisten-Metaphysik im

What I then laid hands on, something terrible and dangerous, a problem with horns, not necessarily a bull itself, but at all events a *new* problem: I should say today it was the *problem of science* itself—science conceived for the first time as problematic, as questionable. But the book, in which my youthful ardour and suspicion then discharged themselves—what an *impossible* book must needs grow out of a task so disagreeable to youth. Constructed of nought but precocious, unripened self-experiences, all of which lay close to the threshold of the communicable, based on the groundwork of *art*—for the problem of science cannot be discerned on the groundwork of science—a book perhaps for artists, with collateral analytical and retrospective aptitudes (that is, an exceptional kind of artists, for whom one must seek and does not even care to seek ...), full of psychological innovations and artists' secrets, with an artists' metaphysics in the background, a work of youth, full of youth's mettle and youth's

Hintergrunde, ein Jugendwerk voller Jugendmut und Jugend-Schwermut, unabhängig, trotzig-selbständig auch noch, wo es sich einer Autorität und eignen Verehrung zu beugen scheint, kurz ein Erstlingswerk auch in jedem schlimmen Sinne des Wortes, trotz seines greisenhaften Problems, mit jedem Fehler der Jugend behaftet, vor allem mit ihrem »Viel zu lang«, ihrem »Sturm und Drang«: andererseits, in Hinsicht auf den Erfolg, den es hatte (insonderheit bei dem großen Künstler, an den es sich wie zu einem Zwiegespräch wendete, bei Richard Wagner) ein *bewiesenes* Buch, ich meine ein solches, das jedenfalls »den Besten seiner Zeit« genuggetan hat. Daraufhin sollte es schon mit einiger Rücksicht und Schweigsamkeit behandelt werden; trotzdem will ich nicht gänzlich unterdrücken, wie unangenehm es mir jetzt erscheint, wie fremd es jetzt nach sechzehn Jahren vor mir steht, – vor einem älteren, hundertmal verwöhnteren, aber keineswegs kälter gewordenen Auge, das auch jener Aufgabe selbst nicht fremder wurde, an welche sich jenes verwegene Buch zum ersten Male herangewagt hat – *die Wissenschaft unter der Optik des Künstlers zu sehen, die Kunst aber unter der des Lebens...*

melancholy, independent, defiantly self-sufficient even when it seems to bow to some authority and self-veneration; in short, a firstling-work, even in every bad sense of the term; in spite of its senile problem, affected with every fault of youth, above all with youth's prolixity and youth's "storm and stress": on the other hand, in view of the success it had (especially with the great artist to whom it addressed itself, as it were, in a duologue, Richard Wagner) a *demonstrated* book, I mean a book which, at any rate, sufficed "for the best of its time." On this account, if for no other reason, it should be treated with some consideration and reserve; yet I shall not altogether conceal how disagreeable it now appears to me, how after sixteen years it stands a total stranger before me—before an eye which is more mature, and a hundred times more fastidious, but which has by no means grown colder nor lost any of its interest in that self-same task essayed for the first time by this daring book—*to* view science through the optics of the artist, and art moreover through the optics of life....

3

Nochmals gesagt, heute ist es mir ein unmögliches Buch, – ich heiße es schlecht geschrieben, schwerfällig, peinlich, bilderwütig und bilderwirrig, gefühlsam, hier und da verzuckert bis zum Femininischen, ungleich im Tempo, ohne Willen zur logischen Sauberkeit, sehr überzeugt und deshalb des Beweisens sich überhebend, mißtrauisch selbst gegen die *Schicklichkeit* des Beweisens, als Buch für Eingeweihte, als »Musik« für solche, die auf Musik getauft, die auf gemeinsame und seltne Kunst-Erfahrungen hin von Anfang der Dinge an verbunden sind, als Erkennungszeichen für Blutsverwandte *in artibus*, – ein hochmütiges und schwärmerisches Buch, das sich gegen das *profanum vulgus* der »Gebildeten« von vornherein noch mehr als gegen das »Volk« abschließt, welches aber, wie seine Wirkung bewies und beweist, sich gut genug auch darauf verstehen muß, sich seine Mitschwärmer zu suchen und sie auf neue Schleichwege und Tanzplätze zu locken. Hier redete jedenfalls – das gestand man sich mit Neugierde ebenso als mit Abneigung ein – eine *fremde* Stimme, der Jünger eines noch »unbekannten Gottes«, der sich einstweilen unter die Kapuze des Gelehrten, unter die Schwere und dialektische Unlustigkeit des Deutschen, selbst unter die

I say again, today it is an impossible book to me—I call it badly written, heavy, painful, image-angling and image-entangling, maudlin, sugared at times even to femininism, uneven in tempo, void of the will to logical cleanliness, very convinced and therefore rising above the necessity of demonstration, distrustful even of the *propriety* of demonstration, as being a book for initiates, as "music" for those who are baptised with the name of Music, who are united from the beginning of things by common ties of rare experiences in art, as a countersign for blood-relations *in artibus.*—a haughty and fantastic book, which from the very first withdraws even more from the *profanum vulgus* of the "cultured" than from the "people," but which also, as its effect has shown and still shows, knows very well how to seek fellow-enthusiasts and lure them to new by-ways and dancing-grounds. Here, at any rate—thus much was acknowledged with curiosity as well as with aversion—a *strange* voice spoke, the disciple of a still "unknown God," who for the time being had hidden himself under the hood of the scholar, under the German's gravity and disinclination for dialectics, even under the bad manners of the

schlechten Manieren des Wagnerianers versteckt hat; hier war ein Geist mit fremden, noch namenlosen Bedürfnissen, ein Gedächtnis strotzend von Fragen, Erfahrungen, Verborgenheiten, welchen der Name Dionysos wie ein Fragezeichen mehr beigeschrieben war; hier sprach – so sagte man sich mit Argwohn – etwas wie eine mystische und beinahe mänadische Seele, die mit Mühsal und willkürlich, fast unschlüssig darüber, ob sie sich mitteilen oder verbergen wolle, gleichsam in einer fremden Zunge stammelt. Sie hätte *singen* sollen, diese »neue Seele« – und nicht reden! Wie schade, daß ich, was ich damals zu sagen hatte, es nicht als Dichter zu sagen wagte: ich hätte es vielleicht gekonnt! Oder mindestens als Philologe: – bleibt doch auch heute noch für den Philologen auf diesem Gebiete beinahe alles zu entdecken und auszugraben! Vor allem das Problem, *daß* hier ein Problem vorliegt, – und daß die Griechen, so lange wir keine Antwort auf die Frage »was ist dionysisch?« haben, nach wie vor gänzlich unerkannt und unvorstellbar sind...

Wagnerian; here was a spirit with strange and still nameless needs, a memory bristling with questions, experiences and obscurities, beside which stood the name Dionysos like one more note of interrogation; here spoke—people said to themselves with misgivings—something like a mystic and almost mænadic soul, which, undecided whether it should disclose or conceal itself, stammers with an effort and capriciously as in a strange tongue. It should have *sung,* this "new soul"—and not spoken! What a pity, that I did not dare to say what I then had to say, as a poet: I could have done so perhaps! Or at least as a philologist:—for even at the present day well-nigh everything in this domain remains to be discovered and disinterred by the philologist! Above all the problem, *that* here there *is* a problem before us—and that, so long as we have no answer to the question "what is Dionysian?" the Greeks are now as ever wholly unknown and inconceivable....

4

Ja, was ist dionysisch? – In diesem Buche steht eine Antwort darauf, – ein »Wissender« redet da, der Eingeweihte und Jünger seines Gottes. Vielleicht würde ich jetzt vorsichtiger und weniger beredt von einer so schweren psychologischen Frage reden, wie sie der Ursprung der Tragödie bei den Griechen ist. Eine Grundfrage ist das Verhältnis des Griechen zum Schmerz, sein Grad von Sensibilität, – blieb dies Verhältnis sich gleich? oder drehte es sich um? – jene Frage, ob wirklich sein immer stärkeres *Verlangen nach Schönheit*, nach Festen, Lustbarkeiten, neuen Kulten aus Mangel, aus Entbehrung, aus Melancholie, aus Schmerz erwachsen ist? Gesetzt nämlich, gerade dies wäre wahr – und Perikles (oder Thukydides) gibt es uns in der großen Leichenrede zu verstehen –: woher müßte dann das entgegengesetzte Verlangen, das der Zeit nach früher hervortrat, stammen, das *Verlangen nach dem Häßlichen*, der gute strenge Wille des älteren Hellenen zum Pessimismus, zum tragischen Mythus, zum Bilde alles Furchtbaren, Bösen, Rätselhaften, Vernichtenden, Verhängnisvollen auf dem Grunde des Daseins, – woher müßte dann die Tragödie stammen? Vielleicht aus der *Lust*, aus der Kraft, aus überströmender Gesundheit, aus übergroßer Fülle? Und welche Bedeutung hat dann, physiologisch gefragt, jener Wahnsinn, aus dem die tragische wie die komische Kunst erwuchs, der dionysische Wahnsinn? Wie? Ist

Yes, what is Dionysian?—In this book may be found an answer—a "knowing one" speaks here, the votary and disciple of his god. Perhaps I should now speak more guardedly and less eloquently of a psychological question so difficult as the origin of tragedy among the Greeks. A fundamental question is the relation of the Greek to pain, his degree of sensibility—did this relation remain constant? or did it veer about?—the question, whether his ever-increasing *longing for beauty,* for festivals, gaieties, new cults, did really grow out of want, privation, melancholy, pain? For suppose even this to be true—and Pericles (or Thucydides) intimates as much in the great Funeral Speech:—whence then the opposite longing, which appeared first in the order of time, the *longing for the ugly,* the good, resolute desire of the Old Hellene for pessimism, for tragic myth, for the picture of all that is terrible, evil, enigmatical, destructive, fatal at the basis of existence—whence then must tragedy have sprung? Perhaps from *joy,* from strength, from exuberant health, from over-fullness. And what then, physiologically speaking, is the meaning of that madness, out of which comic as well as tragic art has grown, the Dionysian madness? What? perhaps madness is not necessarily the symptom of degeneration, of decline, of belated culture?

Wahnsinn vielleicht nicht notwendig das Symptom der Entartung, des Niedergangs, der überspäten Kultur? Gibt es vielleicht – eine Frage für Irrenärzte – Neurosen der *Gesundheit*? der Volks-Jugend und -Jugendlichkeit? Worauf weist jene Synthesis von Gott und Bock im Satyr? Aus welchem Selbsterlebnis, auf welchen Drang hin mußte sich der Grieche den dionysischen Schwärmer und Urmenschen als Satyr denken? Und was den Ursprung des tragischen Chors betrifft: gab es in jenen Jahrhunderten, wo der griechische Leib blühte, die griechische Seele von Leben überschäumte, vielleicht endemische Entzückungen? Visionen und Halluzinationen, welche sich ganzen Gemeinden, ganzen Kultversammlungen mitteilten? Wie? wenn die Griechen, gerade im Reichtum ihrer Jugend, den Willen *zum* Tragischen hatten und Pessimisten waren? wenn es gerade der Wahnsinn war, um ein Wort Platos zu gebrauchen, der die *größten* Segnungen über Hellas gebracht hat? Und wenn, andererseits und umgekehrt, die Griechen gerade in den Zeiten ihrer Auflösung und Schwäche immer optimistischer, oberflächlicher, schauspielerischer, auch nach Logik und Logisierung der Welt brünstiger, also zugleich »heiterer« und »wissenschaftlicher« wurden? Wie? könnte vielleicht, allen »modernen Ideen« und Vorurteilen des demokratischen Geschmacks zum Trotz, der Sieg des *Optimismus*, die vorherrschend gewordene *Vernünftigkeit*, der praktische und theoretische *Utilitarismus*, gleich der Demokratie selbst, mit der er gleichzeitig ist, – ein Symptom der absinkenden Kraft, des nahenden Alters, der physiologischen Ermüdung sein? Und gerade *nicht* – der Pessimismus? War Epikur ein Optimist – gerade als *Leidender*? – – Man sieht, es ist ein ganzes Bündel schwerer Fragen, mit dem sich dieses Buch belastet hat, – fügen wir seine schwerste Frage noch hinzu! Was bedeutet, unter der Optik des *Lebens* gesehn, – die Moral?...

Perhaps there are—a question for alienists—neuroses of *health*? of folk-youth and youthfulness? What does that synthesis of god and goat in the Satyr point to? What self-experience what "stress," made the Greek think of the Dionysian reveller and primitive man as a satyr? And as regards the origin of the tragic chorus: perhaps there were endemic ecstasies in the eras when the Greek body bloomed and the Greek soul brimmed over with life? Visions and hallucinations, which took hold of entire communities, entire cult-assemblies? What if the Greeks in the very wealth of their youth had the will *to be* tragic and were pessimists? What if it was madness itself, to use a word of Plato's, which brought the *greatest* blessings upon Hellas? And what if, on the other hand and conversely, at the very time of their dissolution and weakness, the Greeks became always more optimistic, more superficial, more histrionic, also more ardent for logic and the logicising of the world—consequently at the same time more "cheerful" and more "scientific"? Ay, despite all "modern ideas" and prejudices of the democratic taste, may not the triumph of *optimism*, the *common sense* that has gained the upper hand, the practical and theoretical *utilitarianism*, like democracy itself, with which it is synchronous—be symptomatic of declining vigour, of approaching age, of physiological weariness? And *not* at all—pessimism? Was Epicurus an optimist—because a *sufferer*?... We see it is a whole bundle of weighty questions which this book has taken upon itself—let us not fail to add its weightiest question! Viewed through the optics of *life*, what is the meaning of—morality?...

5

Bereits im Vorwort an Richard Wagner wird die Kunst – und *nicht* die Moral – als die eigentlich *metaphysische* Tätigkeit des Menschen hingestellt; im Buche selbst kehrt der anzügliche Satz mehrfach wieder, daß nur als ästhetisches Phänomen das Dasein der Welt *gerechtfertigt* ist. In der Tat, das ganze Buch kennt nur einen Künstler-Sinn und -Hintersinn hinter allem Geschehen, – einen »Gott«, wenn man will, aber gewiß nur einen gänzlich unbedenklichen und unmoralischen Künstler-Gott, der im Bauen wie im Zerstören, im Guten wie im Schlimmen, seiner

Already in the foreword to Richard Wagner, art—and *not* morality—is set down as the properly *metaphysical* activity of man; in the book itself the piquant proposition recurs time and again, that the existence of the world is *justified* only as an æsthetic phenomenon. Indeed, the entire book recognises only an artist-thought and artist-after-thought behind all occurrences—a "God," if you will, but certainly only an altogether thoughtless and unmoral artist-God, who, in construction as in destruction, in good as in evil,

gleichen Lust und Selbstherrlichkeit innewerden will, der sich, Welten schaffend, von der *Not* der Fülle und *Überfülle*, vom *Leiden* der in ihm gedrängten Gegensätze löst. Die Welt, in jedem Augenblick die *erreichte* Erlösung Gottes, als die ewig wechselnde, ewig neue Vision des Leidendsten, Gegensätzlichsten, Widerspruchreichsten, der nur im *Scheine* sich zu erlösen weiß: diese ganze Artisten-Methaphysik mag man willkürlich, müßig, phantastisch nennen –, das Wesentliche daran ist, daß sie bereits einen Geist verrät, der sich einmal auf jede Gefahr hin gegen die *moralische* Ausdeutung und Bedeutsamkeit des Daseins zur Wehre setzen wird. Hier kündigt sich, vielleicht zum ersten Male, ein Pessimismus »jenseits von Gut und Böse« an, hier kommt jene »Perversität der Gesinnung« zu Wort und Formel, gegen welche Schopenhauer nicht müde geworden ist, im voraus seine zornigsten Flüche und Donnerkeile zu schleudern, – eine Philosophie, welche es wagt, die Moral selbst in die Welt der Erscheinung zu setzen, herabzusetzen und nicht nur unter die »Erscheinungen« (im Sinne des idealistischen *terminus technicus*), sondern unter die »Täuschungen«, als Schein, Wahn, Irrtum, Ausdeutung, Zurechtmachung, Kunst. Vielleicht läßt sich die Tiefe dieses *widermoralischen* Hanges am besten aus dem behutsamen und feindseligen Schweigen ermessen, mit dem in dem ganzen Buche das Christentum behandelt ist, – das Christentum als die ausschweifendste Durchfigurierung des moralischen Themas, welche die Menschheit bisher anzuhören bekommen hat. In Wahrheit, es gibt zu der rein ästhetischen Weltauslegung und Welt-Rechtfertigung, wie sie in diesem Buche gelehrt wird, keinen größeren Gegensatz als die christliche Lehre, welche *nur* moralisch ist und sein will und mit ihren absoluten Maßen, zum Beispiel schon mit ihrer Wahrhaftigkeit Gottes, die Kunst, *jede* Kunst ins Reich der *Lüge* verweist, – das heißt verneint, verdammt, verurteilt. Hinter einer derartigen Denk- und Wertungsweise, welche kunstfeindlich sein muß, solange sie irgendwie echt ist, empfand ich von jeher auch das *Lebensfeindliche*, den ingrimmigen rachsüchtigen Widerwillen gegen das Leben selbst: denn alles Leben ruht auf Schein, Kunst, Täuschung, Optik, Notwendigkeit des Perspektivischen und des Irrtums. Christentum war von Anfang an, wesentlich und gründlich, Ekel und Überdruß des Lebens am Leben, welcher sich unter dem Glauben an ein »anderes« oder »besseres« Leben nur verkleidete, nur versteckte, nur aufputzte. Der Haß auf die »Welt«, der Fluch auf die Affekte, die Furcht vor der Schönheit und Sinnlichkeit, ein Jenseits, erfunden, um das

desires to become conscious of his own equable joy and sovereign glory; who, in creating worlds, frees himself from the *anguish* of fullness and *overfullness,* from the *suffering* of the contradictions concentrated within him. The world, that is, the redemption of God *attained* at every moment, as the perpetually changing, perpetually new vision of the most suffering, most antithetical, most contradictory being, who contrives to redeem himself only in *appearance:* this entire artist-metaphysics, call it arbitrary, idle, fantastic, if you will—the point is, that it already betrays a spirit, which is determined some day, at all hazards, to make a stand against the *moral* interpretation and significance of life. Here, perhaps for the first time, a pessimism "Beyond Good and Evil" announces itself, here that "perverseness of disposition" obtains expression and formulation, against which Schopenhauer never grew tired of hurling beforehand his angriest imprecations and thunderbolts—a philosophy which dares to put, derogatorily put, morality itself in the world of phenomena, and not only among "phenomena" (in the sense of the idealistic *terminus technicus*), but among the "illusions," as appearance, semblance, error, interpretation, accommodation, art. Perhaps the depth of this *antimoral* tendency may be best estimated from the guarded and hostile silence with which Christianity is treated throughout this book—Christianity, as being the most extravagant burlesque of the moral theme to which mankind has hitherto been obliged to listen. In fact, to the purely æsthetic world-interpretation and justification taught in this book, there is no greater antithesis than the Christian dogma, which is *only* and will be only moral, and which, with its absolute standards, for instance, its truthfulness of God, relegates—that is, disowns, convicts, condemns—art, *all* art, to the realm of *falsehood.* Behind such a mode of thought and valuation, which, if at all genuine, must be hostile to art, I always experienced what was *hostile to life,* the wrathful, vindictive counterwill to life itself: for all life rests on appearance, art, illusion, optics, necessity of perspective and error. From the very first Christianity was, essentially and thoroughly, the nausea and surfeit of Life for Life, which only disguised, concealed and decked itself out under the belief in "another" or "better" life. The hatred of the "world," the curse on the affections, the fear of beauty and sensuality, another world, invented for the purpose of slandering this world the more,

Diesseits besser zu verleumden, im Grunde ein Verlangen ins Nichts, ans Ende, ins Ausruhen, hin zum »Sabbat der Sabbate« – dies alles dünkte mich, ebenso wie der unbedingte Wille des Christentums, *nur* moralische Werte gelten zu lassen, immer wie die gefährlichste und unheimlichste Form aller möglichen Formen eines »Willens zum Untergang«, zum mindesten ein Zeichen tiefster Erkrankung, Müdigkeit, Mißmutigkeit, Erschöpfung, Verarmung an Leben, – denn vor der Moral (insonderheit christlichen, das heißt unbedingten Moral) *muß* das Leben beständig und unvermeidlich Unrecht bekommen, weil Leben etwas essentiell Unmoralisches ist, – *muß* endlich das Leben, erdrückt unter dem Gewichte der Verachtung und des ewigen Neins, als begehrens-unwürdig, als unwert an sich empfunden werden. Moral selbst – wie? sollte Moral nicht ein »Wille zur Verneinung des Lebens«, ein heimlicher Instinkt der Vernichtung, ein Verfalls-, Verkleinerungs-, Verleumdungsprinzip, ein Anfang vom Ende sein? Und, folglich, die Gefahr der Gefahren?... *Gegen* die Moral also kehrte sich damals, mit diesem fragwürdigen Buche, mein Instinkt, als ein fürsprechender Instinkt des Lebens, und erfand sich eine grundsätzliche Gegenlehre und Gegenwertung des Lebens, eine rein artistische, eine *antichristliche*. Wie sie nennen? Als Philologe und Mensch der Worte taufte ich sie, nicht ohne einige Freiheit – denn wer wüßte den rechten Namen des Antichrist? – auf den Namen eines griechischen Gottes: ich hieß sie die *dionysische*. –

at bottom a longing for. Nothingness, for the end, for rest, for the "Sabbath of Sabbaths"—all this, as also the unconditional will of Christianity to recognise *only* moral values, has always appeared to me as the most dangerous and ominous of all possible forms of a "will to perish"; at the least, as the symptom of a most fatal disease, of profoundest weariness, despondency, exhaustion, impoverishment of life—for before the tribunal of morality (especially Christian, that is, unconditional morality) life *must* constantly and inevitably be the loser, because life *is* something essentially unmoral—indeed, oppressed with the weight of contempt and the everlasting No, life *must* finally be regarded as unworthy of desire, as in itself unworthy. Morality itself what?—may not morality be a "will to disown life," a secret instinct for annihilation, a principle of decay, of depreciation, of slander, a beginning of the end? And, consequently, the danger of dangers?... It was *against* morality, therefore, that my instinct, as an intercessory-instinct for life, turned in this questionable book, inventing for itself a fundamental counter—dogma and counter-valuation of life, purely artistic, purely *anti-Christian*. What should I call it? As a philologist and man of words I baptised it, not without some liberty—for who could be sure of the proper name of the Antichrist?—with the name of a Greek god: I called it *Dionysian*.

6

Man versteht, an welche Aufgabe ich bereits mit diesem Buche zu rühren wagte?... Wie sehr bedauere ich es jetzt, daß ich damals noch nicht den Mut (oder die Unbescheidenheit?) hatte, um mir in jedem Betrachte für so eigne Anschauungen und Wagnisse auch eine *eigne Sprache* zu erlauben, – daß ich mühselig mit Schopenhauerischen und Kantischen Formeln fremde und neue Wertschätzungen auszudrücken suchte, welche dem Geiste Kantens und Schopenhauers, ebenso wie ihrem Geschmacke, von Grund aus entgegen gingen! Wie dachte doch Schopenhauer über die Tragödie? »Was allem Tragischen den eigentümlichen Schwung zur Erhebung gibt« – sagt er, Welt als Wille und Vorstellung II, 495 – »ist das Aufgehen der Erkenntnis, daß die Welt, das Leben kein rechtes Genügen geben könne, mithin unsrer Anhänglichkeit *nicht wert sei*: darin besteht der tragische Geist –, er

You see which problem I ventured to touch upon in this early work?... How I now regret, that I had not then the courage (or immodesty?) to allow myself, in all respects, the use of an *individual language* for such *individual* contemplations and ventures in the field of thought—that I laboured to express, in Kantian and Schopenhauerian formulæ, strange and new valuations, which ran fundamentally counter to the spirit of Kant and Schopenhauer, as well as to their taste! What, forsooth, were Schopenhauer's views on tragedy? "What gives"—he says in *Welt als Wille und Vorstellung,* II. 495—"to all tragedy that singular swing towards elevation, is the awakening of the knowledge that the world, that life, cannot satisfy us thoroughly, and consequently is *not worthy* of our attachment In this consists the tragic spirit: it therefore leads to *resignation*." Oh, how

leitet demnach zur *Resignation* hin.« O wie anders redete Dionysos zu mir! O wie ferne war mir damals gerade dieser ganze Resignationismus! – Aber es gibt etwas viel Schlimmeres an dem Buche, das ich jetzt noch mehr bedauere, als mit Schopenhauerischen Formeln dionysische Ahnungen verdunkelt und verdorben zu haben: daß ich mir nämlich überhaupt das grandiose *griechische Problem*, wie mir es aufgegangen war, durch Einmischung der modernsten Dinge *verdarb*! Daß ich Hoffnungen anknüpfte, wo nichts zu hoffen war, wo alles allzudeutlich auf ein Ende hinwies! Daß ich, auf Grund der deutschen letzten Musik, vom »deutschen Wesen« zu fabeln begann, wie als ob es eben im Begriff sei, sich selbst zu entdecken und wiederzufinden – und das zu einer Zeit, wo der deutsche Geist, der nicht vor langem noch den Willen zur Herrschaft über Europa, die Kraft zur Führung Europas gehabt hatte, eben letztwillig und endgültig *abdankte* und, unter dem pomphaften Vorwande einer Reichs-Begründung, seinen Übergang zur Vermittelmäßigung, zur Demokratie und den »modernen Ideen« machte! In der Tat, inzwischen lernte ich hoffnungslos und schonungslos genug von diesem »deutschen Wesen« denken, insgleichen von der jetzigen *deutschen Musik*, als welche Romantik durch und durch ist und die ungriechischeste aller möglichen Kunstformen: überdies aber eine Nervenverderberin ersten Ranges, doppelt gefährlich bei einem Volke, das den Trunk liebt und die Unklarheit als Tugend ehrt, nämlich in ihrer doppelten Eigenschaft als berauschendes und zugleich *benebelndes* Narkotikum. – Abseits freilich von allen übereilten Hoffnungen und fehlerhaften Nutzanwendungen auf Gegenwärtigstes, mit denen ich mir damals mein erstes Buch verdarb, bleibt das große dionysische Fragezeichen, wie es darin gesetzt ist, auch in betreff der Musik, fort und fortbestehn: wie müßte eine Musik beschaffen sein, welche nicht mehr romantischen Ursprungs wäre, gleich der deutschen, – sondern *dionysischen*?...

differently Dionysos spoke to me! Oh how far from me then was just this entire resignationism!—But there is something far worse in this book, which I now regret even more than having obscured and spoiled Dionysian anticipations with Schopenhauerian formulæ: to wit, that, in general, I *spoiled* the grand *Hellenic problem,* as it had opened up before me, by the admixture of the most modern things! That I entertained hopes, where nothing was to be hoped for, where everything pointed all-too-clearly to an approaching end! That, on the basis of our latter-day German music, I began to fable about the "spirit of Teutonism," as if it were on the point of discovering and returning to itself—ay, at the very time that the German spirit which not so very long before had had the will to the lordship over Europe, the strength to lead and govern Europe, testamentarily and conclusively *resigned* and, under the pompous pretence of empire-founding, effected its transition to mediocritisation, democracy, and "modern ideas." In very fact, I have since learned to regard this "spirit of Teutonism" as something to be despaired of and unsparingly treated, as also our present *German music,* which is Romanticism through and through and the most un-Grecian of all possible forms of art: and moreover a first-rate nerve-destroyer, doubly dangerous for a people given to drinking and revering the unclear as a virtue, namely, in its twofold capacity of an intoxicating and stupefying narcotic. Of course, apart from all precipitate hopes and faulty applications to matters specially modern, with which I then spoiled my first book, the great Dionysian note of interrogation, as set down therein, continues standing on and on, even with reference to music: how must we conceive of a music, which is no longer of Romantic origin, like the German; but of Dionysian?...

7

– Aber, mein Herr, was in aller Welt ist Romantik, wenn nicht *Ihr* Buch Romantik ist? Läßt sich der tiefe Haß gegen »Jetztzeit«, »Wirklichkeit« und »moderne Ideen« weiter treiben, als es in Ihrer Artisten-Metaphysik geschehen ist? – welche lieber noch an das Nichts, lieber noch an den Teufel als an das »Jetzt« glaubt? Brummt nicht ein Grundbaß von Zorn und Vernichtungslust unter aller Ihrer kontrapunktischen Stimmen-Kunst und Ohren-Verführerei hinweg, eine

—But, my dear Sir, if *your* book is not Romanticism, what in the world is? Can the deep hatred of the present, of "reality" and "modern ideas" be pushed farther than has been done in your artist-metaphysics?—which would rather believe in Nothing, or in the devil, than in the "Now"? Does not a radical bass of wrath and annihilative pleasure growl on beneath all your contrapuntal vocal art and aural seduction, a mad

wütende Entschlossenheit gegen alles, was »jetzt« ist, ein Wille, welcher nicht gar zu ferne vom praktischen Nihilismus ist und zu sagen scheint »lieber mag nichts wahr sein, als daß *ihr* Recht hättet, als daß *eure* Wahrheit Recht behielte!« Hören Sie selbst, mein Herr Pessimist und Kunstvergöttlicher, mit auf geschlossnerem Ohre eine einzige ausgewählte Stelle Ihres Buches an, jene nicht unberedte Drachentöter-Stelle, welche für junge Ohren und Herzen verfänglich-rattenfängerisch klingen mag: wie? ist das nicht das echte rechte Romantiker-Bekenntnis von 1830, unter der Maske des Pessimismus von 1850? hinter dem auch schon das übliche Romantiker-Finale präludiert, – Bruch, Zusammenbruch, Rückkehr und Niedersturz vor einem alten Glauben, vor *dem* alten Gotte... Wie? ist Ihr Pessimisten-Buch nicht selbst ein Stück Antigriechentum und Romantik, selbst etwas »ebenso Berauschendes als Benebelndes«, ein Narkotikum jedenfalls, ein Stück Musik sogar, *deutscher* Musik? Aber man höre:

»Denken wir uns eine heranwachsende Generation mit dieser Unerschrockenheit des Blicks, mit diesem heroischen Zug ins Ungeheure, denken wir uns den kühnen Schritt dieser Drachentöter, die stolze Verwegenheit, mit der sie allen den Schwächlichkeitsdoktrinen des Optimismus den Rücken kehren, um im Ganzen und Vollen ›resolut zu leben‹: *sollte es nicht nötig sein*, daß der tragische Mensch dieser Kultur, bei seiner Selbsterziehung zum Ernst und zum Schrecken, eine neue Kunst, *die Kunst des metaphysischen Trostes*, die Tragödie als die ihm zugehörige Helena begehren und mit Faust ausrufen muß:

Und sollt' ich nicht, sehnsüchtigster Gewalt,
Ins Leben ziehn die einzigste Gestalt?«

»Sollte es nicht *nötig* sein?«... Nein, dreimal nein! ihr jungen Romantiker: es sollte *nicht* nötig sein! Aber es ist sehr wahrscheinlich, daß es so *endet*, daß *ihr* so endet, nämlich »getröstet«, wie geschrieben steht, trotz aller Selbsterziehung zum Ernst und zum Schrecken, »metaphysisch getröstet«, kurz wie Romantiker enden, *christlich*... Nein! Ihr solltet vorerst die Kunst des *diesseitigen* Trostes lernen, – ihr solltet *lachen* lernen, meine jungen Freunde, wenn anders ihr durchaus Pessimisten bleiben wollt; vielleicht daß ihr daraufhin, als Lachende, irgendwann einmal alle metaphysische Trösterei zum Teufel schickt – und die Metaphysik voran! Oder, um es in der Sprache jenes dionysischen Unholds zu sagen, der *Zarathustra* heißt:

determination to oppose all that "now" is, a will which is not so very far removed from practical nihilism and which seems to say: "rather let nothing be true, than that *you* should be in the right, than that *your* truth should prevail!" Hear, yourself, my dear Sir Pessimist and art-deifier, with ever so unlocked ears, a single select passage of your own book, that not ineloquent dragon-slayer passage, which may sound insidiously rat-charming to young ears and hearts. What? is not that the true blue romanticist-confession of 1830 under the mask of the pessimism of 1850? After which, of course, the usual romanticist finale at once strikes up—rupture, collapse, return and prostration before an old belief, before *the* old God.... What? is not your pessimist book itself a piece of anti-Hellenism and Romanticism, something "equally intoxicating and befogging," a narcotic at all events, ay, a piece of music, of *German* music? But listen:

Let us imagine a rising generation with this undauntedness of vision, with this heroic impulse towards the prodigious, let us imagine the bold step of these dragon-slayers, the proud daring with which they turn their backs on all the effeminate doctrines of optimism, in order "to live resolutely" in the Whole and in the Full: *would it not be necessary* for the tragic man of this culture, with his self-discipline to earnestness and terror, to desire a new art, the art of metaphysical comfort, tragedy as the Helen belonging to him, and that he should exclaim with Faust:

And shall I not, most powerful desire,
draw this unique form into life?

"Would it not be *necessary*?" ... No, thrice no! ye young romanticists: it would *not* be necessary! But it is very probable, that things may *end* thus, that *ye* may end thus, namely "comforted," as it is written, in spite of all self-discipline to earnestness and terror; metaphysically comforted, in short, as Romanticists are wont to end, as *Christians*.... No! ye should first of all learn the art of earthly comfort, ye should learn to *laugh,* my young friends, if ye are at all determined to remain pessimists: if so, you will perhaps, as laughing ones, eventually send all metaphysical comfortism to the devil—and metaphysics first of all! Or, to say it in the language of that Dionysian ogre, called *Zarathustra*:

»Erhebt eure Herzen, meine Brüder, hoch, höher! Und vergeßt mir auch die Beine nicht! Erhebt auch eure Beine, ihr guten Tänzer, und besser noch: ihr steht auch auf dem Kopf!
Diese Krone des Lachenden, diese Rosenkranz-Krone: ich selber setzte mir diese Krone auf, ich selber sprach heilig mein Gelächter. Keinen anderen fand ich heute stark genug dazu.
Zarathustra der Tänzer, Zarathustra der Leichte, der mit den Flügeln winkt, ein Flugbereiter, allen Vögeln zuwinkend, bereit und fertig, ein Selig-Leichtfertiger: –
Zarathustra der Wahrsager, Zarathustra der Wahrlacher, kein Ungeduldiger, kein Unbedingter, einer, der Sprünge und Seitensprünge liebt: ich selber setzte mir diese Krone auf!
Diese Krone des Lachenden, diese Rosenkranz-Krone: euch, meinen Brüdern, werfe ich diese Krone zu! Das Lachen sprach ich heilig: ihr höheren Menschen, *lernt* mir – lachen!«

Also sprach Zarathustra, vierter Teil

Lift up your hearts, my brethren, high, higher! And do not forget your legs! Lift up also your legs, ye good dancers—and better still if ye stand also on your heads!
This crown of the laughter, this rose-garland crown—I myself have put on this crown; I myself have consecrated my laughter. No one else have I found today strong enough for this.
Zarathustra the dancer, Zarathustra the light one, who beckoneth with his pinions, one ready for flight, beckoning unto all birds, ready and prepared, a blissfully light-spirited one:—
Zarathustra the soothsayer, Zarathustra the sooth-laugher, no impatient one, no absolute one, one who loveth leaps and side-leaps: I myself have put on this crown!
This crown of the laughter, this rose-garland crown—to you my brethren do I cast this crown! Laughing have I consecrated: ye higher men, *learn,* I pray you—to laugh!

Thus spake Zarathustra, lxxiii. 17, 18, and 20.

SILS-MARIA, OBERENGADIN, *August* 1886.

THE BIRTH OF TRAGEDY FROM THE SPIRIT OF MUSIC

Die Geburt der Tragödie aus dem Geiste der Musik

Vorwort an Richard Wagner

Um mir alle die möglichen Bedenklichkeiten, Aufregungen und Mißverständnisse ferne zu halten, zu denen die in dieser Schrift vereinigten Gedanken bei dem eigentümlichen Charakter unserer ästhetischen Öffentlichkeit Anlaß geben werden, und um auch die Einleitungsworte zu derselben mit der gleichen beschaulichen Wonne schreiben zu können, deren Zeichen sie selbst, als das Petrefakt guter und erhebender Stunden, auf jedem Blatte trägt, vergegenwärtige ich mir den Augenblick, in dem Sie, mein hochverehrter Freund, diese Schrift empfangen werden: wie Sie, vielleicht nach einer abendlichen Wanderung im Winterschnee, den entfesselten Prometheus auf dem Titelblatte betrachten, meinen Namen lesen und sofort überzeugt sind, daß, mag in dieser Schrift stehen, was da wolle, der Verfasser etwas Ernstes und Eindringliches zu sagen hat, ebenfalls daß er, bei allem, was er sich erdachte, mit Ihnen wie mit einem Gegenwärtigen verkehrte und nur etwas dieser Gegenwart Entsprechendes niederschreiben durfte. Sie werden dabei sich erinnern, daß ich zu gleicher Zeit, als Ihre herrliche Festschrift über Beethoven entstand, das heißt in den Schrecken und Erhabenheiten des eben ausgebrochnen Krieges, mich zu diesen Gedanken sammelte. Doch würden diejenigen irren, welche etwa bei dieser Sammlung an den Gegensatz von patriotischer Erregung und ästhetischer Schwelgerei, von tapferem Ernst und heiterem Spiel denken sollten: denen möchte vielmehr, bei einem wirklichen Lesen dieser Schrift, zu ihrem Erstaunen deutlich werden, mit welchem ernsthaft deutschen Problem wir zu tun haben, das von uns recht eigentlich in die Mitte deutscher Hoffnungen, als Wirbel und Wendepunkt, hingestellt wird. Vielleicht aber wird es für eben dieselben überhaupt anstößig sein, ein ästhetisches Problem so ernst genommen zu sehn, falls sie nämlich in der Kunst nicht mehr als ein lustiges Nebenbei, als ein auch wohl zu missendes Schellengeklingel zum »Ernst des Daseins« zu erkennen imstande sind: als ob niemand wüßte, was es bei dieser Gegenüberstellung mit einem solchen »Ernste des Daseins« auf sich habe. Diesen Ernsthaften diene zur Belehrung, daß ich von der Kunst als der höchsten Aufgabe und der eigentlich metaphysischen Tätigkeit dieses Lebens im Sinne des Mannes überzeugt bin, dem ich hier, als meinem erhabenen Vorkämpfer auf dieser Bahn, diese Schrift gewidmet haben will.

Basel, Ende des Jahres 1871

Foreward to Richard Wagner.

In order to keep at a distance all the possible scruples, excitements, and misunderstandings to which the thoughts gathered in this essay will give occasion, considering the peculiar character of our æsthetic publicity, and to be able also Co write the introductory remarks with the same contemplative delight, the impress of which, as the petrifaction of good and elevating hours, it bears on every page, I form a conception of the moment when you, my highly honoured friend, will receive this essay; how you, say after an evening walk in the winter snow, will behold the unbound Prometheus on the title-page, read my name, and be forthwith convinced that, whatever this essay may contain, the author has something earnest and impressive to say, and, moreover, that in all his meditations he communed with you as with one present and could thus write only what befitted your presence. You will thus remember that it was at the same time as your magnificent dissertation on Beethoven originated, viz., amidst the horrors and sublimities of the war which had just then broken out, that I collected myself for these thoughts. But those persons would err, to whom this collection suggests no more perhaps than the antithesis of patriotic excitement and æsthetic revelry, of gallant earnestness and sportive delight. Upon a real perusal of this essay, such readers will, rather to their surprise, discover how earnest is the German problem we have to deal with, which we properly place, as a vortex and turning-point, in the very midst of German hopes. Perhaps, however, this same class of readers will be shocked at seeing an æsthetic problem taken so seriously, especially if they can recognise in art no more than a merry diversion, a readily dispensable court-jester to the "earnestness of existence": as if no one were aware of the real meaning of this confrontation with the "earnestness of existence." These earnest ones may be informed that I am convinced that art is the highest task and the properly metaphysical activity of this life, as it is understood by the man, to whom, as my sublime protagonist on this path, I would now dedicate this essay.

BASEL, end of the year 1871.

1

Wir werden viel für die ästhetische Wissenschaft gewonnen haben, wenn wir nicht nur zur logischen Einsicht, sondern zur unmittelbaren Sicherheit der Anschauung gekommen sind, daß die Fortentwickelung der Kunst an die Duplizität des *Apollinischen* und des *Dionysischen* gebunden ist: in ähnlicher Weise, wie die Generation von der Zweiheit der Geschlechter, bei fortwährendem Kampfe und nur periodisch eintretender Versöhnung, abhängt. Diese Namen entlehnen wir von den Griechen, welche die tiefsinnigen Geheimlehren ihrer Kunstanschauung zwar nicht in Begriffen, aber in den eindringlich deutlichen Gestalten ihrer Götterwelt dem Einsichtigen vernehmbar machen. An ihre beiden Kunstgottheiten, Apollo und Dionysus, knüpft sich unsere Erkenntnis, daß in der griechischen Welt ein ungeheurer Gegensatz, nach Ursprung und Zielen, zwischen der Kunst des Bildners, der apollinischen, und der unbildlichen Kunst der Musik, als der des Dionysus, besteht: beide so verschiedne Triebe gehen nebeneinander her, zumeist im offnen Zwiespalt miteinander und sich gegenseitig zu immer neuen kräftigeren Geburten reizend, um in ihnen den Kampf jenes Gegensatzes zu perpetuieren, den das gemeinsame Wort »Kunst« nur scheinbar überbrückt; bis sie endlich, durch einen metaphysischen Wunderakt des hellenischen »Willens«, miteinander gepaart erscheinen und in dieser Paarung zuletzt das ebenso dionysische als apollinische Kunstwerk der attischen Tragödie erzeugen.

Um uns jene beiden Triebe näherzubringen, denken wir sie uns zunächst als die getrennten Kunstwelten des *Traumes* und des *Rausches*; zwischen welchen physiologischen Erscheinungen ein entsprechender Gegensatz wie zwischen dem Apollinischen und dem Dionysischen zu bemerken ist. Im Traume traten zuerst, nach der Vorstellung des Lukretius, die herrlichen Göttergestalten vor die Seelen der Menschen, im Traume sah der große Bildner den entzückenden Gliederbau übermenschlicher Wesen, und der hellenische Dichter, um die Geheimnisse der poetischen Zeugung befragt, würde ebenfalls an den Traum erinnert und eine ähnliche Belehrung gegeben haben, wie sie Hans Sachs in den Meistersingern gibt:

WE SHALL HAVE GAINED MUCH FOR THE SCIENCE of æsthetics, when once we have perceived not only by logical inference, but by the immediate certainty of intuition, that the continuous development of art is bound up with the duplexity of the *Apollonian* and the *Dionysian:* in like manner as procreation is dependent on the duality of the sexes, involving perpetual conflicts with only periodically intervening reconciliations. These names we borrow from the Greeks, who disclose to the intelligent observer the profound mysteries of their view of art, not indeed in concepts, but in the impressively clear figures of their world of deities. It is in connection with Apollo and Dionysus, the two art-deities of the Greeks, that we learn that there existed in the Grecian world a wide antithesis, in origin and aims, between the art of the shaper, the Apollonian, and the non-pictorial art of music, that of Dionysus: both these instincts, so different, run parallel to each other, for the most part openly at variance, and continually inciting each other to new and more powerful births, to perpetuate in themselves the strife of this antithesis, which is but seemingly bridged over by their mutual term "Art"; till at last, by a metaphysical miracle of the Hellenic "will", they appear paired with each other, and through this pairing eventually generate the equally Dionysian and Apollonian art-work of Attic tragedy.

In order to bring these two tendencies within closer range, let us conceive them first of all as the separate art-worlds of *dreamland* and *drunkenness;* between which physiological phenomena a contrast may be observed analogous to that existing between the Apollonian and the Dionysian. In dreams, according to the conception of Lucretius, the glorious divine figures first appeared to the souls of men, in dreams the great shaper beheld the charming corporeal structure of superhuman beings, and the Hellenic poet, if consulted on the mysteries of poetic inspiration, would likewise have suggested dreams and would have offered an explanation resembling that of Hans Sachs in the Meistersingers:—

Mein Freund, das grad ist Dichters Werk,
daß er sein Träumen deut' und merk'.
Glaubt mir, des Menschen wahrster Wahn
wird ihm im Traume aufgetan:
all Dichtkunst und Poeterei
ist nichts als Wahrtraum-Deuterei.

Der schöne Schein der Traumwelten, in deren Erzeugung jeder Mensch voller Künstler ist, ist die Voraussetzung aller bildenden Kunst, ja auch, wie wir sehen werden, einer wichtigen Hälfte der Poesie. Wir genießen im unmittelbaren Verständnisse der Gestalt, alle Formen sprechen zu uns, es gibt nichts Gleichgültiges und Unnötiges. Bei dem höchsten Leben dieser Traumwirklichkeit haben wir doch noch die durchschimmernde Empfindung ihres *Scheins*: wenigstens ist dies meine Erfahrung, für deren Häufigkeit, ja Normalität, ich manches Zeugnis und die Aussprüche der Dichter beizubringen hätte. Der philosophische Mensch hat sogar das Vorgefühl, daß auch unter dieser Wirklichkeit, in der wir leben und sind, eine zweite ganz andre verborgen liege, daß also auch sie ein Schein sei; und Schopenhauer bezeichnet geradezu die Gabe, daß einem zuzeiten die Menschen und alle Dinge als bloße Phantome oder Traumbilder vorkommen, als das Kennzeichen philosophischer Befähigung. Wie nun der Philosoph zur Wirklichkeit des Daseins, so verhält sich der künstlerisch erregbare Mensch zur Wirklichkeit des Traumes; er sieht genau und gern zu: denn aus diesen Bildern deutet er sich das Leben, an diesen Vorgängen übt er sich für das Leben. Nicht etwa nur die angenehmen und freundlichen Bilder sind es, die er mit jener Allverständlichkeit an sich erfährt: auch das Ernste, Trübe, Traurige, Finstere, die plötzlichen Hemmungen, die Neckereien des Zufalls, die bänglichen Erwartungen, kurz die ganze »göttliche Komödie« des Lebens, mit dem *Inferno*, zieht an ihm vorbei, nicht nur wie ein Schattenspiel – denn er lebt und leidet mit in diesen Szenen – und doch auch nicht ohne jene flüchtige Empfindung des Scheins; und vielleicht erinnert sich mancher, gleich mir, in den Gefährlichkeiten und Schrecken des Traumes sich mitunter ermutigend und mit Erfolg zugerufen zu haben: »Es ist ein Traum! Ich will ihn weiter träumen!« Wie man mir auch von Personen erzählt hat, die die Kausalität eines und desselben Traumes über drei und mehr aufeinanderfolgende Nächte hin fortzusetzen imstande waren: Tatsachen, welche deutlich Zeugnis dafür abgeben, daß unser innerstes Wesen, der gemeinsame Untergrund von uns allen, mit tiefer Lust und freudiger Notwendigkeit den Traum an sich erfährt.

My friend, just this is poet's task:
His dreams to read and to unmask.
Trust me, illusion's truths thrice sealed
In dream to man will be revealed.
All verse-craft and poetisation
Is but soothdream interpretation.

The beauteous appearance of the dream-worlds, in the production of which every man is a perfect artist, is the presupposition of every art of images, and in fact, as we shall see, of an important half of poetry also. We take delight in the immediate apprehension of form; all forms speak to us; there is nothing indifferent, nothing superfluous. But, together with the highest life of this dream-reality we also have, glimmering through it, the sensation of its appearance: such at least is my experience, as to the frequency, ay, normality of which I could adduce many proofs, as also the sayings of the poets. Indeed, the man of philosophic turn has a foreboding that underneath this reality in which we live and have our being, another and altogether different reality lies concealed, and that therefore it is also an appearance; and Schopenhauer actually designates the gift of occasionally regarding men and things as mere phantoms and dream-pictures as the criterion of philosophical ability. Accordingly, the man susceptible to art stands in the same relation to the reality of dreams as the philosopher to the reality of existence; he is a close and willing observer, for from these pictures he reads the meaning of life, and by these processes he trains himself for life. And it is perhaps not only the agreeable and friendly pictures that he realises in himself with such perfect understanding: the earnest, the troubled, the dreary, the gloomy, the sudden checks, the tricks of fortune, the uneasy presentiments, in short, the whole "Divine Comedy" of life, and the Inferno, also pass before him, not merely like pictures on the wall—for he too lives and suffers in these scenes—and yet not without that fleeting sensation of appearance. And perhaps many a one will, like myself, recollect having sometimes called out cheeringly and not without success amid the dangers and terrors of dream-life: "It is a dream! I will dream on!" I have likewise been told of persons capable of continuing the causality of one and the same dream for three and even more successive nights: all of which facts clearly testify that our innermost being, the common substratum of all of us, experiences our dreams with deep joy and cheerful acquiescence.

Diese freudige Notwendigkeit der Traumerfahrung ist gleichfalls von den Griechen in ihrem Apollo ausgedrückt worden: Apollo, als der Gott aller bildnerischen Kräfte, ist zugleich der wahrsagende Gott. Er, der seiner Wurzel nach der »Scheinende«, die Lichtgottheit ist, beherrscht auch den schönen Schein der inneren Phantasie-Welt. Die höhere Wahrheit, die Vollkommenheit dieser Zustände im Gegensatz zu der lückenhaft verständlichen Tageswirklichkeit, sodann das tiefe Bewußtsein von der in Schlaf und Traum heilenden und helfenden Natur ist zugleich das symbolische Analogon der wahrsagenden Fähigkeit und überhaupt der Künste, durch die das Leben möglich und lebenswert gemacht wird. Aber auch jene zarte Linie, die das Traumbild nicht überschreiten darf, um nicht pathologisch zu wirken, widrigenfalls der Schein als plumpe Wirklichkeit uns betrügen würde – darf nicht im Bilde des Apollo fehlen: jene maßvolle Begrenzung, jene Freiheit von den wilderen Regungen, jene weisheitsvolle Ruhe des Bildnergottes. Sein Auge muß »sonnenhaft«, gemäß seinem Ursprunge, sein; auch wenn es zürnt und unmutig blickt, liegt die Weihe des schönen Scheines auf ihm. Und so möchte von Apollo in einem exzentrischen Sinne das gelten, was Schopenhauer von dem im Schleier der Maja befangenen Menschen sagt, Welt als Wille und Vorstellung 1, S. 416: »Wie auf dem tobenden Meere, das, nach allen Seiten unbegrenzt, heulend Wellenberge erhebt und senkt, auf einem Kahn ein Schiffer sitzt, dem schwachen Fahrzeug vertrauend; so sitzt, mitten in einer Welt von Qualen, ruhig der einzelne Mensch, gestützt und vertrauend auf das *principium individuationis.*« Ja es wäre von Apollo zu sagen, daß in ihm das unerschütterte Vertrauen auf jenes *principium* und das ruhige Dasitzen des in ihm Befangenen seinen erhabensten Ausdruck bekommen habe, und man möchte selbst Apollo als das herrliche Götterbild des *principii individuationis* bezeichnen, aus dessen Gebärden und Blicken die ganze Lust und Weisheit des »Scheines« samt seiner Schönheit, zu uns spräche.

An derselben Stelle hat uns Schopenhauer das ungeheure *Grausen* geschildert, welches den Menschen ergreift, wenn er plötzlich an den Erkenntnisformen der Erscheinung irre wird, indem der Satz vom Grunde, in irgendeiner seiner Gestaltungen, eine Ausnahme zu erleiden scheint. Wenn wir zu diesem Grausen die wonnevolle Verzückung hinzunehmen, die bei demselben Zerbrechen des *principii individuationis* aus dem innersten Grunde des Menschen, ja der Natur emporsteigt, so tun wir einen Blick in das Wesen des

This cheerful acquiescence in the dream-experience has likewise been embodied by the Greeks in their Apollo: for Apollo, as the god of all shaping energies, is also the soothsaying god. He, who (as the etymology of the name indicates) is the "shining one," the deity of light, also rules over the fair appearance of the inner world of fantasies. The higher truth, the perfection of these states in contrast to the only partially intelligible everyday world, ay, the deep consciousness of nature, healing and helping in sleep and dream, is at the same time the symbolical analogue of the faculty of soothsaying and, in general, of the arts, through which life is made possible and worth living. But also that delicate line, which the dream-picture must not overstep—lest it act pathologically (in which case appearance, being reality pure and simple, would impose upon us)—must not be wanting in the picture of Apollo: that measured limitation, that freedom from the wilder emotions, that philosophical calmness of the sculptor-god. His eye must be "sunlike," according to his origin; even when it is angry and looks displeased, the sacredness of his beauteous appearance is still there. And so we might apply to Apollo, in an eccentric sense, what Schopenhauer says of the man wrapt in the veil of Mâyâ: *Welt als Wille und Vorstellung,* I. p. 416: "Just as in a stormy sea, unbounded in every direction, rising and falling with howling mountainous waves, a sailor sits in a boat and trusts in his frail barque: so in the midst of a world of sorrows the individual sits quietly supported by and trusting in his *principium individuationis.*" Indeed, we might say of Apollo, that in him the unshaken faith in this *principium* and the quiet sitting of the man wrapt therein have received their sublimest expression; and we might even designate Apollo as the glorious divine image of the *principium individuationis,* from out of the gestures and looks of which all the joy and wisdom of "appearance," together with its beauty, speak to us.

In the same work Schopenhauer has described to us the stupendous *awe* which seizes upon man, when of a sudden he is at a loss to account for the cognitive forms of a phenomenon, in that the principle of reason, in some one of its manifestations, seems to admit of an exception. Add to this awe the blissful ecstasy which rises from the innermost depths of man, ay, of nature, at this same collapse of the *principium individuationis,* and we shall gain an insight into

Dionysischen, das uns am nächsten noch durch die Analogie des *Rausches* gebracht wird. Entweder durch den Einfluß des narkotischen Getränkes, von dem alle ursprünglichen Menschen und Völker in Hymnen sprechen, oder bei dem gewaltigen, die ganze Natur lustvoll durchdringenden Nahen des Frühlingserwachen jene dionysischen Regungen, in deren Steigerung das Subjektive zu völliger Selbstvergessenheit hinschwindet. Auch im deutschen Mittelalter wälzten sich unter der gleichen dionysischen Gewalt immer wachsende Scharen, singend und tanzend, von Ort zu Ort: in diesen Sankt-Johann- und Sankt-Veittänzern erkennen wir die bacchischen Chöre der Griechen wieder, mit ihrer Vorgeschichte in Kleinasien, bis hin zu Babylon und den orgiastischen Sakäen. Es gibt Menschen, die, aus Mangel an Erfahrung oder aus Stumpfsinn, sich von solchen Erscheinungen wie von »Volkskrankheiten«, spöttisch oder bedauernd im Gefühl der eigenen Gesundheit abwenden: die Armen ahnen freilich nicht, wie leichenfarbig und gespenstisch eben diese ihre »Gesundheit« sich ausnimmt, wenn an ihnen das glühende Leben dionysischer Schwärmer vorüberbraust.

the being of the *Dionysian*, which is brought within closest ken perhaps by the analogy of *drunkenness*. It is either under the influence of the narcotic draught, of which the hymns of all primitive men and peoples tell us, or by the powerful approach of spring penetrating all nature with joy, that those Dionysian emotions awake, in the augmentation of which the subjective vanishes to complete self-forgetfulness. So also in the German Middle Ages singing and dancing crowds, ever increasing in number, were borne from place to place under this same Dionysian power. In these St. John's and St. Vitus's dancers we again perceive the Bacchic choruses of the Greeks, with their previous history in Asia Minor, as far back as Babylon and the orgiastic Sacæa. There are some, who, from lack of experience or obtuseness, will turn away from such phenomena as "folk-diseases" with a smile of contempt or pity prompted by the consciousness of their own health: of course, the poor wretches do not divine what a cadaverous-looking and ghastly aspect this very "health" of theirs presents when the glowing life of the Dionysian revellers rushes past them.

Unter dem Zauber des Dionysischen schließt sich nicht nur der Bund zwischen Mensch und Mensch wieder zusammen: auch die entfremdete, feindliche oder unterjochte Natur feiert wieder ihr Versöhnungsfest mit ihrem verlorenen Sohne, dem Menschen. Freiwillig beut die Erde ihre Gaben, und friedfertig nahen die Raubtiere der Felsen und der Wüste. Mit Blumen und Kränzen ist der Wagen des Dionysus überschüttet: unter seinem Joche schreiten Panther und Tiger. Man verwandele das Beethovensche Jubellied der »Freude« in ein Gemälde und bleibe mit seiner Einbildungskraft nicht zurück, wenn die Millionen schauervoll in den Staub sinken: so kann man sich dem Dionysischen nähern. Jetzt ist der Sklave freier Mann, jetzt zerbrechen alle die starren, feindseligen Abgrenzungen, die Not, Willkür oder »freche Mode« zwischen den Menschen festgesetzt haben. Jetzt, bei dem Evangelium der Weltenharmonie, fühlt sich jeder mit seinem Nächsten nicht nur vereinigt, versöhnt, verschmolzen, sondern eins, als ob der Schleier der Maja zerrissen wäre und nur noch in Fetzen vor dem geheimnisvollen Ur-Einen herumflattere. Singend und tanzend äußert sich der Mensch als Mitglied einer höheren Gemeinsamkeit: er hat das Gehen und das Sprechen verlernt und ist auf dem Wege, tanzend in die Lüfte emporzufliegen. Aus seinen Gebärden spricht die Verzauberung. Wie jetzt die Tiere reden, und die Erde

Under the charm of the Dionysian not only is the covenant between man and man again established, but also estranged, hostile or subjugated nature again celebrates her reconciliation with her lost son, man. Of her own accord earth proffers her gifts, and peacefully the beasts of prey approach from the desert and the rocks. The chariot of Dionysus is bedecked with flowers and garlands: panthers and tigers pass beneath his yoke. Change Beethoven's "jubilee-song" into a painting, and, if your imagination be equal to the occasion when the awestruck millions sink into the dust, you will then be able to approach the Dionysian. Now is the slave a free man, now all the stubborn, hostile barriers, which necessity, caprice, or "shameless fashion" has set up between man and man, are broken down. Now, at the evangel of cosmic harmony, each one feels himself not only united, reconciled, blended with his neighbour, but as one with him, as if the veil of Mâyâ has been torn and were now merely fluttering in tatters before the mysterious Primordial Unity. In song and in dance man exhibits himself as a member of a higher community, has forgotten how to walk and speak, and is on the point of taking a dancing flight into the air. His gestures bespeak enchantment. Even as the animals now talk, and as the earth yields milk

Milch und Honig gibt, so tönt auch aus ihm etwas Übernatürliches: als Gott fühlt er sich, er selbst wandelt jetzt so verzückt und erhoben, wie er die Götter im Traume wandeln sah. Der Mensch ist nicht mehr Künstler, er ist Kunstwerk geworden: die Kunstgewalt der ganzen Natur, zur höchsten Wonnebefriedigung des Ur-Einen, offenbart sich hier unter den Schauern des Rausches. Der edelste Ton, der kostbarste Marmor wird hier geknetet und behauen, der Mensch, und zu den Meißelschlägen des dionysischen Weltenkünstlers tönt der eleusinische Mysterienruf:

»Ihr stürzt nieder, Millionen?
Ahnest du den Schöpfer, Welt?« –

and honey, so also something super-natural sounds forth from him: he feels himself a god, he himself now walks about enchanted and elated even as the gods whom he saw walking about in his dreams. Man is no longer an artist, he has become a work of art: the artistic power of all nature here reveals itself in the tremors of drunkenness to the highest gratification of the Primordial Unity. The noblest clay, the costliest marble, namely man, is here kneaded and cut, and the chisel strokes of the Dionysian world-artist are accompanied with the cry of the Eleusinian mysteries:

Do you fall down, all you millions?
Do you see your maker, world?[6]

2

Wir haben bis jetzt das Apollinische und seinen Gegensatz, das Dionysische, als künstlerische Mächte betrachtet, die aus der Natur selbst, *ohne Vermittlung des menschlichen Künstlers*, hervorbrechen, und in denen sich ihre Kunsttriebe zunächst und auf direktem Wege befriedigen: einmal als die Bilderwelt des Traumes, deren Vollkommenheit ohne jeden Zusammenhang mit der intellektuellen Höhe oder künstlerischen Bildung des einzelnen ist, andererseits als rauschvolle Wirklichkeit, die wiederum des einzelnen nicht achtet, sondern sogar das Individuum zu vernichten und durch eine mystische Einheitsempfindung zu erlösen sucht. Diesen unmittelbaren Kunstzuständen der Natur gegenüber ist jeder Künstler »Nachahmer«, und zwar entweder apollonischer Traumkünstler oder dionysischer Rauschkünstler oder endlich – wie beispielsweise in der griechischen Tragödie – zugleich Rausch- und Traumkünstler: als welchen wir uns etwa zu denken haben, wie er, in der dionysischen Trunkenheit und mystischen Selbstentäußerung, einsam und abseits von den schwärmenden Chören niedersinkt und wie sich ihm nun, durch apollinische Traumeinwirkung, sein eigener Zustand, d.h. seine Einheit mit dem innersten Grunde der Welt *in einem gleichnisartigen Traumbilde* offenbart.

Nach diesen allgemeinen Voraussetzungen und Gegenüberstellungen nahen wir uns jetzt den *Griechen*, um zu erkennen, in welchem Grade und bis zu welcher Höhe jene *Kunsttriebe der Natur* in ihnen entwickelt gewesen sind: wodurch wir in den Stand gesetzt

Thus far we have considered the Apollonian and his antithesis, the Dionysian, as artistic powers, which burst forth from nature herself, without the mediation of the human artist, and in which her art-impulses are satisfied in the most immediate and direct way: first, as the pictorial world of dreams, the perfection of which has no connection whatever with the intellectual height or artistic culture of the unit man, and again, as drunken reality, which likewise does not heed the unit man, and again, as drunken reality, which likewise does not heed the unit man, but even seeks to destroy the individual and redeem him by a mystic feeling of Oneness. Anent these immediate art-states of nature every artist is either an "imitator," to wit, either an Apollonian, an artist in dreams, or a Dionysian, an artist in ecstasies, or finally—as for instance in Greek tragedy—an artist in both dreams and ecstasies: so we may perhaps picture him, as in his Dionysian drunkenness and mystical self-abnegation, lonesome and apart from the revelling choruses, he sinks down, and how now, through Apollonian dream-inspiration, his own state, *i.e.*, his oneness with the primal source of the universe, reveals itself to him *in a* symbolical dream-picture.

After these general premisings and contrastings, let us now approach the *Greeks* in order to learn in what degree and to what height these *art-impulses of nature* were developed in them: whereby we shall be enabled to understand and

[6] Cf. Schiller's *Hymn to Joy* (*An die Freude*) and Beethoven, Ninth Symphony.

werden, das Verhältnis des griechischen Künstlers zu seinen Urbildern, oder, nach dem aristotelischen Ausdrucke, »die Nachahmung der Natur« tiefer zu verstehn und zu würdigen. Von den *Träumen* der Griechen ist trotz aller Traumliteratur derselben und zahlreichen Traumanekdoten nur vermutungsweise, aber doch mit ziemlicher Sicherheit zu sprechen: bei der unglaublich bestimmten und sicheren plastischen Befähigung ihres Auges, samt ihrer hellen und aufrichtigen Farbenlust, wird man sich nicht entbrechen können, zur Beschämung aller Spätergeborenen, auch für ihre Träume eine logische Kausalität der Linien und Umrisse, Farben und Gruppen, eine ihren besten Reliefs ähnelnde Folge der Szenen vorauszusetzen, deren Vollkommenheit uns, wenn eine Vergleichung möglich wäre, gewiß berechtigen würde, die träumenden Griechen als Homere und Homer als einen träumenden Griechen zu bezeichnen: in einem tieferen Sinne, als wenn der moderne Mensch sich hinsichtlich seines Traumes mit Shakespeare zu vergleichen wagt.

Dagegen brauchen wir nicht nur vermutungsweise zu sprechen, wenn die ungeheure Kluft aufgedeckt werden soll, welche die *dionysischen Griechen* von den dionysischen Barbaren trennt. Aus allen Enden der alten Welt – um die neuere hier beiseite zu lassen –, von Rom bis Babylon können wir die Existenz dionysischer Feste nachweisen, deren Typus sich, bestenfalls, zu dem Typus der griechischen verhält wie der bärtige Satyr, dem der Bock Namen und Attribute verlieh, zu Dionysus selbst. Fast überall lag das Zentrum dieser Feste in einer überschwänglichen geschlechtlichen Zuchtlosigkeit, deren Wellen über jedes Familientum und dessen ehrwürdige Satzungen hinwegfluteten; gerade die wildesten Bestien der Natur wurden hier entfesselt, bis zu jener abscheulichen Mischung von Wollust und Grausamkeit, die mir immer als der eigentliche »Hexentrank« erschienen ist. Gegen die fieberhaften Regungen jener Feste, deren Kenntnis auf allen Land- und Seewegen zu den Griechen drang, waren sie, scheint es, eine Zeit lang völlig gesichert und geschützt durch die hier in seinem ganzen Stolz sich aufrichtende Gestalt des Apollo, der das Medusenhaupt keiner gefährlicheren Macht entgegenhalten konnte als dieser fratzenhaft ungeschlachten dionysischen. Es ist die dorische Kunst, in der sich jene majestätisch-ablehnende Haltung des Apollo verewigt hat. Bedenklicher und sogar unmöglich wurde dieser Widerstand, als endlich aus der tiefsten Wurzel des Hellenischen heraus sich ähnliche Triebe Bahn brachen: jetzt beschränkte sich das Wirken des delphischen Gottes darauf, dem

appreciate more deeply the relation of the Greek artist to his archetypes, or, according to the Aristotelian expression, "the imitation of nature." In spite of all the dream-literature and the numerous dream-anecdotes of the Greeks, we can speak only conjecturally, though with a fair degree of certainty, of their *dreams*. Considering the incredibly precise and unerring visual power of their eyes, as also their manifest and sincere delight in colours, we can hardly refrain (to the shame of every one born later) from assuming for their very dreams a logical causality of lines and contours, colours and groups, a sequence of scenes resembling their best reliefs, the perfection of which would certainly justify us, if a comparison were possible, in designating the dreaming Greeks as Homers and Homer as a dreaming Greek: in a deeper sense than when modern man, in respect to his dreams, ventures to compare himself with Shakespeare.

On the other hand, we should not have to speak conjecturally, if asked to disclose the immense gap which separated the *Dionysian Greek* from the Dionysian barbarian. From all quarters of the Ancient World—to say nothing of the modern—from Rome as far as Babylon, we can prove the existence of Dionysian festivals, the type of which bears, at best, the same relation to the Greek festivals as the bearded satyr, who borrowed his name and attributes from the goat, does to Dionysus himself. In nearly every instance the centre of these festivals lay in extravagant sexual licentiousness, the waves of which overwhelmed all family life and its venerable traditions; the very wildest beasts of nature were let loose here, including that detestable mixture of lust and cruelty which has always seemed to me the genuine "witches'draught." For some time, however, it would seem that the Greeks were perfectly secure and guarded against the feverish agitations of these festivals (—the knowledge of which entered Greece by all the channels of land and sea) by the figure of Apollo himself rising here in full pride, who could not have held out the Gorgon's head to a more dangerous power than this grotesquely uncouth Dionysian. It is in Doric art that this majestically-rejecting attitude of Apollo perpetuated itself. This opposition became more precarious and even impossible, when, from out of the deepest root of the Hellenic nature, similar impulses finally broke forth and made way for themselves: the Delphic god, by a seasonably

gewaltigen Gegner durch eine zur rechten Zeit abgeschlossene Versöhnung die vernichtenden Waffen aus der Hand zu nehmen. Diese Versöhnung ist der wichtigste Moment in der Geschichte des griechischen Kultus: wohin man blickt, sind die Umwälzungen dieses Ereignisses sichtbar. Es war die Versöhnung zweier Gegner, mit scharfer Bestimmung ihrer von jetzt ab einzuhaltenden Grenzlinien und mit periodischer Übersendung von Ehrengeschenken; im Grunde war die Kluft nicht überbrückt. Sehen wir aber, wie sich unter dem Drucke jenes Friedensschlusses die dionysische Macht offenbarte, so erkennen wir jetzt, im Vergleiche mit jenen babylonischen Sakäen und ihrem Rückschritte des Menschen zum Tiger und Affen, in den dionysischen Orgien der Griechen die Bedeutung von Welterlösungsfesten und Verklärungstagen. Erst bei ihnen erreicht die Natur ihren künstlerischen Jubel, erst bei ihnen wird die Zerreißung des *principii individuationis* ein künstlerisches Phänomen. Jener scheußliche Hexentrank aus Wollust und Grausamkeit war hier ohne Kraft: nur die wundersame Mischung und Doppelheit in den Affekten der dionysischen Schwärmer errinnert an ihn – wie Heilmittel an tödliche Gifte erinnern –, jene Erscheinung, daß Schmerzen Lust erwecken, daß der Jubel der Brust qualvolle Töne entreißt. Aus der höchsten Freude tönt der Schrei des Entsetzens oder der sehnende Klagelaut über einen unersetzlichen Verlust. In jenen griechischen Festen bricht gleichsam ein sentimentalischer Zug der Natur hervor, als ob sie über ihre Zerstückelung in Individuen zu seufzen habe. Der Gesang und die Gebärdensprache solcher zwiefach gestimmter Schwärmer war für die homerisch-griechische Welt etwas Neues und Unerhörtes: und insbesondere erregte ihr die dionysische *Musik* Schrecken und Grausen. Wenn die Musik scheinbar bereits als eine apollinische Kunst bekannt war, so war sie dies doch nur, genau genommen, als Wellenschlag des Rhythmus, dessen bildnerische Kraft zur Darstellung apollinischer Zustände entwickelt wurde. Die Musik des Apollo war dorische Architektonik in Tönen, aber in nur angedeuteten Tönen, wie sie der Kithara zu eigen sind. Behutsam ist gerade das Element, als unapollinisch, ferngehalten, das den Charakter der dionysischen Musik und damit der Musik überhaupt ausmacht, die erschütternde Gewalt des Tones, der einheitliche Strom des Melos und die durchaus unvergleichliche Welt der Harmonie. Im dionysischen Dithyrambus wird der Mensch zur höchsten Steigerung aller seiner symbolischen Fähigkeiten gereizt; etwas Nieempfundenes drängt sich zur Äußerung, die Vernichtung des Schleiers der Maja, das Einssein als Genius der Gattung, ja der Natur. Jetzt

effected reconciliation, was now contented with taking the destructive arms from the hands of his powerful antagonist. This reconciliation marks the most important moment in the history of the Greek cult: wherever we turn our eyes we may observe the revolutions resulting from this event. It was the reconciliation of two antagonists, with the sharp demarcation of the boundary-lines to be thenceforth observed by each, and with periodical transmission of testimonials;—in reality, the chasm was not bridged over. But if we observe how, under the pressure of this conclusion of peace, the Dionysian power manifested itself, we shall now recognise in the Dionysian orgies of the Greeks, as compared with the Babylonian Sacæa and their retrogression of man to the tiger and the ape, the significance of festivals of world-redemption and days of transfiguration. Not till then does nature attain her artistic jubilee; not till then does the rupture of the *principium individuationis* become an artistic phenomenon. That horrible "witches' draught" of sensuality and cruelty was here powerless: only the curious blending and duality in the emotions of the Dionysian revellers reminds one of it—just as medicines remind one of deadly poisons—that phenomenon, to wit, that pains beget joy, that jubilation wrings painful sounds out of the breast. From the highest joy sounds the cry of horror or the yearning wail over an irretrievable loss. In these Greek festivals a sentimental trait, as it were, breaks forth from nature, as if she must sigh over her dismemberment into individuals. The song and pantomime of such dually-minded revellers was something new and unheard-of in the Homeric-Grecian world; and the Dionysian *music* in particular excited awe and horror. If music, as it would seem, was previously known as an Apollonian art, it was, strictly speaking, only as the wave-beat of rhythm, the formative power of which was developed to the representation of Apollonian conditions. The music of Apollo was Doric architectonics in tones, but in merely suggested tones, such as those of the cithara. The very element which forms the essence of Dionysian music (and hence of music in general) is carefully excluded as un-Apollonian; namely, the thrilling power of the tone, the uniform stream of the melos, and the thoroughly incomparable world of harmony. In the Dionysian dithyramb man is incited to the highest exaltation of all his symbolic faculties; something never before experienced struggles for utterance—

soll sich das Wesen der Natur symbolisch ausdrücken; eine neue Welt der Symbole ist nötig, einmal die ganze leibliche Symbolik, nicht nur die Symbolik des Mundes, des Gesichts, des Wortes, sondern die volle, alle Glieder rhythmisch bewegende Tanzgebärde. Sodann wachsen die anderen symbolischen Kräfte, die der Musik, in Rhythmik, Dynamik und Harmonie plötzlich ungestüm. Um diese Gesamtentfesselung aller symbolischen Kräfte zu fassen, muß der Mensch bereits auf jener Höhe der Selbstentäußerung angelangt sein, die in jenen Kräften sich symbolisch aussprechen will: der dithyrambische Dionysusdiener wird somit nur von seinesgleichen verstanden! Mit welchem Erstaunen mußte der apollinische Grieche auf ihn blicken! Mit einem Erstaunen, das um so größer war, als sich ihm das Grausen beimischte, daß ihm jenes alles doch eigentlich so fremd nicht sei, ja, daß sein apollinisches Bewußtsein nur wie ein Schleier diese dionysische Welt vor ihm verdecke.

the annihilation of the veil of Mâyâ, Oneness as genius of the race, ay, of nature. The essence of nature is now to be expressed symbolically; a new world of symbols is required; for once the entire symbolism of the body, not only the symbolism of the lips, face, and speech, but the whole pantomime of dancing which sets all the members into rhythmical motion. Thereupon the other symbolic powers, those of music, in rhythmics, dynamics, and harmony, suddenly become impetuous. To comprehend this collective discharge of all the symbolic powers, a man must have already attained that height of self-abnegation, which wills to express itself symbolically through these powers: the Dithyrambic votary of Dionysus is therefore understood only by those like himself! With what astonishment must the Apollonian Greek have beheld him! With an astonishment, which was all the greater the more it was mingled with the shuddering suspicion that all this was in reality not so very foreign to him, yea, that, like unto a veil, his Apollonian consciousness only hid this Dionysian world from his view.

3

Um dies zu begreifen, müssen wir jenes kunstvolle Gebäude der *apollinischen Kultur* gleichsam Stein um Stein abtragen, bis wir die Fundamente erblicken, auf die es begründet ist. Hier gewahren wir nun zuerst die herrlichen *olympischen* Göttergestalten, die auf den Giebeln dieses Gebäudes stehen, und deren Taten, in weithin leuchtenden Reliefs dargestellt, seine Friese zieren. Wenn unter ihnen auch Apollo steht, als eine einzelne Gottheit neben anderen und ohne den Anspruch einer ersten Stellung, so dürfen wir uns dadurch nicht beirren lassen. Derselbe Trieb, der sich in Apollo versinnlichte, hat überhaupt jene ganze olympische Welt geboren, und in diesem Sinne darf uns Apollo als Vater derselben gelten. Welches war das ungeheure Bedürfnis, aus dem eine so leuchtende Gesellschaft olympischer Wesen entsprang?

Wer, mit einer anderen Religion im Herzen, an diese Olympier herantritt und nun nach sittlicher Höhe, ja Heiligkeit, nach unleiblicher Vergeistigung, nach erbarmungsvollen Liebesblicken bei ihnen sucht, der wird unmutig und enttäuscht ihnen bald den Rücken kehren müssen. Hier erinnert nichts an Askese, Geistigkeit und Pflicht: hier redet nur ein üppiges, ja triumphierendes Dasein zu uns, in dem alles

In order to comprehend this, we must take down the artistic structure, of the *Apollonian culture,* as it were, stone by stone, till we behold the foundations on which it rests. Here we observe first of all the glorious *Olympian* figures of the gods, standing on the gables of this structure, whose deeds, represented in far-shining reliefs, adorn its friezes. Though Apollo stands among them as an individual deity, side by side with others, and without claim to priority of rank, we must not suffer this fact to mislead us. The same impulse which embodied itself in Apollo has, in general, given birth to this whole Olympian world, and in this sense we may regard Apollo as the father thereof. What was the enormous need from which proceeded such an illustrious group of Olympian beings?

Whosoever, with another religion in his heart, approaches these Olympians and seeks among them for moral elevation, even for sanctity, for incorporeal spiritualisation, for sympathetic looks of love, will soon be obliged to turn his back on them, discouraged and disappointed. Here nothing suggests asceticism, spirituality, or duty:

Vorhandene vergöttlicht ist, gleichviel ob es gut oder böse ist. Und so mag der Beschauer recht betroffen vor diesem phantastischen Überschwang des Lebens stehn, um sich zu fragen, mit welchem Zaubertrank im Leibe diese übermütigen Menschen das Leben genossen haben mögen, daß, wohin sie sehen, Helena, das »in süßer Sinnlichkeit schwebende« Idealbild ihrer eigenen Existenz, ihnen entgegenlacht. Diesem bereits rückwärtsgewandten Beschauer müssen wir aber zurufen: Geh nicht von dannen, sondern höre erst, was die griechische Volksweisheit von diesem selben Leben aussagt, das sich hier mit so unerklärlicher Heiterkeit vor dir ausbreitet. Es geht die alte Sage, daß König Midas lange Zeit nach dem weisen *Silen*, dem Begleiter des Dionysus, im Walde gejagt habe, ohne ihn zu fangen. Als er ihm endlich in die Hände gefallen ist, fragt der König, was für den Menschen das Allerbeste und Allervorzüglichste sei. Starr und unbeweglich schweigt der Dämon; bis er, durch den König gezwungen, endlich unter gellem Lachen in diese Worte ausbricht: »Elendes Eintagsgeschlecht, des Zufalls Kinder und der Mühsal, was zwingst du mich dir zu sagen, was nicht zu hören für dich das Ersprießlichste ist? Das Allerbeste ist für dich gänzlich unerreichbar: nicht geboren zu sein, nicht zu *sein*, *nichts* zu sein. Das Zweitbeste aber ist für dich – bald zu sterben.«

Wie verhält sich zu dieser Volksweisheit die olympische Götterwelt? Wie die entzückungsreiche Vision des gefolterten Märtyrers zu seinen Peinigungen.

Jetzt öffnet sich uns gleichsam der olympische Zauberberg und zeigt uns seine Wurzeln. Der Grieche kannte und empfand die Schrecken und Entsetzlichkeiten des Daseins: um überhaupt leben zu können, mußte er vor sie hin die glänzende Traumgeburt der Olympischen stellen. Jenes ungeheure Mißtrauen gegen die titanischen Mächte der Natur, jene über allen Erkenntnissen erbarmungslos thronende Moira, jener Geier des großen Menschenfreundes Prometheus, jenes Schreckenslos des weisen Ödipus, jener Geschlechtsfluch der Atriden, der Orest zum Muttermorde zwingt, kurz jene ganze Philosophie des Waldgottes, samt ihren mythischen Exempeln, an der die schwermütigen Etrurier zugrunde gegangen sind – wurde von den Griechen durch jene künstlerische *Mittelwelt* der Olympier fortwährend von neuem überwunden, jedenfalls verhüllt und dem Anblick entzogen. Um leben zu können, mußten die Griechen diese Götter, aus tiefster Nötigung, schaffen: welchen

here only an exuberant, even triumphant life speaks to us, in which everything existing is deified, whether good or bad. And so the spectator will perhaps stand quite bewildered before this fantastic exuberance of life, and ask himself what magic potion these madly merry men could have used for enjoying life, so that, wherever they turned their eyes, Helena, the ideal image of their own existence "floating in sweet sensuality," smiled upon them. But to this spectator, already turning backwards, we must call out: "depart not hence, but hear rather what Greek folk-wisdom says of this same life, which with such inexplicable cheerfulness spreads out before thee." There is an ancient story that king Midas hunted in the forest a long time for the wise *Silenus*, the companion of Dionysus, without capturing him. When at last he fell into his hands, the king asked what was best of all and most desirable for man. Fixed and immovable, the demon remained silent; till at last, forced by the king, he broke out with shrill laughter into these words: "Oh, wretched race of a day, children of chance and misery, why do ye compel me to say to you what it were most expedient for you not to hear? What is best of all is for ever beyond your reach: not to be born, not to *be*, to be *nothing*. The second best for you, however, is soon to die."

How is the Olympian world of deities related to this folk-wisdom? Even as the rapturous vision of the tortured martyr to his sufferings.

Now the Olympian magic mountain opens, as it were, to our view and shows to us its roots. The Greek knew and felt the terrors and horrors of existence: to be able to live at all, he had to interpose the shining dream-birth of the Olympian world between himself and them. The excessive distrust of the titanic powers of nature, the Moira throning inexorably over all knowledge, the vulture of the great philanthropist Prometheus, the terrible fate of the wise Oedipus, the family curse of the Atridæ which drove Orestes to matricide; in short, that entire philosophy of the sylvan god, with its mythical exemplars, which wrought the ruin of the melancholy Etruscans—was again and again surmounted anew by the Greeks through the artistic *middle world* of the Olympians, or at least veiled and withdrawn from sight. To be able to live, the Greeks had, from direst necessity, to create these gods: which process we may perhaps

Hergang wir uns wohl so vorzustellen haben, daß aus der ursprünglichen titanischen Götterordnung des Schreckens durch jenen apollinischen Schönheitstrieb in langsamen Übergängen die olympische Götterordnung der Freude entwickelt wurde: wie Rosen aus dornigem Gebüsch hervorbrechen. Wie anders hätte jenes so reizbar empfindende, so ungestüm begehrende, zum *Leiden* so einzig befähigte Volk das Dasein ertragen können, wenn ihm nicht dasselbe, von einer höheren Glorie umflossen, in seinen Göttern gezeigt worden wäre. Derselbe Trieb, der die Kunst ins Leben ruft, als die zum Weiterleben verführende Ergänzung und Vollendung des Daseins, ließ auch die olympische Welt entstehen, in der sich der hellenische »Wille« einen verklärenden Spiegel vorhielt. So rechtfertigen die Götter das Menschenleben, indem sie es selbst leben – die allein genügende Theodicee! Das Dasein unter dem hellen Sonnenscheine solcher Götter wird als das an sich Erstrebenswerte empfunden, und der eigentliche *Schmerz* der homerischen Menschen bezieht sich auf das Abscheiden aus ihm, vor allem auf das baldige Abscheiden: so daß man jetzt von ihnen, mit Umkehrung der silenischen Weisheit, sagen könnte, »das Allerschlimmste sei für sie, bald zu sterben, das Zweitschlimmste, überhaupt einmal zu sterben.« Wenn die Klage einmal ertönt, so klingt sie wieder vom kurzlebenden Achilles, von dem blättergleichen Wechsel und Wandel des Menschengeschlechts, von dem Untergang der Heroenzeit. Es ist des größten Helden nicht unwürdig, sich nach dem Weiterleben zu sehnen, sei es selbst als Tagelöhner. So ungestüm verlangt, auf der apollinischen Stufe, der »Wille« nach diesem Dasein, so eins fühlt sich der homerische Mensch mit ihm, daß selbst die Klage zu seinem Preisliede wird.

Hier muß nun ausgesprochen werden, daß diese von den neueren Menschen so sehnsüchtig angeschaute Harmonie, ja Einheit des Menschen mit der Natur, für die Schiller das Kunstwort »naiv« in Geltung gebracht hat, keinesfalls ein so einfacher, sich von selbst ergebender, gleichsam unvermeidlicher Zustand ist, dem wir an der Pforte jeder Kultur, als einem Paradies der Menschheit begegnen *müßten*: dies konnte nur eine Zeit glauben, die den Emil Rousseaus sich auch als Künstler zu denken suchte und in Homer einen solchen am Herzen der Natur erzogenen Künstler Emil gefunden zu haben wähnte. Wo uns das »Naive« in der Kunst begegnet, haben wir die höchste Wirkung der apollinischen Kultur zu erkennen: welche immer erst ein Titanenreich zu stürzen und Ungetüme zu töten hat und durch kräftige Wahnvorspiegelungen und

picture to ourselves in this manner: that out of the original Titan thearchy of terror the Olympian thearchy of joy was evolved, by slow transitions, through the Apollonian impulse to beauty, even as roses break forth from thorny bushes. How else could this so sensitive people, so vehement in its desires, so singularly qualified for *sufferings* have endured existence, if it had not been exhibited to them in their gods, surrounded with a higher glory? The same impulse which calls art into being, as the complement and consummation of existence, seducing to a continuation of life, caused also the Olympian world to arise, in which the Hellenic "will" held up before itself a transfiguring mirror. Thus do the gods justify the life of man, in that they themselves live it—the only satisfactory Theodicy! Existence under the bright sunshine of such gods is regarded as that which is desirable in itself, and the real *grief* of the Homeric men has reference to parting from it, especially to early parting: so that we might now say of them, with a reversion of the Silenian wisdom, that "to die early is worst of all for them, the second worst is—some day to die at all." If once the lamentation is heard, it will ring out again, of the short-lived Achilles, of the leaf-like change and vicissitude of the human race, of the decay of the heroic age. It is not unworthy of the greatest hero to long for a continuation of life, ay, even as a day-labourer. So vehemently does the "will," at the Apollonian stage of development, long for this existence, so completely at one does the Homeric man feel himself with it, that the very lamentation becomes its song of praise.

Here we must observe that this harmony which is so eagerly contemplated by modern man, in fact, this oneness of man with nature, to express which Schiller introduced the technical term "naïve," is by no means such a simple, naturally resulting and, as it were, inevitable condition, which *must* be found at the gate of every culture leading to a paradise of man: this could be believed only by an age which sought to picture to itself Rousseau's Émile also as an artist, and imagined it had found in Homer such an artist Émile, reared at Nature's bosom. Wherever we meet with the "naïve" in art, it behoves us to recognise the highest effect of the Apollonian culture, which in the first place has always to overthrow some Titanic empire and slay monsters, and which, through powerful dazzling representations and pleasurable illusions, must have triumphed over

lustvolle Illusionen über eine schreckliche Tiefe der Weltbetrachtung und reizbarste Leidensfähigkeit Sieger geworden sein muß. Aber wie selten wird das Naive, jenes völlige Verschlungensein in der Schönheit des Scheines, erreicht! Wie unaussprechbar erhaben ist deshalb *Homer*, der sich als einzelner zu jener apollinischen Volkskultur verhält wie der einzelne Traumkünstler zur Traumbefähigung des Volks und der Natur überhaupt. Die homerische »Naivität« ist nur als der vollkommene Sieg der apollinischen Illusion zu begreifen: es ist dies eine solche Illusion, wie sie die Natur, zur Erreichung ihrer Absichten, so häufig verwendet. Das wahre Ziel wird durch ein Wahnbild verdeckt: nach diesem strecken wir die Hände aus, und jenes erreicht die Natur durch unsre Täuschung. In den Griechen wollte der »Wille« sich selbst, in der Verklärung des Genius und der Kunstwelt, anschauen; um sich zu verherrlichen, mußten seine Geschöpfe sich selbst als verherrlichenswert empfinden, sie mußten sich in einer höheren Sphäre wiedersehn, ohne daß diese vollendete Welt der Anschauung als Imperativ oder als Vorwurf wirkte. Dies ist die Sphäre der Schönheit, in der sie ihre Spiegelbilder, die Olympischen, sahen. Mit dieser Schönheitsspiegelung kämpfte der hellenische »Wille« gegen das dem künstlerischen korrelative Talent zum Leiden und zur Weisheit des Leidens: und als Denkmal seines Sieges steht Homer vor uns, der naive Künstler.

a terrible depth of world-contemplation and a most keen susceptibility to suffering. But how seldom is the naïve—that complete absorption, in the beauty of appearance—attained! And hence how inexpressibly sublime is *Homer*, who, as unit being, bears the same relation to this Apollonian folk-culture as the unit dream-artist does to the dream-faculty of the people and of Nature in general. The Homeric "naïveté" can be comprehended only as the complete triumph of the Apollonian illusion: it is the same kind of illusion as Nature so frequently employs to compass her ends. The true goal is veiled by a phantasm: we stretch out our hands for the latter, while Nature attains the former through our illusion. In the Greeks the "will" desired to contemplate itself in the transfiguration of the genius and the world of art; in order to glorify themselves, its creatures had to feel themselves worthy of glory; they had to behold themselves again in a higher sphere, without this consummate world of contemplation acting as an imperative or reproach. Such is the sphere of beauty, in which, as in a mirror, they saw their images, the Olympians. With this mirroring of beauty the Hellenic will combated its talent—correlative to the artistic—for suffering and for the wisdom of suffering: and, as a monument of its victory, Homer, the naïve artist, stands before us.

4

Über diesen naiven Künstler gibt uns die Traumanalogie einige Belehrung. Wenn wir uns den Träumenden vergegenwärtigen, wie er, mitten in der Illusion der Traumwelt und ohne sie zu stören, sich zuruft: »es ist ein Traum, ich will ihn weiter träumen«, wenn wir hieraus auf eine tiefe innere Lust des Traumanschauens zu schließen haben, wenn wir andererseits, um überhaupt mit dieser inneren Lust am Schauen träumen zu können, den Tag und seine schreckliche Zudringlichkeit völlig vergessen haben müssen: so dürfen wir uns alle diese Erscheinungen etwa in folgender Weise, unter der Leitung des traumdeutenden Apollo, interpretieren. So gewiß von den beiden Hälften des Lebens, der wachen und der träumenden Hälfte, uns die erstere als die ungleich bevorzugtere, wichtigere, würdigere, lebenswertere, ja allein gelebte dünkt: so möchte ich doch, bei allem Anscheine einer Paradoxie, für jenen geheimnisvollen Grund unseres Wesens, dessen Erscheinung wir sind, gerade die entgegengesetzte

Concerning this naïve artist the analogy of dreams will enlighten us to some extent. When we realise to ourselves the dreamer, as, in the midst of the illusion of the dream-world and without disturbing it, he calls out to himself: "it is a dream, I will dream on"; when we must thence infer a deep inner joy in dream-contemplation; when, on the other hand, to be at all able to dream with this inner joy in contemplation, we must have completely forgotten the day and its terrible obtrusiveness, we may, under the direction of the dream-reading Apollo, interpret all these phenomena to ourselves somewhat as follows. Though it is certain that of the two halves of life, the waking and the dreaming, the former appeals to us as by far the more preferred, important, excellent and worthy of being lived, indeed, as that which alone is lived: yet, with reference to that mysterious ground of our being of which we are the phenomenon, I should, paradoxical as it may

Wertschätzung des Traumes behaupten. Je mehr ich nämlich in der Natur jene allgewaltigen Kunsttriebe und in ihnen eine inbrünstige Sehnsucht zum Schein, zum Erlöstwerden durch den Schein gewahr werde, um so mehr fühle ich mich zu der metaphysischen Annahme gedrängt, daß das Wahrhaft-Seiende und Ur-Eine, als das Ewig-Leidende und Widerspruchsvolle, zugleich die entzückende Vision, den lustvollen Schein zu seiner steten Erlösung braucht: welchen Schein wir, völlig in ihm befangen und aus ihm bestehend, als das Wahrhaft-Nichtseiende, d.h. als ein fortwährendes Werden in Zeit, Raum und Kausalität, mit anderen Worten, als empirische Realität zu empfinden genötigt sind. Sehen wir also einmal von unsrer eignen »Realität« für einen Augenblick ab, fassen wir unser empirisches Dasein, wie das der Welt überhaupt, als eine in jedem Moment erzeugte Vorstellung des Ur-Einen, so muß uns jetzt der Traum als der *Schein des Scheins*, somit als eine noch höhere Befriedigung der Urbegierde nach dem Schein hin gelten. Aus diesem selben Grunde hat der innerste Kern der Natur jene unbeschreibliche Lust an dem naiven Künstler und dem naiven Kunstwerke, das gleichfalls nur »Schein des Scheins« ist. *Raffael*, selbst einer jener unsterblichen »Naiven«, hat uns in einem gleichnisartigen Gemälde jenes Depotenzieren des Scheins zum Schein, den Urprozeß des naiven Künstlers und zugleich der apollinischen Kultur, dargestellt. In seiner *Transfiguration* zeigt uns die untere Hälfte, mit dem besessenen Knaben, den verzweifelnden Trägern, den ratlos geängstigten Jüngern, die Widerspiegelung des ewigen Urschmerzes, des einzigen Grundes der Welt: der »Schein« ist hier Widerschein des ewigen Widerspruchs, des Vaters der Dinge. Aus diesem Schein steigt nun, wie ein ambrosischer Duft, eine visionsgleiche neue Scheinwelt empor, von der jene im ersten Schein Befangenen nichts sehen – ein leuchtendes Schweben in reinster Wonne und schmerzlosem, aus weiten Augen strahlenden Anschauen. Hier haben wir, in höchster Kunstsymbolik, jene apollinische Schönheitswelt und ihren Untergrund, die schreckliche Weisheit des Silen, vor unseren Blicken und begreifen, durch Intuition, ihre gegenseitige Notwendigkeit. Apollo aber tritt uns wiederum als die Vergöttlichung des *principii individuationis* entgegen, in dem allein das ewig erreichte Ziel des Ur-Einen, seine Erlösung durch den Schein, sich vollzieht: er zeigt uns mit erhabenen Gebärden, wie die ganze Welt der Qual nötig ist, damit durch sie der einzelne zur Erzeugung der erlösenden Vision gedrängt werde und dann, ins

seem, be inclined to maintain the very opposite estimate of the value of dream life. For the more clearly I perceive in nature those all-powerful art impulses, and in them a fervent longing for appearance, for redemption through appearance, the more I feel myself driven to the metaphysical assumption that the Verily-Existent and Primordial Unity, as the Eternally Suffering and Self-Contradictory, requires the rapturous vision, the joyful appearance, for its continuous salvation: which appearance we, who are completely wrapt in it and composed of it, must regard as the Verily Non-existent—*i.e.*, as a perpetual unfolding in time, space and causality—in other words, as empiric reality. If we therefore waive the consideration of our own "reality" for the present, if we conceive our empiric existence, and that of the world generally, as a representation of the Primordial Unity generated every moment, we shall then have to regard the dream as an *appearance of appearance*, hence as a still higher gratification of the primordial desire for appearance. It is for this same reason that the innermost heart of Nature experiences that indescribable joy in the naïve artist and in the naïve work of art, which is likewise only "an appearance of appearance." In a symbolic painting, *Raphael*, himself one of these immortal "naïve" ones, has represented to us this depotentiating of appearance to appearance, the primordial process of the naïve artist and at the same time of Apollonian culture. In his *Transfiguration*, the lower half, with the possessed boy, the despairing bearers, the helpless, terrified disciples, shows to us the reflection of eternal primordial pain, the sole basis of the world: the "appearance" here is the counter-appearance of eternal Contradiction, the father of things. Out of this appearance then arises, like an ambrosial vapour, a visionlike new world of appearances, of which those wrapt in the first appearance see nothing—a radiant floating in purest bliss and painless Contemplation beaming from wide-open eyes. Here there is presented to our view, in the highest symbolism of art, that Apollonian world of beauty and its substratum, the terrible wisdom of Silenus, and we comprehend, by intuition, their necessary interdependence. Apollo, however, again appears to us as the apotheosis of the *principium individuationis*, in which alone the perpetually attained end of the Primordial Unity, its redemption through appearance, is consummated: he shows us, with sublime attitudes, how the entire world of torment is necessary, that thereby the

Anschauen derselben versunken, ruhig auf seinem schwankenden Kahne, inmitten des Meeres, sitze.

individual may be impelled to realise the redeeming vision, and then, sunk in contemplation thereof, quietly sit in his fluctuating barque, in the midst of the sea.

Diese Vergöttlichung der Individuation kennt, wenn sie überhaupt imperativisch und Vorschriften gebend gedacht wird, nur *ein* Gesetz, das Individuum, d.h. die Einhaltung der Grenzen des Individuums, das *Maß* im hellenischen Sinne. Apollo, als ethische Gottheit, fordert von den Seinigen das Maß und, um es einhalten zu können, Selbsterkenntnis. Und so läuft neben der ästhetischen Notwendigkeit der Schönheit die Forderung des »Erkenne dich selbst« und des »Nicht zu viel!« her, während Selbstüberhebung und Übermaß als die eigentlich feindseligen Dämonen der nicht-apollinischen Sphäre, daher als Eigenschaften der vor-apollinischen Zeit, des Titanenzeitalters, und der außer-apollinischen Welt, d.h. der Barbarenwelt, erachtet wurden. Wegen seiner titanenhaften Liebe zu den Menschen mußte Prometheus von den Geiern zerrissen werden, seiner übermäßigen Weisheit halber, die das Rätsel der Sphinx löste, mußte Ödipus in einen verwirrenden Strudel von Untaten stürzen: so interpretierte der delphische Gott die griechische Vergangenheit.

This apotheosis of individuation, if it be at all conceived as imperative and laying down precepts, knows but one law—the individual, *i.e.*, the observance of the boundaries of the individual, *measure* in the Hellenic sense. Apollo, as ethical deity, demands due proportion of his disciples, and, that this may be observed, he demands self-knowledge. And thus, parallel to the æsthetic necessity for beauty, there run the demands "know thyself" and "not too much," while presumption and undueness are regarded as the truly hostile demons of the non-Apollonian sphere, hence as characteristics of the pre-Apollonian age, that of the Titans, and of the extra-Apollonian world, that of the barbarians. Because of his Titan-like love for man, Prometheus had to be torn to pieces by vultures; because of his excessive wisdom, which solved the riddle of the Sphinx, Oedipus had to plunge into a bewildering vortex of monstrous crimes: thus did the Delphic god interpret the Grecian past.

»Titanenhaft« und »barbarisch« dünkte dem apollinischen Griechen auch die Wirkung, die das *Dionysische* erregte: ohne dabei sich verhehlen zu können, daß er selbst doch zugleich auch innerlich mit jenen gestürzten Titanen und Heroen verwandt sei. Ja er mußte noch mehr empfinden: sein ganzes Dasein, mit aller Schönheit und Mäßigung, ruhte auf einem verhüllten Untergrunde des Leidens und der Erkenntnis, der ihm wieder durch jenes Dionysische aufgedeckt wurde. Und siehe! Apollo konnte nicht ohne Dionysus leben! Das »Titanische« und das »Barbarische« war zuletzt eine eben solche Notwendigkeit wie das Apollinische! Und nun denken wir uns, wie in diese auf den Schein und die Mäßigung gebaute und künstlich gedämmte Welt der ekstatische Ton der Dionysusfeier in immer lockenderen Zauberweisen hineinklang, wie in diesen das ganze *Übermaß* der Natur in Lust, Leid und Erkenntnis, bis zum durchdringenden Schrei, laut wurde: denken wir uns, was diesem dämonischen Volksgesange gegenüber der psalmodierende Künstler des Apollo, mit dem gespensterhaften Harfenklange, bedeuten konnte! Die Musen der Künste des »Scheins« verblaßten vor einer Kunst, die in ihrem Rausche die Wahrheit sprach, die Weisheit des Silen rief Wehe! Wehe! aus gegen die heiteren Olympier. Das Individuum, mit allen seinen Grenzen

So also the effects wrought by the *Dionysian* appeared "titanic" and "barbaric" to the Apollonian Greek: while at the same time he could not conceal from himself that he too was inwardly related to these overthrown Titans and heroes. Indeed, he had to recognise still more than this: his entire existence, with all its beauty and moderation, rested on a hidden substratum of suffering and of knowledge, which was again disclosed to him by the Dionysian. And lo! Apollo could not live without Dionysus! The "titanic" and the "barbaric" were in the end not less necessary than the Apollonian. And now let us imagine to ourselves how the ecstatic tone of the Dionysian festival sounded in ever more luring and bewitching strains into this artificially confined world built on appearance and moderation, how in these strains all the *undueness* of nature, in joy, sorrow, and knowledge, even to the transpiercing shriek, became audible: let us ask ourselves what meaning could be attached to the psalmodising artist of Apollo, with the phantom harp-sound, as compared with this demonic folk-song! The muses of the arts of "appearance" paled before an art which, in its intoxication, spoke the truth, the wisdom of Silenus cried "woe! woe!" against the

und Maßen, ging hier in der Selbstvergessenheit der dionysischen Zustände unter und vergaß die apollinischen Satzungen. Das *Übermaß* enthüllte sich als Wahrheit, der Widerspruch, die aus Schmerzengeborene Wonne sprach von sich aus dem Herzen der Natur heraus. Und so war, überall dort, wo das Dionysische durchdrang, das Apollinische aufgehoben und vernichtet. Aber ebenso gewiß ist, daß dort, wo der erste Ansturm ausgehalten wurde, das Ansehen und die Majestät des delphischen Gottes starrer und drohender als je sich äußerte. Ich vermag nämlich den *dorischen* Staat und die dorische Kunst mir nur als ein fortgesetztes Kriegslager des Apollinischen zu erklären: nur in einem unausgesetzten Widerstreben gegen das titanisch-barbarische Wesen des Dionysischen konnte eine so trotzig-spröde, mit Bollwerken umschlossene Kunst, eine so kriegsgemäße und herbe Erziehung, ein so grausames und rücksichtsloses Staatswesen von längerer Dauer sein.

Bis zu diesem Punkte ist des weiteren ausgeführt worden, was ich am Eingange dieser Abhandlung bemerkte: wie das Dionysische und das Apollinische, in immer neuen aufeinanderfolgenden Geburten, und sich gegenseitig steigernd, das hellenische Wesen beherrscht haben: wie aus dem »erzenen« Zeitalter, mit seinen Titanenkämpfen und seiner herben Volksphilosophie, sich unter dem Walten des apollinischen Schönheitstriebes die homerische Welt entwickelt, wie diese »naive« Herrlichkeit wieder von dem einbrechenden Strome des Dionysischen verschlungen wird, und wie dieser neuen Macht gegenüber sich das Apollinische zur starren Majestät der dorischen Kunst und Weltbetrachtung erhebt. Wenn auf diese Weise die ältere hellenische Geschichte, im Kampf jener zwei feindseligen Prinzipien, in vier große Kunststufen zerfällt: so sind wir jetzt gedrängt, weiter nach dem letzten Plane dieses Werdens und Treibens zu fragen, falls uns nicht etwa die letzterreichte Periode, die der dorischen Kunst, als die Spitze und Absicht jener Kunsttriebe gelten sollte: und hier bietet sich unseren Blicken das erhabene und hochgepriesene Kunstwerk der *attischen Tragödie* und des dramatischen Dithyrambus, als das gemeinsame Ziel beider Triebe, deren geheimnisvolles Ehebündnis, nach langem vorhergehenden Kampfe, sich in einem solchen Kinde – das zugleich Antigone und Kassandra ist – verherrlicht hat.

cheerful Olympians. The individual, with all his boundaries and due proportions, went under in the self-oblivion of the Dionysian states and forgot the Apollonian precepts. The *Undueness* revealed itself as truth, contradiction, the bliss born of pain, declared itself but of the heart of nature. And thus, wherever the Dionysian prevailed, the Apollonian was routed and annihilated. But it is quite as certain that, where the first assault was successfully withstood, the authority and majesty of the Delphic god exhibited itself as more rigid and menacing than ever. For I can only explain to myself the *Doric* state and Doric art as a permanent war-camp of the Apollonian: only by incessant opposition to the titanic-barbaric nature of the Dionysian was it possible for an art so defiantly-prim, so encompassed with bulwarks, a training so warlike and rigorous, a constitution so cruel and relentless, to last for any length of time.

Up to this point we have enlarged upon the observation made at the beginning of this essay: how the Dionysian and the Apollonian, in ever new births succeeding and mutually augmenting one another, controlled the Hellenic genius: how from out the age of "bronze," with its Titan struggles and rigorous folk-philosophy, the Homeric world develops under the fostering sway of the Apollonian impulse to beauty, how this "naïve" splendour is again overwhelmed by the inbursting flood of the Dionysian, and how against this new power the Apollonian rises to the austere majesty of Doric art and the Doric view of things. If, then, in this way, in the strife of these two hostile principles, the older Hellenic history falls into four great periods of art, we are now driven to inquire after the ulterior purpose of these unfoldings and processes, unless perchance we should regard the last-attained period, the period of Doric art, as the end and aim of these artistic impulses: and here the sublime and highly celebrated art-work of *Attic tragedy* and dramatic dithyramb presents itself to our view as the common goal of both these impulses, whose mysterious union, after many and long precursory struggles, found its glorious consummation in such a child—which is at once Antigone and Cassandra.

5

Wir nahen uns jetzt dem eigentlichen Ziele unsrer Untersuchung, die auf die Erkenntnis des dionysisch-apollonischen Genius und seines Kunstwerkes, wenigstens auf das ahnungsvolle Verständnis jenes Einleitungsmysteriums gerichtet ist. Hier fragen wir nun zunächst, wo jener neue Keim sich zuerst in der hellenischen Welt bemerkbar macht, der sich nachher bis zur Tragödie und zum dramatischen Dithyrambus entwickelt. Hierüber gibt uns das Altertum selbst bildlich Aufschluß, wenn es als die Urväter und Fackelträger der griechischen Dichtung *Homer* und *Archilochus* auf Bildwerken, Gemmen usw. nebeneinander stellt, in der sicheren Empfindung, daß nur diese beiden gleich völlig originalen Naturen, von denen aus ein Feuerstrom auf die gesamte griechische Nachwelt fortfließe, zu erachten seien. Homer, der in sich versunkene greise Träumer, der Typus des apollinischen, naiven Künstlers, sieht nun staunend den leidenschaftlichen Kopf des wild durchs Dasein getriebenen kriegerischen Musendieners Archilochus: und die neuere Ästhetik wußte nur deutend hinzuzufügen, daß hier dem »objektiven« Künstler der erste »subjektive« entgegengestellt sei. Uns ist mit dieser Deutung wenig gedient, weil wir den subjektiven Künstler nur als schlechten Künstler kennen und in jeder Art und Höhe der Kunst vor allem und zuerst Besiegung des Subjektiven, Erlösung vom »Ich« und Stillschweigen jedes individuellen Willens und Gelüstens fordern, ja ohne Objektivität, ohne reines interesseloses Anschauen nie an die geringste wahrhaft künstlerische Erzeugung glauben können. Darum muß unsre Ästhetik erst jenes Problem lösen, wie der »Lyriker« als Künstler möglich ist: er, der, nach der Erfahrung aller Zeiten, immer »ich« sagt und die ganze chromatische Tonleiter seiner Leidenschaften und Begehrungen vor uns absingt. Gerade dieser Archilochus erschreckt uns, neben Homer, durch den Schrei seines Hasses und Hohnes, durch die trunknen Ausbrüche seiner Begierde; ist er, der erste subjektiv genannte Künstler, nicht damit der eigentliche Nichtkünstler? Woher aber dann die Verehrung, die ihm, dem Dichter, gerade auch das delphische Orakel, der Herd der »objektiven« Kunst, in sehr merkwürdigen Aussprüchen erwiesen hat?

Über den Prozeß seines Dichtens hat uns *Schiller* durch eine ihm selbst unerklärliche, doch nicht bedenklich scheinende psychologische Beobachtung Licht gebracht; er gesteht nämlich, als den vorbereitenden Zustand vor dem Aktus des Dichtens

We now approach the real purpose of our investigation, which aims at acquiring a knowledge of the Dionyso-Apollonian genius and his art-work, or at least an anticipatory understanding of the mystery of the aforesaid union. Here we shall ask first of all where that new germ which subsequently developed into tragedy and dramatic dithyramb first makes itself perceptible in the Hellenic world. The ancients themselves supply the answer in symbolic form, when they place *Homer* and *Archilochus* as the forefathers and torch-bearers of Greek poetry side by side on gems, sculptures, etc., in the sure conviction that only these two thoroughly original compeers, from whom a stream of fire flows over the whole of Greek posterity, should be taken into consideration. Homer, the aged dreamer sunk in himself, the type of the Apollonian naïve artist, beholds now with astonishment the impassioned genius of the warlike votary of the muses, Archilochus, violently tossed to and fro on the billows of existence: and modern æsthetics could only add by way of interpretation, that here the "objective" artist is confronted by the first "subjective" artist. But this interpretation is of little service to us, because we know the subjective artist only as the poor artist, and in every type and elevation of art we demand specially and first of all the conquest of the Subjective, the redemption from the "ego" and the cessation of every individual will and desire; indeed, we find it impossible to believe in any truly artistic production, however insignificant, without objectivity, without pure, interestless contemplation. Hence our æsthetics must first solve the problem as to how the "lyrist" is possible as an artist: he who according to the experience of all ages continually says "I" and sings off to us the entire chromatic scale of his passions and desires. This very Archilochus appals us, alongside of Homer, by his cries of hatred and scorn, by the drunken outbursts of his desire. Is not just he then, who has been called the first subjective artist, the non-artist proper? But whence then the reverence which was shown to him—the poet—in very remarkable utterances by the Delphic oracle itself, the focus of "objective" art?

Schiller has enlightened us concerning his poetic procedure by a psychological observation, inexplicable to himself, yet not apparently open to

nicht etwa eine Reihe von Bildern, mit geordneter Kausalität der Gedanken, vor sich und in sich gehabt zu haben, sondern vielmehr eine *musikalische Stimmung* (»Die Empfindung ist bei mir anfangs ohne bestimmten und klaren Gegenstand; dieser bildet sich erst später. Eine gewisse musikalische Gemütsstimmung geht vorher, und auf diese folgt bei mir erst die poetische Idee«). Nehmen wir jetzt das wichtigste Phänomen der ganzen antiken Lyrik hinzu, die überall als natürlich geltende Vereinigung, ja Identität *des Lyrikers* mit *dem Musiker* – der gegenüber unsre neuere Lyrik wie ein Götterbild ohne Kopf erscheint –, so können wir jetzt, auf Grund unsrer früher dargestellten ästhetischen Metaphysik, uns in folgender Weise den Lyriker erklären. Er ist zuerst, als dionysischer Künstler, gänzlich mit dem Ur-Einen, seinem Schmerz und Widerspruch, eins geworden und produziert das Abbild dieses Ur-Einen als Musik, wenn anders diese mit Recht eine Wiederholung der Welt und ein zweiter Abguß derselben genannt worden ist; jetzt aber wird diese Musik ihm wieder, wie in einem *gleichnisartigen Traumbilde*, unter der apollinischen Traumeinwirkung sichtbar. Jener bild- und begrifflose Widerschein des Urschmerzes in der Musik, mit seiner Erlösung im Scheine, erzeugt jetzt eine zweite Spiegelung, als einzelnes Gleichnis oder Exempel. Seine Subjektivität hat der Künstler bereits in dem dionysischen Prozeß aufgegeben: das Bild, das ihm jetzt seine Einheit mit dem Herzen der Welt zeigt, ist eine Traumszene, die jenen Urwiderspruch und Urschmerz, samt der Urlust des Scheines, versinnlicht. Das »Ich« des Lyrikers tönt also aus dem Abgrunde des Seins: seine »Subjektivität« im Sinne der neueren Ästhetiker ist eine Einbildung. Wenn Archilochus, der erste Lyriker der Griechen, seine rasende Liebe und zugleich seine Verachtung den Töchtern des Lykambes kundgibt, so ist es nicht seine Leidenschaft, die vor uns in orgiastischem Taumel tanzt: wir sehen Dionysus und die Mänaden, wir sehen den berauschten Schwärmer Archilochus zum Schlafe niedergesunken – wie ihn uns Euripides in den Bacchen beschreibt, den Schlaf auf hoher Alpentrift, in der Mittagssonne –: und jetzt tritt Apollo an ihn heran und berührt ihn mit dem Lorbeer. Die dionysisch-musikalische Verzauberung des Schläfers sprüht jetzt gleichsam Bilderfunken um sich, lyrische Gedichte, die in ihrer höchsten Entfaltung Tragödien und dramatische Dithyramben heißen.

any objection. He acknowledges that as the preparatory state to the act of poetising he had not perhaps before him or within him a series of pictures with co-ordinate causality of thoughts, but rather a *musical mood* ("The perception with me is at first without a clear and definite object; this forms itself later. A certain musical mood of mind precedes, and only after this does the poetical idea follow with me.") Add to this the most important phenomenon of all ancient lyric poetry, *the union,* regarded everywhere as natural, *of the lyrist with the musician,* their very identity, indeed—compared with which our modern lyric poetry is like the statue of a god without a head—and we may now, on the basis of our metaphysics of æsthetics set forth above, interpret the lyrist to ourselves as follows. As Dionysian artist he is in the first place become altogether one with the Primordial Unity, its pain and contradiction, and he produces the copy of this Primordial Unity as music, granting that music has been correctly termed a repetition and a recast of the world; but now, under the Apollonian dream-inspiration, this music again becomes visible to him as in a *symbolic dream-picture.* The formless and intangible reflection of the primordial pain in music, with its redemption in appearance, then generates a second mirroring as a concrete symbol or example. The artist has already surrendered his subjectivity in the Dionysian process: the picture which now shows to him his oneness with the heart of the world, is a dream-scene, which embodies the primordial contradiction and primordial pain, together with the primordial joy, of appearance. The "I" of the lyrist sounds therefore from the abyss of being: its "subjectivity," in the sense of the modern æsthetes, is a fiction. When Archilochus, the first lyrist of the Greeks, makes known both his mad love and his contempt to the daughters of Lycambes, it is not his passion which dances before us in orgiastic frenzy: we see Dionysus and the Mænads, we see the drunken reveller Archilochus sunk down to sleep—as Euripides depicts it in the Bacchae, the sleep on the high Alpine pasture, in the noonday sun:—and now Apollo approaches and touches him with the laurel. The Dionyso-musical enchantment of the sleeper now emits, as it were, picture sparks, lyrical poems, which in their highest development are called tragedies and dramatic dithyrambs.

Der Plastiker und zugleich der ihm verwandte Epiker ist in das reine Anschauen der Bilder versunken. Der dionysische Musiker ist ohne jedes Bild völlig nur selbst Urschmerz und Urwiederklang desselben. Der lyrische Genius fühlt aus dem mystischen Selbstentäußerungs- und Einheitszustande eine Bilder- und Gleichniswelt hervorwachsen, die eine ganz andere Färbung, Kausalität und Schnelligkeit hat als jene Welt des Plastikers und Epikers. Während der letztgenannte in diesen Bildern und nur in ihnen mit freudigem Behagen lebt und nicht müde wird, sie bis auf die kleinsten Züge hin liebevoll anzuschauen, während selbst das Bild des zürnenden Achilles für ihn nur ein Bild ist, dessen zürnenden Ausdruck er mit jener Traumlust am Scheine genießt – so daß er, durch diesen Spiegel des Scheines, gegen das Einswerden und Zusammenschmelzen mit seinen Gedanken geschützt ist –, so sind dagegen die Bilder des Lyrikers nichts als *er* selbst und gleichsam nur verschiedene Objektivationen von ihm, weshalb er als bewegender Mittelpunkt jener Welt »ich« sagen darf: nur ist diese Ichheit nicht dieselbe, wie die des wachen, empirisch-realen Menschen, sondern die einzige überhaupt wahrhaft seiende und ewige, im Grunde der Dinge ruhende Ichheit, durch deren Abbilder der lyrische Genius bis auf den Grund der Dinge hindurchsieht. Nun denken wir uns einmal, wie er unter diesen Abbildern auch *sich selbst* als Nichtgenius erblickt, d.h. sein »Subjekt«, das ganze Gewühl subjektiver, auf ein bestimmtes, ihm real dünkendes Ding gerichteter Leidenschaften und Willensregungen; wenn es jetzt scheint, als ob der lyrische Genius und der mit ihm verbundene Nichtgenius eins wäre und als ob der erstere von sich selbst jenes Wörtchen »ich« spräche, so wird uns jetzt dieser Schein nicht mehr verführen können, wie er allerdings diejenigen verführt hat, die den Lyriker als den subjektiven Dichter bezeichnet haben. In Wahrheit ist Archilochus, der leidenschaftlich entbrannte, liebende und hassende Mensch, nur eine Vision des Genius, der bereits nicht mehr Archilochus, sondern Weltgenius ist und der seinen Urschmerz in jenem Gleichnisse vom Menschen Archilochus symbolisch ausspricht: während jener subjektiv wollende und begehrende Mensch Archilochus überhaupt nie und nimmer Dichter sein kann. Es ist aber gar nicht nötig, daß der Lyriker gerade nur das Phänomen des Menschen Archilochus vor sich sieht als Wiederschein des ewigen Seins; und die Tragödie beweist, wie weit sich die Visionswelt des Lyrikers von jenem allerdings zunächst stehenden Phänomen entfernen kann.

The artist of the physical, as also the epic poet, who is related to him, is sunk in the pure contemplation of pictures. The Dionysian musician is, without any picture, himself just primordial pain and the primordial re-echoing thereof. The lyric genius is conscious of a world of pictures and symbols—growing out of the state of mystical self-abnegation and oneness—which has a colouring causality and velocity quite different from that of the world of the physical artist and epic poet. While the latter lives in these pictures, and only in them, with joyful satisfaction, and never grows tired of contemplating them with love, even in their minutest characters, while even the picture of the angry Achilles is to him but a picture, the angry expression of which he enjoys with the dream-joy in appearance—so that, by this mirror of appearance, he is guarded against being unified and blending with his figures;—the pictures of the lyrist on the other hand are nothing but *his very* self and, as it were, only different projections of himself, on account of which he as the moving centre of this world is entitled to say "I": only of course this self is not the same as that of the waking, empirically real man, but the only verily existent and eternal self resting at the basis of things, by means of the images whereof the lyric genius sees through even to this basis of things. Now let us suppose that he beholds *himself* also among these images as non-genius, *i.e.*, his subject, the whole throng of subjective passions and impulses of the will directed to a definite object which appears real to him; if now it seems as if the lyric genius and the allied non-genius were one, and as if the former spoke that little word "I" of his own accord, this appearance will no longer be able to lead us astray, as it certainly led those astray who designated the lyrist as the subjective poet. In truth, Archilochus, the passionately inflamed, loving and hating man, is but a vision of the genius, who by this time is no longer Archilochus, but a genius of the world, who expresses his primordial pain symbolically in the figure of the man Archilochus: while the subjectively willing and desiring man, Archilochus, can never at any time be a poet. It is by no means necessary, however, that the lyrist should see nothing but the phenomenon of the man Archilochus before him as a reflection of eternal being; and tragedy shows how far the visionary world of the lyrist may depart from this phenomenon, to which, of course, it is most intimately related.

Schopenhauer, der sich die Schwierigkeit, die der Lyriker für die philosophische Kunstbetrachtung macht, nicht verhehlt hat, glaubt einen Ausweg gefunden zu haben, den ich nicht mit ihm gehen kann, während ihm allein, in seiner tiefsinnigen Metaphysik der Musik, das Mittel in die Hand gegeben war, mit dem jene Schwierigkeit entscheidend beseitigt werden konnte: wie ich dies, in seinem Geiste und zu seiner Ehre, hier getan zu haben glaube. Dagegen bezeichnet er als das eigentümliche Wesen des Liedes folgendes (Welt als Wille und Vorstellung I, S. 295): »Es ist das Subjekt des Willens, d.h. das eigene Wollen, was das Bewußtsein des Singenden füllt, oft als ein entbundenes, befriedigtes Wollen (Freude), wohl noch öfter aber als ein gehemmtes (Trauer), immer als Affekt, Leidenschaft, bewegter Gemütszustand. Neben diesem jedoch und zugleich damit wird durch den Anblick der umgebenden Natur der Singende sich seiner bewußt als Subjekts des reinen, willenlosen Erkennens, dessen unerschütterliche selige Ruhe nunmehr in Kontrast tritt mit dem Drange des immer beschränkten, immer noch dürftigen Wollens: die Empfindung dieses Kontrastes, dieses Wechselspieles ist eigentlich, was sich im Ganzen des Liedes ausspricht und was überhaupt den lyrischen Zustand ausmacht. In diesem tritt gleichsam das reine Erkennen zu uns heran, um uns vom Wollen und seinem Drange zu erlösen: wir folgen; doch nur auf Augenblicke: immer von neuem entreißt das Wollen, die Erinnerung an unsere persönlichen Zwecke, uns der ruhigen Beschauung; aber auch immer wieder entlockt uns dem Wollen die nächste schöne Umgebung, in welcher sich die reine willenlose Erkenntnis uns darbietet. Darum geht im Liede und der lyrischen Stimmung das Wollen (das persönliche Interesse des Zwecks) und das reine Anschauen der sich darbietenden Umgebung wundersam gemischt durcheinander: es werden Beziehungen zwischen beiden gesucht und imaginiert; die subjektive Stimmung, die Affektion des Willens, teilt der angeschauten Umgebung und diese wiederum jener ihre Farbe im Reflex mit: von diesem ganzen so gemischten und geteilten Gemütszustande ist das echte Lied der Abdruck.«

Wer vermöchte in dieser Schilderung zu verkennen, daß hier die Lyrik als eine unvollkommen erreichte, gleichsam im Sprunge und selten zum Ziel kommende Kunst charakterisiert wird, ja als eine Halbkunst, deren *Wesen* darin bestehen solle, daß das Wollen und das reine Anschauen, d.h. der unästhetische und der ästhetische Zustand, wundersam durcheinandergemischt seien? Wir

Schopenhauer, who did not shut his eyes to the difficulty presented by the lyrist in the philosophical contemplation of art, thought he had found a way out of it, on which, however, I cannot accompany him; while he alone, in his profound metaphysics of music, held in his hands the means whereby this difficulty could be definitely removed: as I believe I have removed it here in his spirit and to his honour. In contrast to our view, he describes the peculiar nature of song as follows (*World as Will and Idea,,* I. 295):— "It is the subject of the will, *i.e.,* his own volition, which fills the consciousness of the singer; often as an unbound and satisfied desire (joy), but still more often as a restricted desire (grief), always as an emotion, a passion, or an agitated frame of mind. Besides this, however, and along with it, by the sight of surrounding nature, the singer becomes conscious of himself as the subject of pure will-less knowing, the unbroken, blissful peace of which now appears, in contrast to the stress of desire, which is always restricted and always needy. The feeling of this contrast, this alternation, is really what the song as a whole expresses and what principally constitutes the lyrical state of mind. In it pure knowing comes to us as it were to deliver us from desire and the stress thereof: we follow, but only for an instant; for desire, the remembrance of our personal ends, tears us anew from peaceful contemplation; yet ever again the next beautiful surrounding in which the pure will-less knowledge presents itself to us, allures us away from desire. Therefore, in song and in the lyrical mood, desire (the personal interest of the ends) and the pure perception of the surrounding which presents itself, are wonderfully mingled with each other; connections between them are sought for and imagined; the subjective disposition, the affection of the will, imparts its own hue to the contemplated surrounding, and conversely, the surroundings communicate the reflex of their colour to the will. The true song is the expression of the whole of this mingled and divided state of mind."

Who could fail to see in this description that lyric poetry is here characterised as an imperfectly attained art, which seldom and only as it were in leaps arrives at its goal, indeed, as a semi-art, the essence of which is said to consist in this, that desire and pure contemplation, *i.e.,* the unæsthetic and the æsthetic condition, are wonderfully mingled with each other? We maintain rather, that

behaupten vielmehr, daß der ganze Gegensatz, nach dem wie nach einem Wertmesser auch noch Schopenhauer die Künste einteilt, der des Subjektiven und des Objektiven, überhaupt in der Ästhetik ungehörig ist, da das Subjekt, das wollende und seine egoistischen Zwecke fördernde Individuum nur als Gegner, nicht als Ursprung der Kunst gedacht werden kann. Insofern aber das Subjekt Künstler ist, ist es bereits von seinem individuellen Willen erlöst und gleichsam Medium geworden, durch das hindurch das eine wahrhaft seiende Subjekt seine Erlösung im Scheine feiert. Denn dies muß uns vor allem, zu unserer Erniedrigung *und* Erhöhung, deutlich sein, daß die ganze Kunstkomödie durchaus nicht für uns, etwa unsrer Besserung und Bildung wegen, aufgeführt wird, ja daß wir ebensowenig die eigentlichen Schöpfer jener Kunstwelt sind: wohl aber dürfen wir von uns selbst annehmen, daß wir für den wahren Schöpfer derselben schon Bilder und künstlerische Projektionen sind und in der Bedeutung von Kunstwerken unsre höchste Würde haben – denn nur als *ästhetisches Phänomen* ist das Dasein und die Welt ewig *gerechtfertigt:* – während freilich unser Bewußtsein über diese unsre Bedeutung kaum ein andres ist, als es die auf Leinwand gemalten Krieger von der auf ihr dargestellten Schlacht haben. Somit ist unser ganzes Kunstwissen im Grunde ein völlig illusorisches, weil wir als Wissende mir jenem Wesen nicht eins und identisch sind, das sich, als einziger Schöpfer und Zuschauer jener Kunstkomödie, einen ewigen Genuß bereitet. Nur soweit der Genius im Aktus der künstlerischen Zeugung mit jenem Urkünstler der Welt verschmilzt, weiß er etwas über das ewige Wesen der Kunst; denn in jenem Zustande ist er, wunderbarerweise, dem unheimlichen Bild des Märchens gleich, das die Augen drehn und sich selber anschaun kann; jetzt ist er zugleich Subjekt und Objekt, zugleich Dichter, Schauspieler und Zuschauer.

this entire antithesis, according to which, as according to some standard of value, Schopenhauer, too, still classifies the arts, the antithesis between the subjective and the objective, is quite out of place in æsthetics, inasmuch as the subject *i.e.*, the desiring individual who furthers his own egoistic ends, can be conceived only as the adversary, not as the origin of art. In so far as the subject is the artist, however, he has already been released from his individual will, and has become as it were the medium, through which the one verily existent Subject celebrates his redemption in appearance. For this one thing must above all be clear to us, to our humiliation *and* exaltation, that the entire comedy of art is not at all performed, say, for our betterment and culture, and that we are just as little the true authors of this art-world: rather we may assume with regard to ourselves, that its true author uses us as pictures and artistic projections, and that we have our highest dignity in our significance as works of art—for only as an *æsthetic phenomenon* is existence and the world eternally *justified:*—while of course our consciousness of this our specific significance hardly differs from the kind of consciousness which the soldiers painted on canvas have of the battle represented thereon. Hence all our knowledge of art is at bottom quite illusory, because, as knowing persons we are not one and identical with the Being who, as the sole author and spectator of this comedy of art, prepares a perpetual entertainment for himself. Only in so far as the genius in the act of artistic production coalesces with this primordial artist of the world, does he get a glimpse of the eternal essence of art, for in this state he is, in a marvellous manner, like the weird picture of the fairy-tale which can at will turn its eyes and behold itself; he is now at once subject and object, at once poet, actor, and spectator.

6

In betreff des Archilochus hat die gelehrte Forschung entdeckt, daß er das *Volkslied* in die Literatur eingeführt habe, und daß ihm, dieser Tat halber, jene einzige Stellung neben Homer in der allgemeinen Schätzung der Griechen zukomme. Was aber ist das Volkslied im Gegensatz zu dem völlig apollinischen Epos? Was anders als das *perpetuum vestigium* einer Vereinigung des Apollinischen und des Dionysischen; seine ungeheure, über alle Völker sich

With reference to Archilochus, it has been established by critical research that he introduced the *folk-song* into literature, and, on account thereof, deserved, according to the general estimate of the Greeks, his unique position alongside of Homer. But what is this popular folk-song in contrast to the wholly Apollonian epos? What else but the *perpetuum vestigium* of a union of the Apollonian and the Dionysian? Its enormous diffusion among

erstreckende und in immer neuen Geburten sich steigernde Verbreitung ist uns ein Zeugnis dafür, wie stark jener künstlerische Doppeltrieb der Natur ist: der in analoger Weise seine Spuren im Volkslied hinterläßt, wie die orgiastischen Bewegungen eines Volkes sich in seiner Musik verewigen. Ja es müßte auch historisch nachweisbar sein, wie jede an Volksliedern reich produktive Periode zugleich auf das stärkste durch dionysische Strömungen erregt worden ist, welche wir immer als Untergrund und Voraussetzung des Volksliedes zu betrachten haben.

Das Volkslied aber gilt uns zuallernächst als musikalischer Weltspiegel, als ursprüngliche Melodie, die sich jetzt eine parallele Traumerscheinung sucht und diese in der Dichtung ausspricht. *Die Melodie ist also das Erste und Allgemeine*, das deshalb auch mehrere Objektivationen, in mehreren Texten, an sich erleiden kann. Sie ist auch das bei weitem Wichtigere und Notwendigere in der naiven Schätzung des Volkes. Die Melodie gebiert die Dichtung aus sich, und zwar immer wieder von neuem; nichts andres will uns *die Strophenform des Volksliedes* sagen: welches Phänomen ich immer mit Erstaunen betrachtet habe, bis ich endlich diese Erklärung fand. Wer eine Sammlung von Volksliedern, z.B. des Knaben Wunderhorn, auf diese Theorie hin ansieht, der wird unzählige Beispiele finden, wie die fortwährend gebärende Melodie Bilderfunken um sich aussprüht, die in ihrer Buntheit, ihrem jähen Wechsel, ja ihrem tollen Sichüberstürzen eine dem epischen Scheine und seinem ruhigen Fortströmen wildfremde Kraft offenbaren. Vom Standpunkte des Epos ist diese ungleiche und unregelmäßige Bilderwelt der Lyrik einfach zu verurteilen: und dies haben gewiß die feierlichen epischen Rhapsoden der apollinischen Feste im Zeitalter des Terpander getan.

In der Dichtung des Volksliedes sehen wir also die Sprache auf das stärkste angespannt, *die Musik nachzuahmen*: deshalb beginnt mit Archilochus eine neue Welt der Poesie, die der homerischen in ihrem tiefsten Grunde widerspricht. Hiermit haben wir das einzig mögliche Verhältnis zwischen Poesie und Musik, Wort und Ton bezeichnet: das Wort, das Bild, der Begriff sucht einen der Musik analogen Ausdruck und erleidet jetzt die Gewalt der Musik an sich. In diesem Sinne dürfen wir in der Sprachgeschichte des griechischen Volkes zwei Hauptströmungen unterscheiden, je nachdem die Sprache die Erscheinungs- und Bilderwelt oder die Musikwelt nachahmte. Man denke nur einmal tiefer über die

all peoples, still further enhanced by ever new births, testifies to the power of this artistic double impulse of nature: which leaves its vestiges in the popular song in like manner as the orgiastic movements of a people perpetuate themselves in its music. Indeed, one might also furnish historical proofs, that every period which is highly productive in popular songs has been most violently stirred by Dionysian currents, which we must always regard as the substratum and prerequisite of the popular song.

First of all, however, we regard the popular song as the musical mirror of the world, as the Original melody, which now seeks for itself a parallel dream-phenomenon and expresses it in poetry. *Melody is therefore primary and universal,* and as such may admit of several objectivations, in several texts. Likewise, in the naïve estimation of the people, it is regarded as by far the more important and necessary. Melody generates the poem out of itself by an ever-recurring process. The strophic form of the popular song points to the same phenomenon, which I always beheld with astonishment, till at last I found this explanation. Any one who in accordance with this theory examines a collection of popular songs, such as "Des Knaben Wunderhorn," will find innumerable instances of the perpetually productive melody scattering picture sparks all around: which in their variegation, their abrupt change, their mad precipitance, manifest a power quite unknown to the epic appearance and its steady flow. From the point of view of the epos, this unequal and irregular pictorial world of lyric poetry must be simply condemned: and the solemn epic rhapsodists of the Apollonian festivals in the age of Terpander have certainly done so.

Accordingly, we observe that in the poetising of the popular song, language is strained to its utmost *to imitate music;* and hence a new world of poetry begins with Archilochus, which is fundamentally opposed to the Homeric. And in saying this we have pointed out the only possible relation between poetry and music, between word and tone: the word, the picture, the concept here seeks an expression analogous to music and now experiences in itself the power of music. In this sense we may discriminate between two main currents in the history of the language of the Greek people, according as their language imitated either the world of phenomena and of pictures, or the world of music. One has only to reflect seriously on the linguistic difference with regard to colour, syntactical structure, and

sprachliche Differenz der Farbe, des syntaktischen Baus, des Wortmaterials bei Homer und Pindar nach, um die Bedeutung dieses Gegensatzes zu begreifen; ja es wird einem dabei handgreiflich deutlich, daß zwischen Homer und Pindar die *orgiastischen Flötenweisen des Olympus* erklungen sein müssen, die noch im Zeitalter des Aristoteles, inmitten einer unendlich entwickelteren Musik, zu trunkner Begeisterung hinrissen und gewiß in ihrer ursprünglichen Wirkung alle dichterischen Ausdrucksmittel der gleichzeitigen Menschen zur Nachahmung aufgereizt haben. Ich erinnere hier an ein bekanntes, unserer Ästhetik nur anstößig dünkendes Phänomen unserer Tage. Wir erleben es immer wieder, wie eine Beethovensche Symphonie die einzelnen Zuhörer zu einer Bilderrede nötigt, sei es auch, daß eine Zusammenstellung der verschiedenen, durch ein Tonstück erzeugten Bilderwelten sich recht phantastisch bunt, ja widersprechend ausnimmt: an solchen Zusammenstellungen ihren armen Witz zu üben und das doch wahrlich erklärenswerte Phänomen zu übersehen, ist recht in der Art jener Ästhetik. Ja selbst wenn der Tondichter in Bildern über eine Komposition geredet hat, etwa wenn er eine Symphonie als pastorale und einen Satz als »Szene am Bach«, einen anderen als »lustiges Zusammensein der Landleute« bezeichnet, so sind das ebenfalls nur gleichnisartige, aus der Musik geborne Vorstellungen – und nicht etwa die nachgeahmten Gegenstände der Musik – Vorstellungen, die über den *dionysischen* Inhalt der Musik uns nach keiner Seite hin belehren können, ja die keinen ausschließlichen Wert neben andern Bildern haben. Diesen Prozeß einer Entladung der Musik in Bildern haben wir uns nun auf eine jugendfrische, sprachlich schöpferische Volksmenge zu übertragen, um zur Ahnung zu kommen, wie das strophische Volkslied entsteht, und wie das ganze Sprachvermögen durch das neue Prinzip der Nachahmung der Musik aufgeregt wird.

Dürfen wir also die lyrische Dichtung als die nachahmende Effulguration der Musik in Bildern und Begriffen betrachten, so können wir jetzt fragen: »als was *erscheint* die Musik im Spiegel der Bildlichkeit und der Begriffe?« *Sie erscheint als Wille*, das Wort im Schopenhauerischen Sinne genommen, d.h. als Gegensatz der ästhetischen, rein beschaulichen willenlosen Stimmung. Hier unterscheide man nun so scharf als möglich den Begriff des Wesens von dem der Erscheinung: denn die Musik kann, ihrem Wesen nach, unmöglich Wille sein, weil sie als solcher gänzlich aus dem Bereich der

vocabulary in Homer and Pindar, in order to comprehend the significance of this contrast; indeed, it becomes palpably clear to us that in the period between Homer and Pindar the *orgiastic flute tones of Olympus* must have sounded forth, which, in an age as late as Aristotle's, when music was infinitely more developed, transported people to drunken enthusiasm, and which, when their influence was first felt, undoubtedly incited all the poetic means of expression of contemporaneous man to imitation. I here call attention to a familiar phenomenon of our own times, against which our æsthetics raises many objections. We again and again have occasion to observe how a symphony of Beethoven compels the individual hearers to use figurative speech, though the appearance presented by a collocation of the different pictorial world generated by a piece of music may be never so fantastically diversified and even contradictory. To practise its small wit on such compositions, and to overlook a phenomenon which is certainly worth explaining, is quite in keeping with this æsthetics. Indeed, even if the tone-poet has spoken in pictures concerning a composition, when for instance he designates a certain symphony as the "pastoral" symphony, or a passage therein as "the scene by the brook," or another as the "merry gathering of rustics," these are likewise only symbolical representations born out of music—and not perhaps the imitated objects of music—representations which can give us no information whatever concerning the *Dionysian* content of music, and which in fact have no distinctive value of their own alongside of other pictorical expressions. This process of a discharge of music in pictures we have now to transfer to some youthful, linguistically productive people, to get a notion as to how the strophic popular song originates, and how the entire faculty of speech is stimulated by this new principle of imitation of music.

If, therefore, we may regard lyric poetry as the effulguration of music in pictures and concepts, we can now ask: "how does music *appear* in the mirror of symbolism and conception?" *It appears as will*, taking the word in the Schopenhauerian sense, *i.e.*, as the antithesis of the æsthetic, purely contemplative, and passive frame of mind. Here, however, we must discriminate as sharply as possible between the concept of essentiality and the concept of phenominality; for music, according to its essence, cannot be will, because as such it would have to be wholly banished from the domain of art—for the will is the unæsthetic-in-itself;—yet it appears

Kunst zu bannen wäre – denn der Wille ist das an sich Unästhetische –; aber sie erscheint als Wille. Denn um ihre Erscheinung in Bildern auszudrücken, braucht der Lyriker alle Regungen der Leidenschaft, vom Flüstern der Neigung bis zum Grollen des Wahnsinns; unter dem Triebe, in apollinischen Gleichnissen von der Musik zu reden, versteht er die ganze Natur und sich in ihr nur als das ewig Wollende, Begehrende, Sehnende. Insofern er aber die Musik in Bildern deutet, ruht er selbst in der stillen Meeresruhe der apollinischen Betrachtung, so sehr auch alles, was er durch das Medium der Musik anschaut, um ihn herum in drängender und treibender Bewegung ist. Ja wenn er sich selbst durch dasselbe Medium erblickt, so zeigt sich ihm sein eignes Bild im Zustande des unbefriedigten Gefühls: sein eignes Wollen, Sehnen, Stöhnen, Jauchzen ist ihm ein Gleichnis, mit dem er die Musik sich deutet. Dies ist das Phänomen des Lyrikers: als apollinischer Genius interpretiert er die Musik durch das Bild des Willens, während er selbst, völlig losgelöst von der Gier des Willens, reines ungetrübtes Sonnenauge ist.

Diese ganze Erörterung hält daran fest, daß die Lyrik ebenso abhängig ist vom Geiste der Musik, als die Musik selbst, in ihrer völligen Unumschränktheit, das Bild und den Begriff nicht *braucht*, sondern ihn nur neben sich *erträgt*. Die Dichtung des Lyrikers kann nichts aussagen, was nicht in der ungeheuersten Allgemeinheit und Allgültigkeit bereits in der Musik lag, die ihn zur Bilderrede nötigte. Der Weltsymbolik der Musik ist eben deshalb mit der Sprache auf keine Weise erschöpfend beizukommen, weil sie sich auf den Urwiderspruch und Urschmerz im Herzen des Ur-Einen symbolisch bezieht, somit eine Sphäre symbolisiert, die über alle Erscheinung und vor aller Erscheinung ist. Ihr gegenüber ist vielmehr jede Erscheinung nur Gleichnis: daher kann die *Sprache*, als Organ und Symbol der Erscheinungen, nie und nirgends das tiefste Innere der Musik nach außen kehren, sondern bleibt immer, sobald sie sich auf Nachahmung der Musik einläßt, nur in einer äußerlichen Berührung mit der Musik, während deren tiefster Sinn, durch alle lyrische Beredsamkeit, uns auch keinen Schritt näher gebracht werden kann.

as will. For in order to express the phenomenon of music in pictures, the lyrist requires all the stirrings of passion, from the whispering of infant desire to the roaring of madness. Under the impulse to speak of music in Apollonian symbols, he conceives of all nature, and himself therein, only as the eternally willing, desiring, longing existence. But in so far as he interprets music by means of pictures, he himself rests in the quiet calm of Apollonian contemplation, however much all around him which he beholds through the medium of music is in a state of confused and violent motion. Indeed, when he beholds himself through this same medium, his own image appears to him in a state of unsatisfied feeling: his own willing, longing, moaning and rejoicing are to him symbols by which he interprets music. Such is the phenomenon of the lyrist: as Apollonian genius he interprets music through the image of the will, while he himself, completely released from the avidity of the will, is the pure, undimmed eye of day.

Our whole disquisition insists on this, that lyric poetry is dependent on the spirit of music just as music itself in its absolute sovereignty does not *require* the picture and the concept, but only *endures* them as accompaniments. The poems of the lyrist can express nothing which has not already been contained in the vast universality and absoluteness of the music which compelled him to use figurative speech. By no means is it possible for language adequately to render the cosmic symbolism of music, for the very reason that music stands in symbolic relation to the primordial contradiction and primordial pain in the heart of the Primordial Unity, and therefore symbolises a sphere which is above all appearance and before all phenomena. Rather should we say that all phenomena, compared with it, are but symbols: hence *language*, as the organ and symbol of phenomena, cannot at all disclose the innermost essence, of music; language can only be in superficial contact with music when it attempts to imitate music; while the profoundest significance of the latter cannot be brought one step nearer to us by all the eloquence of lyric poetry.

7

Alle die bisher erörterten Kunstprinzipien müssen wir jetzt zu Hilfe nehmen, um uns in dem Labyrinth zurechtzufinden, als welches wir *den Ursprung der griechischen Tragödie* bezeichnen müssen. Ich denke nichts Ungereimtes zu behaupten, wenn ich sage, daß das Problem dieses Ursprungs bis jetzt noch nicht einmal ernsthaft aufgestellt, geschweige denn gelöst ist, so oft auch die zerflatternden Fetzen der antiken Überlieferung schon kombinatorisch aneinandergenäht und wieder auseinandergerissen sind. Diese Überlieferung sagt uns mit voller Entschiedenheit, *daß die Tragödie aus dem tragischen Chore entstanden ist* und ursprünglich nur Chor und nichts als Chor war: woher wir die Verpflichtung nehmen, diesem tragischen Chore als dem eigentlichen Urdrama ins Herz zu sehen, ohne uns an den geläufigen Kunstredensarten – daß er der idealische Zuschauer sei oder das Volk gegenüber der fürstlichen Region der Szene zu vertreten habe – irgendwie genügen zu lassen. Jener zuletzt erwähnte, für manchen Politiker erhaben klingende Erläuterungsgedanke – als ob das unwandelbare Sittengesetz von den demokratischen Athenern in dem Volkschore dargestellt sei, der über die leidenschaftlichen Ausschreitungen und Ausschweifungen der Könige hinaus immer Recht behalte – mag noch so sehr durch ein Wort des Aristoteles nahegelegt sein: auf die ursprüngliche Formation der Tragödie ist er ohne Einfluß, da von jenen rein religiösen Ursprüngen der ganze Gegensatz von Volk und Fürst, überhaupt jegliche politisch-soziale Sphäre ausgeschlossen ist; aber wir möchten es auch in Hinsicht auf die uns bekannte klassische Form des Chors bei Äschylus und Sophokles für Blasphemie erachten, hier von der Ahnung einer »konstitutionellen Volksvertretung« zu reden, vor welcher Blasphemie andere nicht zurückgeschrocken sind. Eine konstitutionelle Volksvertretung kennen die antiken Staatsverfassungen *in praxi* nicht und haben sie hoffentlich auch in ihrer Tragödie nicht einmal »geahnt«.

Viel berühmter als diese politische Erklärung des Chors ist der Gedanke A. W. Schlegels, der uns den Chor gewissermaßen als den Inbegriff und Extrakt der Zuschauermenge, als den »idealischen Zuschauer« zu betrachten anempfiehlt. Diese Ansicht, zusammengehalten mit jener historischen Überlieferung, daß ursprünglich die Tragödie nur Chor war, erweist sich als das, was sie ist, als eine rohe, unwissenschaftliche, doch glänzende Behauptung, die

We shall now have to avail ourselves of all the principles of art hitherto considered, in order to find our way through the labyrinth, as we must designate *the origin of Greek tragedy.* I shall not be charged with absurdity in saying that the problem of this origin has as yet not even been seriously stated, not to say solved, however often the fluttering tatters of ancient tradition have been sewed together in sundry combinations and torn asunder again. This tradition tells us in the most unequivocal terms, *that tragedy sprang from the tragic chorus,* and was originally only chorus and nothing but chorus: and hence we feel it our duty to look into the heart of this tragic chorus as being the real proto-drama, without in the least contenting ourselves with current art-phraseology—according to which the chorus is the ideal spectator, or represents the people in contrast to the regal side of the scene. The latter explanatory notion, which sounds sublime to many a politician—that the immutable moral law was embodied by the democratic Athenians in the popular chorus, which always carries its point over the passionate excesses and extravagances of kings—may be ever so forcibly suggested by an observation of Aristotle: still it has no bearing on the original formation of tragedy, inasmuch as the entire antithesis of king and people, and, in general, the whole politico-social sphere, is excluded from the purely religious beginnings of tragedy; but, considering the well-known classical form of the chorus in Aeschylus and Sophocles, we should even deem it blasphemy to speak here of the anticipation of a "constitutional representation of the people," from which blasphemy others have not shrunk, however. The ancient governments knew of no constitutional representation of the people *in praxi,* and it is to be hoped that they did not even so much as "anticipate" it in tragedy.

Much more celebrated than this political explanation of the chorus is the notion of A. W. Schlegel, who advises us to regard the chorus, in a manner, as the essence and extract of the crowd of spectators—as the "ideal spectator." This view when compared with the historical tradition that tragedy was originally only chorus, reveals itself in its true character, as a crude, unscientific, yet brilliant assertion, which, however, has acquired its brilliancy only through its concentrated form

ihren Glanz aber nur durch ihre konzentrierte Form des Ausdrucks, durch die echt germanische Voreingenommenheit für alles, was »idealisch« genannt wird, und durch unser momentanes Erstauntsein erhalten hat. Wir sind nämlich erstaunt, sobald wir das uns gut bekannte Theaterpublikum mit jenem Chore vergleichen und uns fragen, ob es wohl möglich sei, aus diesem Publikum je etwas dem tragischen Chore Analoges herauszuidealisieren. Wir leugnen dies im stillen und wundern uns jetzt ebenso über die Kühnheit der Schlegelschen Behauptung wie über die total verschiedene Natur des griechischen Publikums. Wir hatten nämlich doch immer gemeint, daß der rechte Zuschauer, er sei wer er wolle, sich immer bewußt bleiben müsse, ein Kunstwerk vor sich zu haben, nicht eine empirische Realität: während der tragische Chor der Griechen in den Gestalten der Bühne leibhafte Existenzen zu erkennen genötigt ist. Der Okeanidenchor glaubt wirklich den Titan Prometheus vor sich zu sehen und hält sich selbst für ebenso real wie den Gott der Szene. Und das sollte die höchste und reinste Art des Zuschauers sein, gleich den Okeaniden den Prometheus für leiblich vorhanden und real zu halten? Und es wäre das Zeichen des idealischen Zuschauers auf die Bühne zu laufen und den Gott von seinen Martern zu befreien? Wir hatten an ein ästhetisches Publikum geglaubt und den einzelnen Zuschauer um so befähigter gehalten, je mehr er imstande war, das Kunstwerk als Kunst, d.h. ästhetisch zu nehmen; und jetzt deutete uns der Schlegelsche Ausdruck an, daß der vollkommne idealische Zuschauer die Welt der Szene gar nicht ästhetisch, sondern leibhaft empirisch auf sich wirken lasse. O über diese Griechen! seufzten wir; sie werfen uns unsre Ästhetik um! Daran aber gewöhnt, wiederholten wir den Schlegelschen Spruch, so oft der Chor zur Sprache kam.

Aber jene so ausdrückliche Überlieferung redet hier gegen Schlegel: der Chor an sich, ohne Bühne, also die primitive Gestalt der Tragödie und jener Chor idealischer Zuschauer vertragen sich nicht miteinander. Was wäre das für eine Kunstgattung, die aus dem Begriff des Zuschauers herausgezogen wäre, als deren eigentliche Form der »Zuschauer an sich« zu gelten hätte. Der Zuschauer ohne Schauspiel ist ein widersinniger Begriff. Wir fürchten, daß die Geburt der Tragödie weder aus der Hochachtung vor der sittlichen Intelligenz der Masse, noch aus dem Begriff des schauspiellosen Zuschauers zu erklären sei, und halten dies Problem für zu tief, um von so flachen Betrachtungsarten auch nur berührt zu werden.

of expression, through the truly Germanic bias in favour of whatever is called "ideal," and through our momentary astonishment. For we are indeed astonished the moment we compare our well-known theatrical public with this chorus, and ask ourselves if it could ever be possible to idealise something analogous to the Greek chorus out of such a public. We tacitly deny this, and now wonder as much at the boldness of Schlegel's assertion as at the totally different nature of the Greek public. For hitherto we always believed that the true spectator, be he who he may, had always to remain conscious of having before him a work of art, and not an empiric reality: whereas the tragic chorus of the Greeks is compelled to recognise real beings in the figures of the stage. The chorus of the Oceanides really believes that it sees before it the Titan Prometheus, and considers itself as real as the god of the scene. And are we to own that he is the highest and purest type of spectator, who, like the Oceanides, regards Prometheus as real and present in body? And is it characteristic of the ideal spectator that he should run on the stage and free the god from his torments? We had believed in an æsthetic public, and considered the individual spectator the better qualified the more he was capable of viewing a work of art as art, that is, æsthetically; but now the Schlegelian expression has intimated to us, that the perfect ideal spectator does not at all suffer the world of the scenes to act æsthetically on him, but corporeo-empirically. Oh, these Greeks! we have sighed; they will upset our æsthetics! But once accustomed to it, we have reiterated the saying of Schlegel, as often as the subject of the chorus has been broached.

But the tradition which is so explicit here speaks against Schlegel: the chorus as such, without the stage—the primitive form of tragedy—and the chorus of ideal spectators do not harmonise. What kind of art would that be which was extracted from the concept of the spectator, and whereof we are to regard the "spectator as such" as the true form? The spectator without the play is something absurd. We fear that the birth of tragedy can be explained neither by the high esteem for the moral intelligence of the multitude nor by the concept of the spectator without the play; and we regard the problem as too deep to be even so much as touched by such superficial modes of contemplation.

Eine unendlich wertvollere Einsicht über die Bedeutung des Chors hatte bereits Schiller in der berühmten Vorrede zur Braut von Messina verraten, der den Chor als eine lebendige Mauer betrachtete, die die Tragödie um sich herum zieht, um sich von der wirklichen Welt rein abzuschließen und sich ihren idealen Boden und ihre poetische Freiheit zu bewahren.

An infinitely more valuable insight into the signification of the chorus had already been displayed by Schiller in the celebrated Preface to his Bride of Messina, where he regarded the chorus as a living wall which tragedy draws round herself to guard her from contact with the world of reality, and to preserve her ideal domain and poetical freedom.

Schiller kämpft mit dieser seiner Hauptwaffe gegen den gemeinen Begriff des Natürlichen, gegen die bei der dramatischen Poesie gemeinhin geheischte Illusion. Während der Tag selbst auf dem Theater nur ein künstlicher, die Architektur nur eine symbolische sei und die metrische Sprache einen idealen Charakter trage, herrsche immer noch der Irrtum im ganzen: es sei nicht genug, daß man *das* nur als eine poetische Freiheit dulde, was doch das Wesen aller Poesie sei. Die Einführung des Chores sei der entscheidende Schritt, mit dem jedem Naturalismus in der Kunst offen und ehrlich der Krieg erklärt werde. – Eine solche Betrachtungsart ist es, scheint mir, für die unser sich überlegen wähnendes Zeitalter das wegwerfende Schlagwort »Pseudoidealismus« gebraucht. Ich fürchte, wir sind dagegen mit unserer jetzigen Verehrung des Natürlichen und Wirklichen am Gegenpol alles Idealismus angelangt, nämlich in der Region der Wachsfigurenkabinette. Auch in ihnen gibt es eine Kunst, wie bei gewissen beliebten Romanen der Gegenwart: nur quäle man uns nicht mit dem Anspruch, daß mit dieser Kunst der Schiller-Goethesche »Pseudoidealismus« überwunden sei.

It is with this, his chief weapon, that Schiller combats the ordinary conception of the natural, the illusion ordinarily required in dramatic poetry. He contends that while indeed the day on the stage is merely artificial, the architecture only symbolical, and the metrical dialogue purely ideal in character, nevertheless an erroneous view still prevails in the main: that it is not enough to tolerate merely as a poetical license *that* which is in reality the essence of all poetry. The introduction of the chorus is, he says, the decisive step by which war is declared openly and honestly against all naturalism in art.—It is, methinks, for disparaging this mode of contemplation that our would-be superior age has coined the disdainful catchword "pseudo-idealism." I fear, however, that we on the other hand with our present worship of the natural and the real have landed at the nadir of all idealism, namely in the region of cabinets of wax-figures. An art indeed exists also here, as in certain novels much in vogue at present: but let no one pester us with the claim that by this art the Schiller-Goethian "Pseudo-idealism" has been vanquished.

Freilich ist es ein »idealer« Boden, auf dem, nach der richtigen Einsicht Schillers, der griechische Satyrchor, der Chor der ursprünglichen Tragödie, zu wandeln pflegt, ein Boden, hoch emporgehoben über die wirkliche Wandelbahn der Sterblichen. Der Grieche hat sich für diesen Chor die Schwebegerüste eines fingierten *Naturzustandes* gezimmert und auf sie hin fingierte *Naturwesen* gestellt. Die Tragödie ist auf diesem Fundamente emporgewachsen und freilich schon deshalb von Anbeginn an einem peinlichen Abkonterfeien der Wirklichkeit enthoben gewesen. Dabei ist es doch keine willkürlich zwischen Himmel und Erde hineinphantasierte Welt; vielmehr eine Welt von gleicher Realität und Glaubwürdigkeit, wie sie der Olymp samt seinen Insassen für den gläubigen Hellenen besaß. Der Satyr als der dionysische Choreut lebt in einer religiös zugestandenen Wirklichkeit unter der Sanktion des Mythus und des Kultus. Daß mit ihm die Tragödie beginnt, daß aus ihm die dionysische Weisheit der Tragödie spricht, ist ein hier uns ebenso

It is indeed an "ideal" domain, as Schiller rightly perceived, upon—which the Greek satyric chorus, the chorus of primitive tragedy, was wont to walk, a domain raised far above the actual path of mortals. The Greek framed for this chorus the suspended scaffolding of a fictitious *natural state* and placed thereon fictitious *natural beings*. It is on this foundation that tragedy grew up, and so it could of course dispense from the very first with a painful portrayal of reality. Yet it is, not an arbitrary world placed by fancy betwixt heaven and earth; rather is it a world possessing the same reality and trustworthiness that Olympus with its dwellers possessed for the believing Hellene. The satyr, as being the Dionysian chorist, lives in a religiously acknowledged reality under the sanction of the myth and cult. That tragedy begins with him, that the Dionysian wisdom of tragedy speaks through him, is just as surprising a

befremdendes Phänomen, wie überhaupt die Entstehung der Tragödie aus dem Chore. Vielleicht gewinnen wir einen Ausgangspunkt der Betrachtung, wenn ich die Behauptung hinstelle, daß sich der Satyr, das fingierte Naturwesen, zu dem Kulturmenschen in gleicher Weise verhält, wie die dionysische Musik zur Zivilisation. Von letzterer sagt Richard Wagner, daß sie von der Musik aufgehoben werde wie der Lampenschein vom Tageslicht. In gleicher Weise, glaube ich, fühlte sich der griechische Kulturmensch im Angesicht des Satyrchors aufgehoben: und dies ist die nächste Wirkung der dionysischen Tragödie, daß der Staat und die Gesellschaft, überhaupt die Klüfte zwischen Mensch und Mensch einem übermächtigen Einheitsgefühle weichen, welches an das Herz der Natur zurückführt. Der metaphysische Trost – mit welchem, wie ich schon hier andeute, uns jede wahre Tragödie entläßt – daß das Leben im Grunde der Dinge, trotz allem Wechsel der Erscheinungen unzerstörbar mächtig und lustvoll sei, dieser Trost erscheint in leibhafter Deutlichkeit als Satyrchor, als Chor von Naturwesen, die gleichsam hinter aller Zivilisation unvertilgbar leben und trotz allem Wechsel der Generationen und der Völkergeschichte ewig dieselben bleiben.

Mit diesem Chore tröstet sich der tiefsinnige und zum zartesten und schwersten Leiden einzig befähigte Hellene, der mit schneidigem Blicke mitten in das furchtbare Vernichtungstreiben der sogenannten Weltgeschichte, ebenso wie in die Grausamkeit der Natur geschaut hat und in Gefahr ist, sich nach einer buddhistischen Verneinung des Willens zu sehnen. Ihn rettet die Kunst, und durch die Kunst rettet ihn sich – das Leben.

Die Verzückung des dionysischen Zustandes mit seiner Vernichtung der gewöhnlichen Schranken und Grenzen des Daseins enthält nämlich während seiner Dauer ein *lethargisches* Element, in das sich alles persönlich in der Vergangenheit Erlebte eintaucht. So scheidet sich durch diese Kluft der Vergessenheit die Welt der alltäglichen und der dionysischen Wirklichkeit voneinander ab. Sobald aber jene alltägliche Wirklichkeit wieder ins Bewußtsein tritt, wird sie mit Ekel als solche empfunden; eine asketische, willenverneinende Stimmung ist die Frucht jener Zustände. In diesem Sinne hat der dionysische Mensch Ähnlichkeit mit Hamlet: beide haben einmal einen wahren Blick in das Wesen der Dinge getan, sie haben *erkannt*, und es ekelt sie zu handeln; denn ihre Handlung kann nichts am ewigen Wesen der Dinge ändern, sie empfinden es als lächerlich oder

phenomenon to us as, in general, the derivation of tragedy from the chorus. Perhaps we shall get a starting-point for our inquiry, if I put forward the proposition that the satyr, the fictitious natural being, is to the man of culture what Dionysian music is to civilisation. Concerning this latter, Richard Wagner says that it is neutralised by music even as lamplight by daylight. In like manner, I believe, the Greek man of culture felt himself neutralised in the presence of the satyric chorus: and this is the most immediate effect of the Dionysian tragedy, that the state and society, and, in general, the gaps between man and man give way to an overwhelming feeling of oneness, which leads back to the heart of nature. The metaphysical comfort—with which, as I have here intimated, every true tragedy dismisses us—that, in spite of the perpetual change of phenomena, life at bottom is indestructibly powerful and pleasurable, this comfort appears with corporeal lucidity as the satyric chorus, as the chorus of natural beings, who live ineradicable as it were behind all civilisation, and who, in spite of the ceaseless change of generations and the history of nations, remain for ever the same.

With this chorus the deep-minded Hellene, who is so singularly qualified for the most delicate and severe suffering, consoles himself:—he who has glanced with piercing eye into the very heart of the terrible destructive processes of so-called universal history, as also into the cruelty of nature, and is in danger of longing for a Buddhistic negation of the will. Art saves him, and through art life saves him—for herself.

For we must know that in the rapture of the Dionysian state, with its annihilation of the ordinary bounds and limits of existence, there is a *lethargic* element, wherein all personal experiences of the past are submerged. It is by this gulf of oblivion that the everyday world and the world of Dionysian reality are separated from each other. But as soon as this everyday reality rises again in consciousness, it is felt as such, and nauseates us; an ascetic will-paralysing mood is the fruit of these states. In this sense the Dionysian man may be said to resemble Hamlet: both have for once seen into the true nature of things—they have *perceived*, but they are loath to act; for their action cannot change the eternal nature of things; they regard it as shameful or ridiculous that one should require of them to set

schmachvoll, daß ihnen zugemutet wird, die Welt, die aus den Fugen ist, wieder einzurichten. Die Erkenntnis tötet das Handeln, zum Handeln gehört das Umschleiertsein durch die Illusion – das ist die Hamletlehre, nicht jene wohlfeile Weisheit von Hans dem Träumer, der aus zu viel Reflexion, gleichsam aus einem Überschuß von Möglichkeiten, nicht zum Handeln kommt; nicht das Reflektieren, nein! – die wahre Erkenntnis, der Einblick in die grauenhafte Wahrheit überwiegt jedes zum Handeln antreibende Motiv, bei Hamlet sowohl als bei dem dionysischen Menschen. Jetzt verfängt kein Trost mehr, die Sehnsucht geht über eine Welt nach dem Tode, über die Götter selbst hinaus, das Dasein wird, samt seiner gleißenden Wiederspiegelung in den Göttern oder in einem unsterblichen Jenseits, verneint. In der Bewußtheit der einmal geschauten Wahrheit sieht jetzt der Mensch überall nur das Entsetzliche oder Absurde des Seins, jetzt versteht er das Symbolische im Schicksal der Ophelia, jetzt erkennt er die Weisheit des Waldgottes Silen: es ekelt ihn.

Hier, in dieser höchsten Gefahr des Willens, naht sich, als rettende, heilkundige Zauberin, die *Kunst*: sie allein vermag jene Ekelgedanken über das Entsetzliche oder Absurde des Daseins in Vorstellungen umzubiegen, mit denen sich leben läßt: diese sind das *Erhabene* als die künstlerische Bändigung des Entsetzlichen und das *Komische* als die künstlerische Entladung vom Ekel des Absurden. Der Satyrchor des Dithyrambus ist die rettende Tat der griechischen Kunst; an der Mittelwelt dieser dionysischen Begleiter erschöpften sich jene vorhin beschriebenen Anwandlungen.

aright the time which is out of joint. Knowledge kills action, action requires the veil of illusion—it is this lesson which Hamlet teaches, and not the cheap wisdom of John-a-Dreams who from too much reflection, as it were from a surplus of possibilities, does not arrive at action at all. Not reflection, no!—true knowledge, insight into appalling truth, preponderates over all motives inciting to action, in Hamlet as well as in the Dionysian man. No comfort avails any longer; his longing goes beyond a world after death, beyond the gods themselves; existence with its glittering reflection in the gods, or in an immortal other world is abjured. In the consciousness of the truth he has perceived, man now sees everywhere only the awfulness or the absurdity of existence, he now understands the symbolism in the fate of Ophelia, he now discerns the wisdom of the sylvan god Silenus: and loathing seizes him.

Here, in this extremest danger of the will, *art* approaches, as a saving and healing enchantress; she alone is able to transform these nauseating reflections on the awfulness or absurdity of existence into representations wherewith it is possible to live: these are the representations of the *sublime* as the artistic subjugation of the awful, and the *comic* as the artistic delivery from the nausea of the absurd. The satyric chorus of dithyramb is the saving deed of Greek art; the paroxysms described above spent their force in the intermediary world of these Dionysian followers.

8

Der Satyr wie der idyllische Schäfer unserer neueren Zeit sind beide Ausgeburten einer auf das Ursprüngliche und Natürliche gerichteten Sehnsucht; aber mit welchem festen unerschrocknen Griffe faßte der Grieche nach seinem Waldmenschen, wie verschämt und weichlich tändelt der moderne Mensch mit dem Schmeichelbild eines zärtlichen, flötenden, weichgearteten Hirten! Die Natur, an der noch keine Erkenntnis gearbeitet, in der die Riegel der Kultur noch unerbrochen sind – das sah der Grieche in seinem Satyr, der ihm deshalb noch nicht mit dem Affen zusammenfiel. Im Gegenteil: es war das Urbild des Menschen, der Ausdruck seiner höchsten und stärksten Regungen, als begeisterter Schwärmer, den die Nähe des Gottes entzückt, als

The satyr, like the idyllic shepherd of our more recent time, is the offspring of a longing after the Primitive and the Natural; but mark with what firmness and fearlessness the Greek embraced the man of the woods, and again, how coyly and mawkishly the modern man dallied with the flattering picture of a tender, flute-playing, soft-natured shepherd! Nature, on which as yet no knowledge has been at work, which maintains unbroken barriers to culture—this is what the Greek saw in his satyr, which still was not on this account supposed to coincide with the ape. On the contrary: it was the archetype of man, the embodiment of his highest and strongest emotions, as the enthusiastic reveller enraptured By the

mitleidender Genosse, in dem sich das Leiden des Gottes wiederholt, als Weisheitsverkünder aus der tiefsten Brust der Natur heraus, als Sinnbild der geschlechtlichen Allgewalt der Natur, die der Grieche gewöhnt ist mit ehrfürchtigem Staunen zu betrachten. Der Satyr war etwas Erhabenes und Göttliches: so mußte er besonders dem schmerzlich gebrochnen Blick des dionysischen Menschen dünken. Ihn hätte der geputzte, erlogene Schäfer beleidigt: auf den unverhüllten und unverkümmert großartigen Schriftzügen der Natur weilte sein Auge in erhabener Befriedigung; hier war die Illusion der Kultur von dem Urbilde des Menschen weggewischt, hier enthüllte sich der wahre Mensch, der bärtige Satyr, der zu seinem Gotte aufjubelt. Vor ihm schrumpfte der Kulturmensch zur lügenhaften Karikatur zusammen. Auch für diese Anfänge der tragischen Kunst hat Schiller Recht: der Chor ist eine lebendige Mauer gegen die anstürmende Wirklichkeit, weil er – der Satyrchor – das Dasein wahrhaftiger, wirklicher, vollständiger abbildet als der gemeinhin sich als einzige Realität achtende Kulturmensch. Die Sphäre der Poesie liegt nicht außerhalb der Welt, als eine phantastische Unmöglichkeit eines Dichterhirns: sie will das gerade Gegenteil sein, der ungeschminkte Ausdruck der Wahrheit, und muß eben deshalb den lügenhaften Aufputz jener vermeinten Wirklichkeit des Kulturmenschen von sich werfen. Der Kontrast dieser eigentlichen Naturwahrheit und der sich als einzige Realität gebärdenden Kulturlüge ist ein ähnlicher wie zwischen dem ewigen Kern der Dinge, dem Ding an sich, und der gesamten Erscheinungswelt: und wie die Tragödie mit ihrem metaphysischen Troste auf das ewige Leben jenes Daseinskernes, bei dem fortwährenden Untergange der Erscheinungen, hinweist, so spricht bereits die Symbolik des Satyrchors in einem Gleichnis jenes Urverhältnis zwischen Ding an sich und Erscheinung aus. Jener idyllische Schäfer des modernen Menschen ist nur ein Konterfei der ihm als Natur geltenden Summe von Bildungsillusionen; der dionysische Grieche will die Wahrheit und die Natur in ihrer höchsten Kraft – er sieht sich zum Satyr verzaubert.

Unter solchen Stimmungen und Erkenntnissen jubelt die schwärmende Schar der Dionysusdiener: deren Macht sie selbst vor ihren eignen Augen verwandelt, so daß sie sich als wiederhergestellte Naturgenien, als Satyrn, zu erblicken wähnen. Die spätere Konstitution des Tragödienchors ist die künstlerische Nachahmung jenes natürlichen Phänomens; bei der nun allerdings eine Scheidung

proximity of his god, as the fellow-suffering companion in whom the suffering of the god repeats itself, as the herald of wisdom speaking from the very depths of nature, as the emblem of the sexual omnipotence of nature, which the Greek was wont to contemplate with reverential awe. The satyr was something sublime and godlike: he could not but appear so, especially to the sad and wearied eye of the Dionysian man. He would have been offended by our spurious tricked-up shepherd, while his eye dwelt with sublime satisfaction on the naked and unstuntedly magnificent characters of nature: here the illusion of culture was brushed away from the archetype of man; here the true man, the bearded satyr, revealed himself, who shouts joyfully to his god. Before him the cultured man shrank to a lying caricature. Schiller is right also with reference to these beginnings of tragic art: the chorus is a living bulwark against the onsets of reality, because it—the satyric chorus—portrays existence more truthfully, more realistically, more perfectly than the cultured man who ordinarily considers himself as the only reality. The sphere of poetry does not lie outside the world, like some fantastic impossibility of a poet's imagination: it seeks to be the very opposite, the unvarnished expression of truth, and must for this very reason cast aside the false finery of that supposed reality of the cultured man. The contrast between this intrinsic truth of nature and the falsehood of culture, which poses as the only reality, is similar to that existing between the eternal kernel of things, the thing in itself, and the collective world of phenomena. And even as tragedy, with its metaphysical comfort, points to the eternal life of this kernel of existence, notwithstanding the perpetual dissolution of phenomena, so the symbolism of the satyric chorus already expresses figuratively this primordial relation between the thing in itself and phenomenon. The idyllic shepherd of the modern man is but a copy of the sum of the illusions of culture which he calls nature; the Dionysian Greek desires truth and nature in their most potent form;—he sees himself metamorphosed into the satyr.

The revelling crowd of the votaries of Dionysus rejoices, swayed by such moods and perceptions, the power of which transforms them before their own eyes, so that they imagine they behold themselves as reconstituted genii of nature, as satyrs. The later constitution of the tragic chorus is the artistic imitation of this natural phenomenon,

von dionysischen Zuschauern und dionysischen Verzauberten nötig wurde. Nur muß man sich immer gegenwärtig halten, daß das Publikum der attischen Tragödie sich selbst in dem Chore der Orchestra wiederfand, daß es im Grunde keinen Gegensatz von Publikum und Chor gab: denn alles ist nur ein großer erhabener Chor von tanzenden und singenden Satyrn oder von solchen, welche sich durch diese Satyrn repräsentieren lassen. Das Schlegelsche Wort muß sich uns hier in einem tieferen Sinne erschließen. Der Chor ist der »idealische Zuschauer«, insofern er der einzige *Schauer* ist, der Schauer der Visionswelt der Szene. Ein Publikum von Zuschauern, wie wir es kennen, war den Griechen unbekannt: in ihren Theatern war es jedem, bei dem in konzentrischen Bogen sich erhebenden Terrassenbau des Zuschauerraumes, möglich, die gesamte Kulturwelt um sich herum ganz eigentlich zu *übersehen* und in gesättigtem Hinschauen selbst Choreut sich zu wähnen. Nach dieser Einsicht dürfen wir den Chor, auf seiner primitiven Stufe in der Urtragödie, eine Selbstspiegelung des dionysischen Menschen nennen: welches Phänomen am deutlichsten durch den Prozeß des Schauspielers zu machen ist, der, bei wahrhafter Begabung, sein von ihm darzustellendes Rollenbild zum Greifen wahrnehmbar vor seinen Augen schweben sieht. Der Satyrchor ist zu allererst eine Vision der dionysischen Masse, wie wiederum die Welt der Bühne eine Vision dieses Satyrchors ist: die Kraft dieser Vision ist stark genug, um gegen den Eindruck der »Realität«, gegen die rings auf den Sitzreihen gelagerten Bildungsmenschen den Blick stumpf und unempfindlich zu machen. Die Form des griechischen Theaters erinnert an ein einsames Gebirgstal: die Architektur der Szene erscheint wie ein leuchtendes Wolkenbild, welches die im Gebirge herumschwärmenden Bacchen von der Höhe aus erblicken, als die herrliche Umrahmung, in deren Mitte ihnen das Bild des Dionysus offenbar wird.

Jene künstlerische Urerscheinung, die wir hier zur Erklärung des Tragödienchors zur Sprache bringen, ist, bei unserer gelehrtenhaften Anschauung über die elementaren künstlerischen Prozesse, fast anstößig; während nichts ausgemachter sein kann, als daß der Dichter nur dadurch Dichter ist, daß er von Gestalten sich umringt sieht, die vor ihm leben und handeln, und in deren innerstes Wesen er hineinblickt. Durch eine eigentümliche Schwäche der modernen Begabung sind wir geneigt, uns das ästhetische Urphänomen zu kompliziert und abstrakt vorzustellen. Die Metapher ist für den echten Dichter

which of course required a separation of the Dionysian spectators from the enchanted Dionysians. However, we must never lose sight of the fact that the public of the Attic tragedy rediscovered itself in the chorus of the orchestra, that there was in reality no antithesis of public and chorus: for all was but one great sublime chorus of dancing and singing satyrs, or of such as allowed themselves to be represented by the satyrs. The Schlegelian observation must here reveal itself to us in a deeper sense. The chorus is the "ideal spectator" in so far as it is the only *beholder*, the beholder of the visionary world of the scene. A public of spectators, as known to us, was unknown to the Greeks. In their theatres the terraced structure of the spectators' space rising in concentric arcs enabled every one, in the strictest sense, to *overlook* the entire world of culture around him, and in surfeited contemplation to imagine himself a chorist. According to this view, then, we may call the chorus in its primitive stage in proto-tragedy, a self-mirroring of the Dionysian man: a phenomenon which may be best exemplified by the process of the actor, who, if he be truly gifted, sees hovering before his eyes with almost tangible perceptibility the character he is to represent. The satyric chorus is first of all a vision of the Dionysian throng, just as the world of the stage is, in turn, a vision of the satyric chorus: the power of this vision is great enough to render the eye dull and insensible to the impression of "reality," to the presence of the cultured men occupying the tiers of seats on every side. The form of the Greek theatre reminds one of a lonesome mountain-valley: the architecture of the scene appears like a luminous cloud-picture which the Bacchants swarming on the mountains behold from the heights, as the splendid encirclement in the midst of which the image of Dionysus is revealed to them.

Owing to our learned conception of the elementary artistic processes, this artistic proto-phenomenon, which is here introduced to explain the tragic chorus, is almost shocking: while nothing can be more certain than that the poet is a poet only in that he beholds himself surrounded by forms which live and act before him, into the innermost being of which his glance penetrates. By reason of a strange defeat in our capacities, we modern men are apt to represent to ourselves the æsthetic proto-phenomenon as too complex and abstract. For the true poet the metaphor is not

nicht eine rhetorische Figur, sondern ein stellvertretendes Bild, das ihm wirklich, an Stelle eines Begriffes, vorschwebt. Der Charakter ist für ihn nicht etwas aus zusammengesuchten Einzelzügen komponiertes Ganzes, sondern eine vor seinen Augen aufdringlich lebendige Person, die von der gleichen Vision des Malers sich nur durch das fortwährende Weiterleben und Weiterhandeln unterscheidet. Wodurch schildert Homer so viel anschaulicher als alle Dichter? Weil er um so viel mehr anschaut. Wir reden über Poesie so abstrakt, weil wir alle schlechte Dichter zu sein pflegen. Im Grunde ist das ästhetische Phänomen einfach; man habe nur die Fähigkeit, fortwährend ein lebendiges Spiel zu sehen und immerfort von Geisterscharen umringt zu leben, so ist man Dichter; man fühle nur den Trieb, sich selbst zu verwandeln und aus anderen Leibern und Seelen herauszureden, so ist man Dramatiker.

a rhetorical figure, but a vicarious image which actually hovers before him in place of a concept. The character is not for him an aggregate composed of a studied collection of particular traits, but an irrepressibly live person appearing before his eyes, and differing only from the corresponding vision of the painter by its ever continued life and action. Why is it that Homer sketches much more vividly than all the other poets? Because he contemplates much more. We talk so abstractly about poetry, because we are all wont to be bad poets. At bottom the æsthetic phenomenon is simple: let a man but have the faculty of perpetually seeing a lively play and of constantly living surrounded by hosts of spirits, then he is a poet: let him but feel the impulse to transform himself and to talk from out the bodies and souls of others, then he is a dramatist.

Die dionysische Erregung ist imstande, einer ganzen Masse diese künstlerische Begabung mitzuteilen, sich von einer solchen Geisterschar umringt zu sehen, mit der sie sich innerlich eins weiß. Dieser Prozeß des Tragödienchors ist das *dramatische* Urphänomen: sich selbst vor sich verwandelt zu sehen und jetzt zu handeln, als ob man wirklich in einen andern Leib, in einen andern Charakter eingegangen wäre. Dieser Prozeß steht an dem Anfang der Entwicklung des Dramas. Hier ist etwas anderes als der Rhapsode, der mit seinen Bildern nicht verschmilzt, sondern sie, dem Maler ähnlich, mit betrachtendem Auge außer sich sieht; hier ist bereits ein Aufgeben des Individuums durch Einkehr in eine fremde Natur. Und zwar tritt dieses Phänomen epidemisch auf: eine ganze Schar fühlt sich in dieser Weise verzaubert. Der Dithyramb ist deshalb wesentlich von jedem anderen Chorgesange unterschieden. Die Jungfrauen, die, mit Lorbeerzweigen in der Hand, feierlich zum Tempel des Apollo ziehn und dabei ein Prozessionslied singen, bleiben, wer sie sind, und behalten ihren bürgerlichen Namen: der dithyrambische Chor ist ein Chor von Verwandelten, bei denen ihre bürgerliche Vergangenheit, ihre soziale Stellung völlig vergessen ist: sie sind die zeitlosen, außerhalb aller Gesellschaftssphären lebenden Diener ihres Gottes geworden. Alle andere Chorlyrik der Hellenen ist nur eine ungeheure Steigerung des apollinischen Einzelsängers; während im Dithyramb eine Gemeinde von unbewußten Schauspielern vor uns steht, die sich selbst untereinander als verwandelt ansehen.

The Dionysian excitement is able to impart to a whole mass of men this artistic faculty of seeing themselves surrounded by such a host of spirits, with whom they know themselves to be inwardly one. This function of the tragic chorus is the *dramatic* proto-phenomenon: to see one's self transformed before one's self, and then to act as if one had really entered into another body, into another character. This function stands at the beginning of the development of the drama. Here we have something different from the rhapsodist, who does not blend with his pictures, but only sees them, like the painter, with contemplative eye outside of him; here we actually have a surrender of the individual by his entering into another nature. Moreover this phenomenon appears in the form of an epidemic: a whole throng feels itself metamorphosed in this wise. Hence it is that the dithyramb is essentially different from every other variety of the choric song. The virgins, who with laurel twigs in their hands solemnly proceed to the temple of Apollo and sing a processional hymn, remain what they are and retain their civic names: the dithyrambic chorus is a chorus of transformed beings, whose civic past and social rank are totally forgotten: they have become the timeless servants of their god that live aloof from all the spheres of society. Every other variety of the choric lyric of the Hellenes is but an enormous enhancement of the Apollonian unit-singer: while in the dithyramb we have before us a community of unconscious actors, who mutually regard themselves as transformed among one another.

Die Verzauberung ist die Voraussetzung aller dramatischen Kunst. In dieser Verzauberung sieht sich der dionysische Schwärmer als Satyr *und als Satyr wiederum schaut er den Gott*, d.h. er sieht in seiner Verwandlung eine neue Vision außer sich, als apollinische Vollendung seines Zustandes. Mit dieser neuen Vision ist das Drama vollständig.

This enchantment is the prerequisite of all dramatic art. In this enchantment the Dionysian reveller sees himself as a satyr, *and as satyr he in turn beholds the god,* that is, in his transformation he sees a new vision outside him as the Apollonian consummation of his state. With this new vision the drama is complete.

Nach dieser Erkenntnis haben wir die griechische Tragödie als den dionysischen Chor zu verstehen, der sich immer von neuem wieder in einer apollinischen Bilderwelt entladet. Jene Chorpartien, mit denen die Tragödie durchflochten ist, sind also gewissermaßen der Mutterschoß des ganzen sogenannten Dialogs, d.h. der gesamten Bühnenwelt, des eigentlichen Dramas. In mehreren aufeinanderfolgenden Entladungen strahlt dieser Urgrund der Tragödie jene Vision des Dramas aus: die durchaus Traumerscheinung und insofern epischer Natur ist, andrerseits aber, als Objektivation eines dionysischen Zustandes, nicht die apollinische Erlösung im Scheine, sondern im Gegenteil das Zerbrechen des Individuums und sein Einswerden mit dem Ursein darstellt. Somit ist das Drama die apollinische Versinnlichung dionysischer Erkenntnisse und Wirkungen und dadurch wie durch eine ungeheure Kluft vom Epos abgeschieden.

According to this view, we must understand Greek tragedy as the Dionysian chorus, which always disburdens itself anew in an Apollonian world of pictures. The choric parts, therefore, with which tragedy is interlaced, are in a manner the mother-womb of the entire so-called dialogue, that is, of the whole stage-world, of the drama proper. In several successive outbursts does this primordial basis of tragedy beam forth the vision of the drama, which is a dream-phenomenon throughout, and, as such, epic in character: on the other hand, however, as objectivation of a Dionysian state, it does not represent the Apollonian redemption in appearance, but, conversely, the dissolution of the individual and his unification with primordial existence. Accordingly, the drama is the Apollonian embodiment of Dionysian perceptions and influences, and is thereby separated from the epic as by an immense gap.

Der *Chor* der griechischen Tragödie, das Symbol der gesamten dionysisch erregten Masse, findet an dieser unserer Auffassung seine volle Erklärung. Während wir, mit der Gewöhnung an die Stellung eines Chors auf der modernen Bühne, zumal eines Opernchors, gar nicht begreifen konnten, wie jener tragische Chor der Griechen älter, ursprünglicher, ja wichtiger sein sollte, als die eigentliche »Aktion« – wie dies doch so deutlich überliefert war –, während wir wiederum mit jener überlieferten hohen Wichtigkeit und Ursprünglichkeit nicht reimen konnten, warum er doch nur aus niedrigen dienenden Wesen, ja zuerst nur aus bocksartigen Satyrn zusammengesetzt worden sei, während uns die Orchestra vor der Szene immer ein Rätsel blieb, sind wir jetzt zu der Einsicht gekommen, daß die Szene samt der Aktion im Grunde und ursprünglich nur als *Vision* gedacht wurde, daß die einzige »Realität« eben der Chor ist, der die Vision aus sich erzeugt und von ihr mit der ganzen Symbolik des Tanzes, des Tones und des Wortes redet. Dieser Chor schaut in seiner Vision seinen Herrn und Meister Dionysus und ist darum ewig der *dienende* Chor: er sieht, wie dieser, der Gott, leidet und sich verherrlicht, und *handelt* deshalb selbst nicht. Bei

The *chorus* of Greek tragedy, the symbol of the mass of the people moved by Dionysian excitement, is thus fully explained by our conception of it as here set forth. Whereas, being accustomed to the position of a chorus on the modern stage, especially an operatic chorus, we could never comprehend why the tragic chorus of the Greeks should be older, more primitive, indeed, more important than the "action" proper—as has been so plainly declared by the voice of tradition; whereas, furthermore, we could not reconcile with this traditional paramount importance and primitiveness the fact of the chorus' being composed only of humble, ministering beings; indeed, at first only of goatlike satyrs; whereas, finally, the orchestra before the scene was always a riddle to us; we have learned to comprehend at length that the scene, together with the action, was fundamentally and originally conceived only as a *vision,* that the only reality is just the chorus, which of itself generates the vision and speaks thereof with the entire symbolism of dancing, tone, and word. This chorus beholds in the vision its lord and master Dionysus, and is thus for ever the *serving* chorus: it sees how he, the god, suffers and glorifies

dieser, dem Gotte gegenüber durchaus dienenden Stellung ist er doch der höchste, nämlich dionysische Ausdruck der *Natur* und redet darum, wie diese, in der Begeisterung Orakel- und Weisheitssprüche: als der *mitleidende* ist er zugleich der *weise*, aus dem Herzen der Welt die Wahrheit verkündende. So entsteht denn jene phantastische und so anstößig scheinende Figur des weisen und begeisterten Satyrs, der zugleich »der tumbe Mensch« im Gegensatz zum Gotte ist: Abbild der Natur und ihrer stärksten Triebe, ja Symbol derselben und zugleich Verkünder ihrer Weisheit und Kunst: Musiker, Dichter, Tänzer, Geisterseher in *einer* Person.

Dionysus, der eigentliche Bühnenheld und Mittelpunkt der Vision, ist gemäß dieser Erkenntnis und gemäß der Überlieferung, zuerst, in der allerältesten Periode der Tragödie, nicht wahrhaft vorhanden, sondern wird nur als vorhanden vorgestellt: d.h. ursprünglich ist die Tragödie nur »Chor« und nicht »Drama«. Später wird nun der Versuch gemacht, den Gott als einen realen zu zeigen und die Visionsgestalt samt der verklärenden Umrahmung als jedem Auge sichtbar darzustellen: damit beginnt das »Drama« im engeren Sinne. Jetzt bekommt der dithyrambische Chor die Aufgabe, die Stimmung der Zuhörer bis zu dem Grade dionysisch anzuregen, daß sie, wenn der tragische Held auf der Bühne erscheint, nicht etwa den unförmlich maskierten Menschen sehen, sondern eine gleichsam aus ihrer eignen Verzückung geborene Visionsgestalt. Denken wir uns Admet mit tiefem Sinnen seiner jüngst abgeschiedenen Gattin Alcestis gedenkend und ganz im geistigen Anschauen derselben sich verzehrend – wie ihm nun plötzlich ein ähnlich gestaltetes, ähnlich schreitendes Frauenbild in Verhüllung entgegengeführt wird: denken wir uns seine plötzliche zitternde Unruhe, sein stürmisches Vergleichen, seine instinktive Überzeugung – so haben wir ein Analogon zu der Empfindung, mit der der dionysisch erregte Zuschauer den Gott auf der Bühne heranschreiten sah, mit dessen Leiden er bereits eins geworden ist. Unwillkürlich übertrug er das ganze magisch vor seiner Seele zitternde Bild des Gottes auf jene maskierte Gestalt und löste ihre Realität gleichsam in eine geisterhafte Unwirklichkeit auf. Dies ist der apollinische Traumeszustand, in dem die Welt des Tages sich verschleiert und eine neue Welt, deutlicher, verständlicher, ergreifender als jene und doch schattengleicher, in fortwährendem Wechsel sich unserem Auge neu gebiert. Demgemäß erkennen wir in der Tragödie einen durchgreifenden Stilgegensatz: Sprache, Farbe, Beweglichkeit,

himself, and therefore does not itself *act*. But though its attitude towards the god is throughout the attitude of ministration, this is nevertheless the highest expression, the Dionysian expression of *Nature*, and therefore, like Nature herself, the chorus utters oracles and wise sayings when transported with enthusiasm: as *fellow-sufferer* it is also the *sage* proclaiming truth from out the heart of Nature. Thus, then, originates the fantastic figure, which seems so shocking, of the wise and enthusiastic satyr, who is at the same time "the dumb man" in contrast to the god: the image of Nature and her strongest impulses, yea, the symbol of Nature, and at the same time the herald of her art and wisdom: musician, poet, dancer, and visionary in one person.

Agreeably to this view, and agreeably to tradition, *Dionysus*, the proper stage-hero and focus of vision, is not at first actually present in the oldest period of tragedy, but is only imagined as present: *i.e.*, tragedy is originally only "chorus" and not "drama." Later on the attempt is made to exhibit the god as real and to display the visionary figure together with its glorifying encirclement before the eyes of all; it is here that the "drama" in the narrow sense of the term begins. To the dithyrambic chorus is now assigned the task of exciting the minds of the hearers to such a pitch of Dionysian frenzy, that, when the tragic hero appears on the stage, they do not behold in him, say, the unshapely masked man, but a visionary figure, born as it were of their own ecstasy. Let us picture Admetes thinking in profound meditation of his lately departed wife Alcestis, and quite consuming himself in spiritual contemplation thereof—when suddenly the veiled figure of a woman resembling her in form and gait is led towards him: let us picture his sudden trembling anxiety, his agitated comparisons, his instinctive conviction—and we shall have an analogon to the sensation with which the spectator, excited to Dionysian frenzy, saw the god approaching on the stage, a god with whose sufferings he had already become identified. He involuntarily transferred the entire picture of the god, fluttering magically before his soul, to this masked figure and resolved its reality as it were into a phantasmal unreality. This is the Apollonian dream-state, in which the world of day is veiled, and a new world, clearer, more intelligible, more striking than the former, and nevertheless more shadowy, is ever born anew in perpetual change before our eyes. We accordingly recognise in

Dynamik der Rede treten in der dionysischen Lyrik des Chors und andrerseits in der apollinischen Traumwelt der Szene als völlig gesonderte Sphären des Ausdrucks auseinander. Die apollinischen Erscheinungen, in denen sich Dionysus objektiviert, sind nicht mehr »ein ewiges Meer, ein wechselnd Weben, ein glühend Leben«, wie es die Musik des Chors ist, nicht mehr jene nur empfundenen, nicht zum Bilde verdichteten Kräfte, in denen der begeisterte Dionysusdiener die Nähe des Gottes spürt: jetzt spricht, von der Szene aus, die Deutlichkeit und Festigkeit der epischen Gestaltung zu ihm, jetzt redet Dionysus nicht mehr durch Kräfte, sondern als epischer Held, fast mit der Sprache Homers.

tragedy a thorough-going stylistic contrast: the language, colour, flexibility and dynamics of the dialogue fall apart in the Dionysian lyrics of the chorus on the one hand, and in the Apollonian dream-world of the scene on the other, into entirely separate spheres of expression. The Apollonian appearances, in which Dionysus objectifies himself, are no longer "An eternal sea, A weaving, flowing, Life, all glowing,"[7] as is the music of the chorus, they are no longer the forces merely felt, but not condensed into a picture, by which the inspired votary of Dionysus divines the proximity of his god: the clearness and firmness of epic form now speak to him from the scene, Dionysus now no longer speaks through forces, but as an epic hero, almost in the language of Homer

9

Alles, was im apollinischen Teile der griechischen Tragödie, im Dialoge, auf die Oberfläche kommt, sieht einfach, durchsichtig, schön aus. In diesem Sinne ist der Dialog ein Abbild des Hellenen, dessen Natur sich im Tanze offenbart, weil im Tanze die größte Kraft nur potenziell ist, aber sich in der Geschmeidigkeit und Üppigkeit der Bewegung verrät. So überrascht uns die Sprache der sophokleischen Helden durch ihre apollinische Bestimmtheit und Helligkeit, so daß wir sofort bis in den innersten Grund ihres Wesens zu blicken wähnen, mit einigem Erstaunen, daß der Weg bis zu diesem Grunde so kurz ist. Sehen wir aber einmal von dem auf die Oberfläche kommenden und sichtbar werdenden Charakter des Helden ab – der im Grunde nichts mehr ist als das auf eine dunkle Wand geworfene Lichtbild, d.h. Erscheinung durch und durch –, dringen wir vielmehr in den Mythus ein, der in diesen hellen Spiegelungen sich projiziert, so erleben wir plötzlich ein Phänomen, das ein umgekehrtes Verhältnis zu einem bekannten optischen hat. Wenn wir bei einem kräftigen Versuch, die Sonne ins Auge zu fassen, uns geblendet abwenden, so haben wir dunkle farbige Flecken gleichsam als Heilmittel vor den Augen: umgekehrt sind jene Lichtbildererscheinungen des sophokleischen Helden, kurz das Apollinische der Maske, notwendige Erzeugungen eines Blickes ins Innere und Schreckliche der Natur, gleichsam leuchtende Flecken zur Heilung des von grausiger Nacht versehrten Blickes. Nur in diesem Sinne dürfen wir glauben, den ernsthaften und bedeutenden Begriff

Whatever rises to the surface in the dialogue of the Apollonian part of Greek tragedy, appears simple, transparent, beautiful. In this sense the dialogue is a copy of the Hellene, whose nature reveals itself in the dance, because in the dance the greatest energy is merely potential, but betrays itself nevertheless in flexible and vivacious movements. The language of the Sophoclean heroes, for instance, surprises us by its Apollonian precision and clearness, so that we at once imagine we see into the innermost recesses of their being, and marvel not a little that the way to these recesses is so short. But if for the moment we disregard the character of the hero which rises to the surface and grows visible—and which at bottom is nothing but the light-picture cast on a dark wall, that is, appearance through and through—if rather we enter into the myth which projects itself in these bright mirrorings, we shall of a sudden experience a phenomenon which bears a reverse relation to one familiar in optics. When, after a vigorous effort to gaze into the sun, we turn away blinded, we have dark-coloured spots before our eyes as restoratives, so to speak; while, on the contrary, those light-picture phenomena of the Sophoclean hero—in short, the Apollonian of the mask—are the necessary productions of a glance into the secret and terrible things of nature, as it were shining spots to heal the eye which dire night has seared. Only in this sense can we hope to be able to grasp the true meaning of the serious and significant notion of

[7] *Faust, sc.1.*

der »griechischen Heiterkeit« richtig zu fassen; während wir allerdings den falsch verstandenen Begriff dieser Heiterkeit im Zustande ungefährdeten Behagens auf allen Wegen und Stegen der Gegenwart antreffen.

Die leidvollste Gestalt der griechischen Bühne, der unglückselige *Ödipus*, ist von Sophokles als der edle Mensch verstanden worden, der zum Irrtum und zum Elend trotz seiner Weisheit bestimmt ist, der aber am Ende durch sein ungeheures Leiden eine magische segensreiche Kraft um sich ausübt, die noch über sein Verscheiden hinaus wirksam ist. Der edle Mensch sündigt nicht, will uns der tiefsinnige Dichter sagen: durch sein Handeln mag jedes Gesetz, jede natürliche Ordnung, ja die sittliche Welt zugrunde gehen, eben durch dieses Handeln wird ein höherer magischer Kreis von Wirkungen gezogen, die eine neue Welt auf den Ruinen der umgestürzten alten gründen. Das will uns der Dichter, insofern er zugleich religiöser Denker ist, sagen: als Dichter zeigt er uns zuerst einen wunderbar geschürzten Prozeßknoten, den der Richter langsam, Glied für Glied, zu seinem eigenen Verderben löst; die echt hellenische Freude an dieser dialektischen Lösung ist so groß, daß hierdurch ein Zug von überlegener Heiterkeit über das ganze Werk kommt, der den schauderhaften Voraussetzungen jenes Prozesses überall die Spitze abbricht. Im »Ödipus auf Kolonos« treffen wir diese selbe Heiterkeit, aber in eine unendliche Verklärung emporgehoben; dem vom Übermaße des Elends betroffenen Greise gegenüber, der allem, was ihn betrifft, rein als *Leidender* preisgegeben ist – steht die überirdische Heiterkeit, die aus göttlicher Sphäre herniederkommt und uns andeutet, daß der Held in seinem rein passiven Verhalten seine höchste Aktivität erlangt, die weit über sein Leben hinausgreift, während sein bewußtes Dichten und Trachten im früheren Leben ihn nur zur Passivität geführt hat. So wird der für das sterbliche Auge unauflöslich verschlungene Prozeßknoten der Ödipusfabel langsam entwirrt – und die tiefste menschliche Freude überkommt uns bei diesem göttlichen Gegenstück der Dialektik. Wenn wir mit dieser Erklärung dem Dichter gerecht geworden sind, so kann doch immer noch gefragt werden, ob damit der Inhalt des Mythus erschöpft ist: und hier zeigt sich, daß die ganze Auffassung des Dichters nichts ist als eben jenes Lichtbild, welches uns, nach einem Blick in den Abgrund, die heilende Natur vorhält. Ödipus der Mörder seines Vaters, der Gatte seiner Mutter, Ödipus der Rätsellöser der Sphinx! Was sagt uns die geheimnisvolle Dreiheit dieser

"Greek cheerfulness"; while of course we encounter the misunderstood notion of this cheerfulness, as resulting from a state of unendangered comfort, on all the ways and paths of the present time.

The most sorrowful figure of the Greek stage, the hapless *Oedipus,* was understood by Sophocles as the noble man, who in spite of his wisdom was destined to error and misery, but nevertheless through his extraordinary sufferings ultimately exerted a magical, wholesome influence on all around him, which continues effective even after his death. The noble man does not sin; this is what the thoughtful poet wishes to tell us: all laws, all natural order, yea, the moral world itself, may be destroyed through his action, but through this very action a higher magic circle of influences is brought into play, which establish a new world on the ruins of the old that has been overthrown. This is what the poet, in so far as he is at the same time a religious thinker, wishes to tell us: as poet, he shows us first of all a wonderfully complicated legal mystery, which the judge slowly unravels, link by link, to his own destruction. The truly Hellenic delight at this dialectical loosening is so great, that a touch of surpassing cheerfulness is thereby communicated to the entire play, which everywhere blunts the edge of the horrible presuppositions of the procedure. In the "Oedipus at Colonus" we find the same cheerfulness, elevated, however, to an infinite transfiguration: in contrast to the aged king, subjected to an excess of misery, and exposed solely as a *sufferer* to all that befalls him, we have here a supermundane cheerfulness, which descends from a divine sphere and intimates to us that in his purely passive attitude the hero attains his highest activity, the influence of which extends far beyond his life, while his earlier conscious musing and striving led him only to passivity. Thus, then, the legal knot of the fable of Oedipus, which to mortal eyes appears indissolubly entangled, is slowly unravelled—and the profoundest human joy comes upon us in the presence of this divine counterpart of dialectics. If this explanation does justice to the poet, it may still be asked whether the substance of the myth is thereby exhausted; and here it turns out that the entire conception of the poet is nothing but the light-picture which healing nature holds up to us after a glance into the abyss. Oedipus, the murderer of his father, the husband of his mother, Oedipus, the interpreter of the

Schicksalstaten? Es gibt einen uralten, besonders persischen Volksglauben, daß ein weiser Magier nur aus Inzest geboren werden könne: was wir uns, im Hinblick auf den rätsellösenden und seine Mutter freienden Ödipus, sofort so zu interpretieren haben, daß dort, wo durch weissagende und magische Kräfte der Bann von Gegenwart und Zukunft, das starre Gesetz der Individuation und überhaupt der eigentliche Zauber der Natur gebrochen ist, eine ungeheure Naturwidrigkeit – wie dort der Inzest – als Ursache vorausgegangen sein muß; denn wie könnte man die Natur zum Preisgeben ihrer Geheimnisse zwingen, wenn nicht dadurch, daß man ihr siegreich widerstrebt, d.h. durch das Unnatürliche? Diese Erkenntnis sehe ich in jener entsetzlichen Dreiheit der Ödipusschicksale ausgeprägt: derselbe, der das Rätsel der Natur – jener doppelgearteten Sphinx – löst, muß auch als Mörder des Vaters und Gatte der Mutter die heiligsten Naturordnungen zerbrechen. Ja der Mythus scheint uns zuraunen zu wollen, daß die Weisheit und gerade die dionysische Weisheit ein naturwidriger Greuel sei, daß der, welcher durch sein Wissen die Natur in den Abgrund der Vernichtung stürzt, auch an sich selbst die Auflösung der Natur zu erfahren habe. »Die Spitze der Weisheit kehrt sich gegen den Weisen; Weisheit ist ein Verbrechen an der Natur«: solche schreckliche Sätze ruft uns der Mythus zu: der hellenische Dichter aber berührt wie ein Sonnenstrahl die erhabene und furchtbare Memnonssäule des Mythus, so daß er plötzlich zu tönen beginnt – in sophokleischen Melodien!

Der Glorie der Passivität stelle ich jetzt die Glorie der Aktivität gegenüber, welche den *Prometheus* des Äschylus umleuchtet. Was uns hier der Denker Äschylus zu sagen hatte, was er aber als Dichter durch sein gleichnisartiges Bild uns nur ahnen läßt, das hat uns der jugendliche Goethe in den verwegenen Worten seines Prometheus zu enthüllen gewußt:

»Hier sitz ich, forme Menschen
Nach meinem Bilde,
Ein Geschlecht, das mir gleich sei,
Zu leiden, zu weinen,
Zu genießen und zu freuen sich,
Und dein nicht zu achten,
Wie ich!«

Der Mensch, ins Titanische sich steigernd, erkämpft sich selbst seine Kultur und zwingt die Götter, sich mit ihm zu verbinden, weil er in seiner selbsteignen Weisheit die Existenz und die Schranken derselben in seiner Hand hat. Das Wunderbarste an jenem

riddle of the Sphinx! What does the mysterious triad of these deeds of destiny tell us? There is a primitive popular belief, especially in Persia, that a wise Magian can be born only of incest: which we have forthwith to interpret to ourselves with reference to the riddle-solving and mother-marrying Oedipus, to the effect that when the boundary of the present and future, the rigid law of individuation and, in general, the intrinsic spell of nature, are broken by prophetic and magical powers, an extraordinary counter-naturalness—as, in this case, incest—must have preceded as a cause; for how else could one force nature to surrender her secrets but by victoriously opposing her, *i.e.*, by means of the Unnatural? It is this intuition which I see imprinted in the awful triad of the destiny of Oedipus: the very man who solves the riddle of nature—that double-constituted Sphinx—must also, as the murderer of his father and husband of his mother, break the holiest laws of nature. Indeed, it seems as if the myth sought to whisper into our ears that wisdom, especially Dionysian wisdom, is an unnatural abomination, and that whoever, through his knowledge, plunges nature into an abyss of annihilation, must also experience the dissolution of nature in himself. "The sharpness of wisdom turns round upon the sage: wisdom is a crime against nature": such terrible expressions does the myth call out to us: but the Hellenic poet touches like a sunbeam the sublime and formidable Memnonian statue of the myth, so that it suddenly begins to sound—in Sophoclean melodies.

With the glory of passivity I now contrast the glory of activity which illuminates the *Prometheus* of Aeschylus. That which Aeschylus the thinker had to tell us here, but which as a poet he only allows us to surmise by his symbolic picture, the youthful Goethe succeeded in disclosing to us in the daring words of his Prometheus: —

Here I sit, forming mankind
in my image,
a race that is the same as me,
to suffer, to cry,
to have joy and be happy,
and have no thought of you,
like me!"

Man, elevating himself to the rank of the Titans, acquires his culture by his own efforts, and compels the gods to unite with him, because in his

Prometheusgedicht, das seinem Grundgedanken nach der eigentliche Hymnus der Unfrömmigkeit ist, ist aber der tiefe äschyleische Zug nach *Gerechtigkeit*: das unermeßliche Leid des kühnen »Einzelnen« auf der einen Seite, und die göttliche Not, ja Ahnung einer Götterdämmerung auf der andern, die zur Versöhnung, zum metaphysischen Einssein zwingende Macht jener beiden Leidenswelten – dies alles erinnert auf das stärkste an den Mittelpunkt und Hauptsatz der äschyleischen Weltbetrachtung, die über Göttern und Menschen die Moira als ewige Gerechtigkeit thronen sieht. Bei der erstaunlichen Kühnheit, mit der Äschylus die olympische Welt auf seine Gerechtigkeitswagschalen stellt, müssen wir uns vergegenwärtigen, daß der tiefsinnige Grieche einen unverrückbar festen Untergrund des metaphysischen Denkens in seinen Mysterien hatte, und daß sich an den Olympiern alle seine skeptischen Anwandlungen entladen konnten. Der griechische Künstler insbesondere empfand im Hinblick auf die Gottheiten ein dunkles Gefühl wechselseitiger Abhängigkeit: und gerade im Prometheus des Äschylus ist dieses Gefühl symbolisiert. Der titanische Künstler fand in sich den trotzigen Glauben, Menschen schaffen und olympische Götter wenigstens vernichten zu können: und dies durch seine höhere Weisheit, die er freilich durch ewiges Leiden zu büßen gezwungen war. Das herrliche »Können« des großen Genius, das selbst mit ewigem Leide zu gering bezahlt ist, der herbe Stolz des *Künstlers* – das ist Inhalt und Seele der äschyleischen Dichtung, während Sophokles in seinem Ödipus das Siegeslied des *Heiligen* präludierend anstimmt. Aber auch mit jener Deutung, die Äschylus dem Mythus gegeben hat, ist dessen erstaunliche Schreckenstiefe nicht ausgemessen: vielmehr ist die Werdelust des Künstlers, die jedem Unheil trotzende Heiterkeit des künstlerischen Schaffens nur ein lichtes Wolken- und Himmelsbild, das sich auf einem schwarzen See der Traurigkeit spiegelt. Die Prometheussage ist ein ursprüngliches Eigentum der gesamten arischen Völkergemeinde und ein Dokument für deren Begabung zum Tiefsinnig-Tragischen, ja es möchte nicht ohne Wahrscheinlichkeit sein, daß diesem Mythus für das arische Wesen eben dieselbe charakteristische Bedeutung innewohnt, die der Sündenfallmythus für das semitische hat, und daß zwischen beiden Mythen ein Verwandtschaftsgrad existiert, wie zwischen Bruder und Schwester. Die Voraussetzung jenes Prometheusmythus ist der überschwängliche Wert, den eine naive Menschheit dem *Feuer* beilegt als dem wahren Palladium jeder aufsteigenden Kultur: daß aber der Mensch frei über das Feuer waltet und es nicht nur durch ein Geschenk

self-sufficient wisdom he has their existence and their limits in his hand. What is most wonderful, however, in this Promethean form, which according to its fundamental conception is the specific hymn of impiety, is the profound Aeschylean yearning for *justice*: the untold sorrow of the bold “single-handed being” on the one hand, and the divine need, ay, the foreboding of a twilight of the gods, on the other, the power of these two worlds of suffering constraining to reconciliation, to metaphysical oneness—all this suggests most forcibly the central and main position of the Aeschylean view of things, which sees Moira as eternal justice enthroned above gods and men. In view of the astonishing boldness with which Aeschylus places the Olympian world on his scales of justice, it must be remembered that the deep-minded Greek had an immovably firm substratum of metaphysical thought in his mysteries, and that all his sceptical paroxysms could be discharged upon the Olympians. With reference to these deities, the Greek artist, in particular, had an obscure feeling as to mutual dependency: and it is just in the Prometheus of Aeschylus that this feeling is symbolised. The Titanic artist found in himself the daring belief that he could create men and at least destroy Olympian deities: namely, by his superior wisdom, for which, to be sure, he had to atone by eternal suffering. The splendid “can-ing” of the great genius, bought too cheaply even at the price of eternal suffering, the stern pride of the *artist*: this is the essence and soul of Aeschylean poetry, while Sophocles in his Oedipus preludingly strikes up the victory-song of the *saint*. But even this interpretation which Aeschylus has given to the myth does not fathom its astounding depth of terror; the fact is rather that the artist’s delight in unfolding, the cheerfulness of artistic creating bidding defiance to all calamity, is but a shining stellar and nebular image reflected in a black sea of sadness. The tale of Prometheus is an original possession of the entire Aryan family of races, and documentary evidence of their capacity for the profoundly tragic; indeed, it is not improbable that this myth has the same characteristic significance for the Aryan race that the myth of the fall of man has for the Semitic, and that there is a relationship between the two myths like that of brother and sister. The presupposition of the Promethean myth is the transcendent value which a naïve humanity attach to *fire* as the true palladium of every ascending culture: that man, however,

vom Himmel, als zündenden Blitzstrahl oder wärmenden Sonnenbrand, empfängt, erschien jenen beschaulichen Ur-Menschen als ein Frevel, als ein Raub an der göttlichen Natur. Und so stellt gleich das erste philosophische Problem einen peinlichen unlösbaren Widerspruch zwischen Mensch und Gott hin und rückt ihn wie einen Felsblock an die Pforte jeder Kultur. Das Beste und Höchste, dessen die Menschheit teilhaftig werden kann, erringt sie durch einen Frevel und muß nun wieder seine Folgen dahinnehmen, nämlich die ganze Flut von Leiden und von Kümmernissen, mit denen die beleidigten Himmlischen das edel emporstrebende Menschengeschlecht heimsuchen – müssen: ein herber Gedanke, der durch die *Würde*, die er dem Frevel erteilt, seltsam gegen den semitischen Sündenfallmythus absticht, in welchem die Neugierde, die lügnerische Vorspiegelung, die Verführbarkeit, die Lüsternheit, kurz eine Reihe vornehmlich weiblicher Affektionen als der Ursprung des Übels angesehen wurde. Das, was die arische Vorstellung auszeichnet, ist die erhabene Ansicht von der *aktiven Sünde* als der eigentlich prometheischen Tugend: womit zugleich der ethische Untergrund der pessimistischen Tragödie gefunden ist, als die *Rechtfertigung* des menschlichen Übels, und zwar sowohl der menschlichen Schuld als des dadurch verwirkten Leidens. Das Unheil im Wesen der Dinge – das der beschauliche Arier nicht geneigt ist wegzudeuteln –, der Widerspruch im Herzen der Welt offenbart sich ihm als ein Durcheinander verschiedener Welten, z.B. einer göttlichen und einer menschlichen, von denen jede als Individuum im Recht ist, aber als einzelne neben einer anderen für ihre Individuation zu leiden hat. Bei dem heroischen Drange des einzelnen ins Allgemeine, bei dem Versuche, über den Bann der Individuation hinauszuschreiten und das eine Weltwesen selbst sein zu wollen, erleidet er an sich den in den Dingen verborgenen Urwiderspruch, d.h. er frevelt und leidet. So wird von den Ariern der Frevel als Mann, von den Semiten die Sünde als Weib verstanden, so wie auch der Urfrevel vom Manne, die Ursünde vom Weibe begangen wird. Übrigens sagt der Hexenchor:

»Wir nehmen das nicht so genau:
Mit tausend Schritten machts die Frau;
Doch wie sie auch sich eilen kann,
Mit einem Sprunge machts der Mann.«

should dispose at will of this fire, and should not receive it only as a gift from heaven, as the igniting lightning or the warming solar flame, appeared to the contemplative primordial men as crime and robbery of the divine nature. And thus the first philosophical problem at once causes a painful, irreconcilable antagonism between man and God, and puts as it were a mass of rock at the gate of every culture. The best and highest that men can acquire they obtain by a crime, and must now in their turn take upon themselves its consequences, namely the whole flood of sufferings and sorrows with which the offended celestials *must* visit the nobly aspiring race of man: a bitter reflection, which, by the *dignity* it confers on crime, contrasts strangely with the Semitic myth of the fall of man, in which curiosity, beguilement, seducibility, wantonness—in short, a whole series of pre-eminently feminine passions—were regarded as the origin of evil. What distinguishes the Aryan representation is the sublime view of *active sin* as the properly Promethean virtue, which suggests at the same time the ethical basis of pessimistic tragedy as the *justification* of human evil—of human guilt as well as of the suffering incurred thereby. The misery in the essence of things—which the contemplative Aryan is not disposed to explain away—the antagonism in the heart of the world, manifests itself to him as a medley of different worlds, for instance, a Divine and a human world, each of which is in the right individually, but as a separate existence alongside of another has to suffer for its individuation. With the heroic effort made by the individual for universality, in his attempt to pass beyond the bounds of individuation and become the *one* universal being, he experiences in himself the primordial contradiction concealed in the essence of things, *i.e.*, he trespasses and suffers. Accordingly crime is understood by the Aryans to be a man, sin by the Semites a woman; as also, the original crime is committed by man, the original sin by woman. Besides, the witches' chorus says:

We don't take that too seriously:
a woman does it with a thousand steps,
but no matter how much she hurries,
a man can do it with one leap.

—*Faust.*

Wer jenen innersten Kern der Prometheussage versteht – nämlich die dem titanisch strebenden Individuum gebotene Notwendigkeit des Frevels –, der muß auch zugleich das Unapollinische dieser pessimistischen Vorstellung empfinden; denn Apollo will die Einzelwesen gerade dadurch zur Ruhe bringen, daß er Grenzlinien zwischen ihnen zieht und daß er immer wieder an diese als an die heiligsten Weltgesetze mit seinen Forderungen der Selbsterkenntnis und des Maßes erinnert. Damit aber bei dieser apollinischen Tendenz die Form nicht zu ägyptischer Steifigkeit und Kälte erstarre, damit nicht unter dem Bemühen, der einzelnen Welle ihre Bahn und ihr Bereich vorzuschreiben, die Bewegung des ganzen Sees ersterbe, zerstörte von Zeit zu Zeit wieder die hohe Flut des Dionysischen alle jene kleinen Zirkel, in die der einseitig apollinische »Wille« das Hellenentum zu bannen suchte. Jene plötzlich anschwellende Flut des Dionysischen nimmt dann die einzelnen kleinen Wellenberge der Individuen auf ihren Rücken, wie der Bruder des Prometheus, der Titan Atlas, die Erde. Dieser titanische Drang, gleichsam der Atlas aller einzelnen zu werden und sie mit breitem Rücken höher und höher, weiter und weiter zu tragen, ist das Gemeinsame zwischen dem Prometheischen und dem Dionysischen. Der äschyleische Prometheus ist in diesem Betracht eine dionysische Maske, während in jenem vorhin erwähnten tiefen Zuge nach Gerechtigkeit Äschylus seine väterliche Abstammung von Apollo, dem Gotte der Individuation und der Gerechtigkeitsgrenzen, dem Einsichtigen verrät. Und so möchte das Doppelwesen des äschyleischen Prometheus, seine zugleich dionysische und apollinische Natur in begrifflicher Formel so ausgedrückt werden können: »Alles Vorhandene ist gerecht und ungerecht und in beidem gleich berechtigt.«

Das ist deine Welt! Das heißt eine Welt! –
—*Faust.*

He who understands this innermost core of the tale of Prometheus—namely the necessity of crime imposed on the titanically striving individual—will at once be conscious of the un-Apollonian nature of this pessimistic representation: for Apollo seeks to pacify individual beings precisely by drawing boundary lines between them, and by again and again calling attention thereto, with his requirements of self-knowledge and due proportion, as the holiest laws of the universe. In order, however, to prevent the form from congealing to Egyptian rigidity and coldness in consequence of this Apollonian tendency, in order to prevent the extinction of the motion of the entire lake in the effort to prescribe to the individual wave its path and compass, the high tide of the Dionysian tendency destroyed from time to time all the little circles in which the one-sided Apollonian "will" sought to confine the Hellenic world. The suddenly swelling tide of the Dionysian then takes the separate little wave-mountains of individuals on its back, just as the brother of Prometheus, the Titan Atlas, does with the earth. This Titanic impulse, to become as it were the Atlas of all individuals, and to carry them on broad shoulders higher and higher, farther and farther, is what the Promethean and the Dionysian have in common. In this respect the Aeschylean Prometheus is a Dionysian mask, while, in the afore-mentioned profound yearning for justice, Aeschylus betrays to the intelligent observer his paternal descent from Apollo, the god of individuation and of the boundaries of justice. And so the double-being of the Aeschylean Prometheus, his conjoint Dionysian and Apollonian nature, might be thus expressed in an abstract formula: "Whatever exists is alike just and unjust, and equally justified in both."

This is your world, and what a world!

10

Es ist eine unanfechtbare Überlieferung, daß die griechische Tragödie in ihrer ältesten Gestalt nur die Leiden des Dionysus zum Gegenstand hatte, und daß der längere Zeit hindurch einzig vorhandene Bühnenheld eben Dionysus war. Aber mit der gleichen Sicherheit darf behauptet werden, daß niemals bis auf Euripides Dionysus aufgehört hat, der tragische Held zu sein, sondern daß alle die berühmten Figuren der griechischen Bühne, Prometheus, Ödipus usw. nur

It is an indisputable tradition that Greek tragedy in its earliest form had for its theme only the sufferings of Dionysus, and that for some time the only stage-hero therein was simply Dionysus himself. With the same confidence, however, we can maintain that not until Euripides did Dionysus cease to be the tragic hero, and that in fact all the celebrated figures of the Greek stage—Prometheus, Oedipus, etc.—are but masks of this

Masken jenes ursprünglichen Helden Dionysus sind. Daß hinter allen diesen Masken eine Gottheit steckt, das ist der eine wesentliche Grund für die so oft angestaunte typische »Idealität« jener berühmten Figuren. Es hat ich weiß nicht wer behauptet, daß alle Individuen als Individuen komisch und damit untragisch seien: woraus zu entnehmen wäre, daß die Griechen überhaupt Individuen auf der tragischen Bühne nicht ertragen *konnten*. In der Tat scheinen sie so empfunden zu haben: wie überhaupt jene platonische Unterscheidung und Wertabschätzung der »Idee« im Gegensatze zum »Idol«, zum Abbild, tief im hellenischen Wesen begründet liegt. Um uns aber der Terminologie Platos zu bedienen, so wäre von den tragischen Gestalten der hellenischen Bühne etwa so zu reden: der eine wahrhaft reale Dionysus erscheint in einer Vielheit der Gestalten, in der Maske eines kämpfenden Helden und gleichsam in das Netz des Einzelwillens verstrickt. So wie jetzt der erscheinende Gott redet und handelt, ähnelt er einem irrenden strebenden leidenden Individuum: und daß er überhaupt mit dieser epischen Bestimmtheit und Deutlichkeit *erscheint*, ist die Wirkung des Traumdeuters Apollo, der dem Chore seinen dionysischen Zustand durch jene gleichnisartige Erscheinung deutet. In Wahrheit aber ist jener Held der leidende Dionysus der Mysterien, jener die Leiden der Individuation an sich erfahrende Gott, von dem wundervolle Mythen erzählen, wie er als Knabe von den Titanen zerstückelt worden sei und nun in diesem Zustande als Zagreus verehrt werde: wobei angedeutet wird, daß diese Zerstückelung, das eigentlich dionysische *Leiden*, gleich einer Umwandlung in Luft, Wasser, Erde und Feuer sei, daß wir also den Zustand der Individuation als den Quell und Urgrund alles Leidens, als etwas an sich Verwerfliches, zu betrachten hätten. Aus dem Lächeln dieses Dionysus sind die olympischen Götter, aus seinen Tränen die Menschen entstanden. In jener Existenz als zerstückelter Gott hat Dionysus die Doppelnatur eines grausamen verwilderten Dämons und eines milden sanftmütigen Herrschers. Die Hoffnung der Epopten ging aber auf eine Wiedergeburt des Dionysus, die wir jetzt als das Ende der Individuation ahnungsvoll zu begreifen haben: diesem kommenden dritten Dionysus erscholl der brausende Jubelgesang der Epopten. Und nur in dieser Hoffnung gibt es einen Strahl von Freude auf dem Antlitze der zerrissenen, in Individuen zertrümmerten Welt: wie es der Mythus durch die in ewige Trauer versenkte Demeter verbildlicht, welche zum ersten Male wieder sich *freut*, als man ihr sagt, sie könne den Dionysus *noch einmal* gebären. In den angeführten Anschauungen haben wir bereits alle

original hero, Dionysus. The presence of a god behind all these masks is the one essential cause of the typical "ideality," so oft exciting wonder, of these celebrated figures. Some one, I know not whom, has maintained that all individuals are comic as individuals and are consequently un-tragic: from whence it might be inferred that the Greeks in general *could* not endure individuals on the tragic stage. And they really seem to have had these sentiments: as, in general, it is to be observed that the Platonic discrimination and valuation of the "idea" in contrast to the "eidolon," the image, is deeply rooted in thc Hellenic being. Availing ourselves of Plato's terminology, however, we should have to speak of the tragic figures of the Hellenic stage somewhat as follows. The one truly real Dionysus appears in a multiplicity of forms, in the mask of a fighting hero and entangled, as it were, in the net of an individual will. As the visibly appearing god now talks and acts, he resembles an erring, striving, suffering individual: and that, in general, he *appears* with such epic precision and clearness, is due to the dream-reading Apollo, who reads to the chorus its Dionysian state through this symbolic appearance. In reality, however, this hero is the suffering Dionysus of the mysteries, a god experiencing in himself the sufferings of individuation, of whom wonderful myths tell that as a boy he was dismembered by the Titans and has been worshipped in this state as Zagreus: whereby is intimated that this dismemberment, the properly Dionysian *suffering*, is like a transformation into air, water, earth, and fire, that we must therefore regard the state of individuation as the source and primal cause of all suffering, as something objectionable in itself. From the smile of this Dionysus sprang the Olympian gods, from his tears sprang man. In his existence as a dismembered god, Dionysus has the dual nature of a cruel barbarised demon, and a mild pacific ruler. But the hope of the epopts looked for a new birth of Dionysus, which we have now to conceive of in anticipation as the end of individuation: it was for this coming third Dionysus that the stormy jubilation-hymns of the epopts resounded. And it is only this hope that sheds a ray of joy upon the features of a world torn asunder and shattered into individuals: as is symbolised in the myth by Demeter sunk in eternal sadness, who *rejoices* again only whcn told that she may *once more* give birth to Dionysus In the views of things here given we already have all

Bestandteile einer tiefsinnigen und pessimistischen Weltbetrachtung und zugleich damit *die Mysterienlehre der Tragödie* zusammen: die Grunderkenntnis von der Einheit alles Vorhandenen, die Betrachtung der Individuation als des Urgrundes des Übels, die Kunst als die freudige Hoffnung, daß der Bann der Individuation zu zerbrechen sei, als die Ahnung einer wiederhergestellten Einheit. –

the elements of a profound and pessimistic contemplation of the world, and along with these we have the *mystery doctrine of tragedy*: the fundamental knowledge of the oneness of all existing things, the consideration of individuation as the primal cause of evil, and art as the joyous hope that the spell of individuation may be broken, as the augury of a restored oneness.

Es ist früher angedeutet worden, daß das homerische Epos die Dichtung der olympischen Kultur ist, mit der sie ihr eignes Siegeslied über die Schrecken des Titanenkampfes gesungen hat. Jetzt, unter dem übermächtigen Einflusse der tragischen Dichtung, werden die homerischen Mythen von neuem umgeboren und zeigen in dieser Metempsychose, daß inzwischen auch die olympische Kultur von einer noch tieferen Weltbetrachtung besiegt worden ist. Der trotzige Titan Prometheus hat es seinem olympischen Peiniger angekündigt, daß einst seiner Herrschaft die höchste Gefahr drohe, falls er nicht zur rechten Zeit sich mit ihm verbinden werde. In Äschylus erkennen wir das Bündnis des erschreckten, vor seinem Ende bangenden Zeus mit dem Titanen. So wird das frühere Titanenzeitalter nachträglich wieder aus dem Tartarus ans Licht geholt. Die Philosophie der wilden und nackten Natur schaut die vorübertanzenden Mythen der homerischen Welt mit der unverhüllten Miene der Wahrheit an: sie erbleichen, sie zittern vor dem blitzartigen Auge dieser Göttin – bis sie die mächtige Faust des dionysischen Künstlers in den Dienst der neuen Gottheit zwingt. Die dionysische Wahrheit übernimmt das gesamte Bereich des Mythus als Symbolik *ihrer* Erkenntnisse und spricht diese teils in dem öffentlichen Kultus der Tragödie, teils in den geheimen Begehungen dramatischer Mysterienfeste, aber immer unter der alten mythischen Hülle aus. Welche Kraft war dies, die den Prometheus von seinen Geiern befreite und den Mythus zum Vehikel dionysischer Weisheit umwandelte? Dies ist die heraklesmäßige Kraft der Musik: als welche, in der Tragödie zu ihrer höchsten Erscheinung gekommen, den Mythus mit neuer tiefsinnigster Bedeutsamkeit zu interpretieren weiß; wie wir dies als das mächtigste Vermögen der Musik früher schon zu charakterisieren hatten. Denn es ist das Los jedes Mythus, allmählich in die Enge einer angeblich historischen Wirklichkeit hineinzukriechen und von irgendeiner späteren Zeit als einmaliges Faktum mit historischen Ansprüchen behandelt zu werden: und die Griechen waren bereits völlig auf dem Wege, ihren ganzen mythischen

It has already been intimated that the Homeric epos is the poem of Olympian culture, wherewith this culture has sung its own song of triumph over the terrors of the war of the Titans. Under the predominating influence of tragic poetry, these Homeric myths are now reproduced anew, and show by this metempsychosis that meantime the Olympian culture also has been vanquished by a still deeper view of things. The haughty Titan Prometheus has announced to his Olympian tormentor that the extremest danger will one day menace his rule, unless he ally with him betimes. In Aeschylus we perceive the terrified Zeus, apprehensive of his end, in alliance with the Titan. Thus, the former age of the Titans is subsequently brought from Tartarus once more to the light of day. The philosophy of wild and naked nature beholds with the undissembled mien of truth the myths of the Homeric world as they dance past: they turn pale, they tremble before the lightning glance of this goddess—till the powerful fist[8] of the Dionysian artist forces them into the service of the new deity. Dionysian truth takes over the entire domain of myth as symbolism of *its* knowledge, which it makes known partly in the public cult of tragedy and partly in the secret celebration of the dramatic mysteries, always, however, in the old mythical garb. What was the power, which freed Prometheus from his vultures and transformed the myth into a vehicle of Dionysian wisdom? It is the Heracleian power of music: which, having reached its highest manifestness in tragedy, can invest myths with a new and most profound significance, which we have already had occasion to characterise as the most powerful faculty of music. For it is the fate of every myth to insinuate itself into the narrow limits of some alleged historical reality, and to be treated by some later generation as a solitary fact with historical claims: and the Greeks were already fairly on the way to restamp the whole of their mythical juvenile

[8] Die mächtige Faust.—Cf. *Faust*, Chorus of Spirits.

Jugendtraum mit Scharfsinn und Willkür in eine historisch-pragmatische *Jugendgeschichte* umzustempeln. Denn dies ist die Art, wie Religionen abzusterben pflegen: wenn nämlich die mythischen Voraussetzungen einer Religion unter den strengen, verstandesmäßigen Augen eines rechtgläubigen Dogmatismus als eine fertige Summe von historischen Ereignissen systematisiert werden und man anfängt, ängstlich die Glaubwürdigkeit der Mythen zu verteidigen, aber gegen jedes natürliche Weiterleben und Weiterwuchern derselben sich zu sträuben, wenn also das Gefühl für den Mythus abstirbt und an seine Stelle der Anspruch der Religion auf historische Grundlagen tritt. Diesen absterbenden Mythus ergriff jetzt der neugeborne Genius der dionysischen Musik: und in seiner Hand blühte er noch einmal, mit Farben, wie er sie noch nie gezeigt, mit einem Duft, der eine sehnsüchtige Ahnung einer metaphysischen Welt erregte. Nach diesem letzten Aufglänzen fällt er zusammen, seine Blätter werden welk, und bald haschen die spöttischen Luciane des Altertums nach den von allen Winden fortgetragenen, entfärbten und verwüsteten Blumen. Durch die Tragödie kommt der Mythus zu seinem tiefsten Inhalt, seiner ausdrucksvollsten Form; noch einmal erhebt er sich, wie ein verwundeter Held, und der ganze Überschuß von Kraft, samt der weisheitsvollen Ruhe des Sterbenden, brennt in seinem Auge mit letztem, mächtigem Leuchten.

Was wolltest du, frevelnder Euripides, als du diesen Sterbenden noch einmal zu deinem Frondienste zu zwingen suchtest? Er starb unter deinen gewaltsamen Händen: und jetzt brauchtest du einen nachgemachten, maskierten Mythus, der sich wie der Affe des Herakles mit dem alten Prunke nur noch aufzuputzen wußte. Und wie dir der Mythus starb, so starb dir auch der Genius der Musik: mochtest du auch mit gierigem Zugreifen alle Gärten der Musik plündern, auch so brachtest du es nur zu einer nachgemachten maskierten Musik. Und weil du Dionysus verlassen, so verließ dich auch Apollo; jage alle Leidenschaften von ihrem Lager auf und banne sie in deinen Kreis, spitze und feile dir für die Reden deiner Helden eine sophistische Dialektik zurecht – auch deine Helden haben nur nachgeahmte maskierte Leidenschaften und sprechen nur nachgeahmte maskierte Reden.

dream sagaciously and arbitrarily into a historico-pragmatical *juvenile history*. For this is the manner in which religions are wont to die out: when of course under the stern, intelligent eyes of an orthodox dogmatism, the mythical presuppositions of a religion are systematised as a completed sum of historical events, and when one begins apprehensively to defend the credibility of the myth, while at the same time opposing all continuation of their natural vitality and luxuriance; when, accordingly, the feeling for myth dies out, and its place is taken by the claim of religion to historical foundations. This dying myth was now seized by the new-born genius of Dionysian music, in whose hands it bloomed once more, with such colours as it had never yet displayed, with a fragrance that awakened a longing anticipation of a metaphysical world. After this final effulgence it collapses, its leaves wither, and soon the scoffing Lucians of antiquity catch at the discoloured and faded flowers which the winds carry off in every direction. Through tragedy the myth attains its profoundest significance, its most expressive form; it rises once more like a wounded hero, and the whole surplus of vitality, together with the philosophical calmness of the Dying, burns in its eyes with a last powerful gleam.

What did you mean, o impious Euripides, in seeking once more to enthral this dying one? It died under your ruthless hands: and then you made use of counterfeit, masked myth, which like the ape of Heracles could only trick itself out in the old finery. And as myth died in your hands, so also died the genius of music; though you covetously plundered all the gardens of music—you could only make a counterfeit, masked music. And because you had forsaken Dionysus. you were forsaken by Apollo also; rouse up all the passions from their haunts and conjure them into your sphere, sharpen and polish a sophistical dialectics for the speeches of your heroes—your very heroes have only counterfeit, masked passions, and speak only counterfeit, masked music.

11

Die griechische Tragödie ist anders zugrunde gegangen als sämtliche ältere schwesterliche Kunstgattungen: sie starb durch Selbstmord, infolge eines unlösbaren Konfliktes, also tragisch, während jene alle in hohem Alter des schönsten und ruhigsten Todes verblichen sind. Wenn es nämlich einem glücklichen Naturzustande gemäß ist, mit schöner Nachkommenschaft und ohne Krampf vom Leben zu scheiden, so zeigt uns das Ende jener älteren Kunstgattungen einen solchen glücklichen Naturzustand: sie tauchen langsam unter, und vor ihren ersterbenden Blicken steht schon ihr schönerer Nachwuchs und reckt mit mutiger Gebärde ungeduldig das Haupt. Mit dem Tode der griechischen Tragödie dagegen entstand eine ungeheure, überall tief empfundene Leere; wie einmal griechische Schiffer zu Zeiten des Tiberius an einem einsamen Eiland den erschütternden Schrei hörten »der große Pan ist tot«: so klang es jetzt wie ein schmerzlicher Klageton durch die hellenische Welt: »die Tragödie ist tot! Die Poesie selbst ist mit ihr verlorengegangen! Fort, fort mit euch verkümmerten, abgemagerten Epigonen! Fort in den Hades, damit ihr euch dort an den Brosamen der vormaligen Meister einmal sattessen könnt!«

Als aber nun doch noch eine neue Kunstgattung aufblühte, die in der Tragödie ihre Vorgängerin und Meisterin verehrte, da war mit Schrecken wahrzunehmen, daß sie allerdings die Züge ihrer Mutter trage, aber dieselben, die jene in ihrem langen Todeskampfe gezeigt hatte. Diesen Todeskampf der Tragödie kämpfte *Euripides;* jene spätere Kunstgattung ist als *neuere attische Komödie* bekannt. In ihr lebte die entartete Gestalt der Tragödie fort, zum Denkmale ihres überaus mühseligen und gewaltsamen Hinscheidens.

Bei diesem Zusammenhange ist die leidenschaftliche Zuneigung begreiflich, welche die Dichter der neueren Komödie zu Euripides empfanden; so daß der Wunsch des Philemon nicht weiter befremdet, der sich sogleich aufhängen lassen mochte, nur um den Euripides in der Unterwelt aufsuchen zu können: wenn er nur überhaupt überzeugt sein dürfte, daß der Verstorbene auch jetzt noch bei Verstande sei. Will man aber in aller Kürze und ohne den Anspruch, damit etwas Erschöpfendes zu sagen, dasjenige bezeichnen, was Euripides mit Menander und Philemon gemein hat und was für jene so aufregend vorbildlich wirkte: so genügt es zu sagen, daß *der Zuschauer* von Euripides auf die Bühne gebracht worden ist. Wer erkannt hat,

Greek tragedy had a fate different from that of all her older sister arts: she died by suicide, in consequence of an irreconcilable conflict; accordingly she died tragically, while they all passed away very calmly and beautifully in ripe old age. For if it be in accordance with a happy state of things to depart this life without a struggle, leaving behind a fair posterity, the closing period of these older arts exhibits such a happy state of things: slowly they sink out of sight, and before their dying eyes already stand their fairer progeny, who impatiently lift up their heads with courageous mien. The death of Greek tragedy, on the other hand, left an immense void, deeply felt everywhere. Even as certain Greek sailors in the time of Tiberius once heard upon a lonesome island the thrilling cry, "great Pan is dead": so now as it were sorrowful wailing sounded through the Hellenic world: "Tragedy is dead! Poetry itself has perished with her! Begone, begone, ye stunted, emaciated epigones! Begone to Hades, that ye may for once eat your fill of the crumbs of your former masters!"

But when after all a new Art blossomed forth which revered tragedy as her ancestress and mistress, it was observed with horror that she did indeed bear the features of her mother, but those very features the latter had exhibited in her long death-struggle. It was *Euripides* who fought this death-struggle of tragedy; the later art is known as the *New Attic Comedy.* In it the degenerate form of tragedy lived on as a monument of the most painful and violent death of tragedy proper.

This connection between the two serves to explain the passionate attachment to Euripides evinced by the poets of the New Comedy, and hence we are no longer surprised at the wish of Philemon, who would have got himself hanged at once, with the sole design of being able to visit Euripides in the lower regions: if only he could be assured generally that the deceased still had his wits. But if we desire, as briefly as possible, and without professing to say aught exhaustive on the subject, to characterise what Euripides has in common with Menander and Philemon, and what appealed to them so strongly as worthy of imitation: it will suffice to say that the *spectator* was brought upon the stage by Euripides. He who has perceived the material of which the

aus welchem Stoffe die prometheischen Tragiker vor Euripides ihre Helden formten und wie ferne ihnen die Absicht lag, die treue Maske der Wirklichkeit auf die Bühne zu bringen, der wird auch über die gänzlich abweichende Tendenz des Euripides im klaren sein. Der Mensch des alltäglichen Lebens drang durch ihn aus den Zuschauerräumen auf die Szene, der Spiegel, in dem früher nur die großen und kühnen Züge zum Ausdruck kamen, zeigte jetzt jene peinliche Treue, die auch die mißlungenen Linien der Natur gewissenhaft wiedergibt. Odysseus, der typische Hellene der älteren Kunst, sank jetzt unter den Händen der neueren Dichter zur Figur des Graeculus herab, der von jetzt ab als gutmütig-verschmitzter Haussklave im Mittelpunkte des dramatischen Interesses steht. Was Euripides sich in den aristophanischen »Fröschen« zum Verdienst anrechnet, daß er die tragische Kunst durch seine Hausmittel von ihrer pomphaften Beleibtheit befreit habe, das ist vor allem an seinen tragischen Helden zu spüren. Im wesentlichen sah und hörte jetzt der Zuschauer seinen Doppelgänger auf der euripideischen Bühne und freute sich, daß jener so gut zu reden verstehe. Bei dieser Freude blieb es aber nicht: man lernte selbst bei Euripides sprechen, und dessen rühmt er sich selbst im Wettkampfe mit Äschylus: wie durch ihn jetzt das Volk kunstmäßig und mit den schlausten Sophistikationen zu beobachten, zu verhandeln und Folgerungen zu ziehen gelernt habe. Durch diesen Umschwung der öffentlichen Sprache hat er überhaupt die neuere Komödie möglich gemacht. Denn von jetzt ab war es kein Geheimnis mehr, wie und mit welchen Sentenzen die Alltäglichkeit sich auf der Bühne vertreten könne. Die bürgerliche Mittelmäßigkeit, auf die Euripides alle seine politischen Hoffnungen aufbaute, kam jetzt zu Wort, nachdem bis dahin in der Tragödie der Halbgott, in der Komödie der betrunkene Satyr oder der Halbmensch den Sprachcharakter bestimmt hatten. Und so hebt der aristophanische Euripides zu seinem Preise hervor, wie er das allgemeine, allbekannte, alltägliche Leben und Treiben dargestellt habe, über das ein jeder zu urteilen befähigt sei. Wenn jetzt die ganze Masse philosophiere, mit unerhörter Klugheit Land und Gut verwalte und ihre Prozesse führe, so sei dies sein Verdienst und der Erfolg der von ihm dem Volke eingeimpften Weisheit.

An eine derartig zubereitete und aufgeklärte Masse durfte sich jetzt die neuere Komödie wenden, für die Euripides gewissermaßen der Chorlehrer geworden ist; nur daß diesmal der Chor der Zuschauer eingeübt werden mußte. Sobald dieser in der euripideischen Tonart zu singen geübt war, erhob sich jene

Promethean tragic writers prior to Euripides formed their heroes, and how remote from their purpose it was to bring the true mask of reality on the stage, will also know what to make of the wholly divergent tendency of Euripides. Through him the commonplace individual forced his way from the spectators' benches to the stage itself; the mirror in which formerly only great and bold traits found expression now showed the painful exactness that conscientiously reproduces even the abortive lines of nature. Odysseus, the typical Hellene of the Old Art, sank, in the hands of the new poets, to the figure of the Græculus, who, as the good-naturedly cunning domestic slave, stands henceforth in the centre of dramatic interest. What Euripides takes credit for in the Aristophanean "Frogs," namely, that by his household remedies he freed tragic art from its pompous corpulency, is apparent above all in his tragic heroes. The spectator now virtually saw and heard his double on the Euripidean stage, and rejoiced that he could talk so well. But this joy was not all: one even learned of Euripides how to speak: he prides himself upon this in his contest with Aeschylus: how the people have learned from him how to observe, debate, and draw conclusions according to the rules of art and with the cleverest sophistications. In general it may be said that through this revolution of the popular language he made the New Comedy possible. For it was henceforth no longer a secret, how—and with what saws—the commonplace could represent and express itself on the stage. Civic mediocrity, on which Euripides built all his political hopes, was now suffered to speak, while heretofore the demigod in tragedy and the drunken satyr, or demiman, in comedy, had determined the character of the language. And so the Aristophanean Euripides prides himself on having portrayed the common, familiar, everyday life and dealings of the people, concerning which all are qualified to pass judgment. If now the entire populace philosophises, manages land and goods with unheard-of circumspection, and conducts law-suits, he takes all the credit to himself, and glories in the splendid results of the wisdom with which he inoculated the rabble.

It was to a populace prepared and enlightened in this manner that the New Comedy could now address itself, of which Euripides had become as it were the chorus-master; only that in this case the chorus of spectators had to be trained. As soon as

schachspielartige Gattung des Schauspiels, die neuere Komödie, mit ihrem fortwährenden Triumphe der Schlauheit und Verschlagenheit. Euripides aber – der Chorlehrer – wurde unaufhörlich gepriesen: ja man würde sich getötet haben, um noch mehr von ihm zu lernen, wenn man nicht gewußt hätte, daß die tragischen Dichter eben so tot seien wie die Tragödie. Mit ihr aber hatte der Hellene den Glauben an seine Unsterblichkeit aufgegeben, nicht nur den Glauben an eine ideale Vergangenheit, sondern auch den Glauben an eine ideale Zukunft. Das Wort aus der bekannten Grabschrift »als Greis leichtsinnig und grillig« gilt auch vom greisen Hellenentume. Der Augenblick, der Witz, der Leichtsinn, die Laune sind seine höchsten Gottheiten; der fünfte Stand, der des Sklaven, kommt, wenigstens der Gesinnung nach, jetzt zur Herrschaft: und wenn jetzt überhaupt noch von »griechischer Heiterkeit« die Rede sein darf, so ist es die Heiterkeit des Sklaven, der nichts Schweres zu verantworten, nichts Großes zu erstreben, nichts Vergangenes oder Zukünftiges höher zu schätzen weiß als das Gegenwärtige. Dieser Schein der »griechischen Heiterkeit« war es, der die tiefsinnigen und furchtbaren Naturen der vier ersten Jahrhunderte des Christentums so empörte: ihnen erschien diese weibische Flucht vor dem Ernst und dem Schrecken, dieses feige Sichgenügenlassen am bequemen Genuß – nicht nur verächtlich, sondern als die eigentlich antichristliche Gesinnung. Und ihrem Einfluß ist es zuzuschreiben, daß die durch Jahrhunderte fortlebende Anschauung des griechischen Altertums mit fast unüberwindlicher Zähigkeit jene blaßrote Heiterkeitsfarbe festhielt – als ob es nie ein sechstes Jahrhundert mit seiner Geburt der Tragödie, seinen Mysterien, seinen Pythagoras und Heraklit gegeben hätte, ja als ob die Kunstwerke der großen Zeit gar nicht vorhanden wären, die doch – jedes für sich – aus dem Boden einer solchen greisenhaften und sklavenmäßigen Daseinslust und Heiterkeit gar nicht zu erklären sind und auf eine völlig andere Weltbetrachtung als ihren Existenzgrund hinweisen.

Wenn zuletzt behauptet wurde, daß Euripides den Zuschauer auf die Bühne gebracht habe, um zugleich damit den Zuschauer zum Urteil über das Drama erst wahrhaft zu befähigen, so entsteht der Schein, als ob die ältere tragische Kunst aus einem Mißverhältnis zum Zuschauer nicht herausgekommen sei: und man möchte versucht sein, die radikale Tendenz des Euripides, ein entsprechendes Verhältnis zwischen Kunstwerk und Publikum zu erzielen, als einen Fortschritt über Sophokles hinaus zu preisen. Nun aber ist »Publikum« nur ein Wort und durchaus keine

this chorus was trained to sing in the Euripidean key, there arose that chesslike variety of the drama, the New Comedy, with its perpetual triumphs of cunning and artfulness. But Euripides—the chorus-master—was praised incessantly: indeed, people would have killed themselves in order to learn yet more from him, had they not known that tragic poets were quite as dead as tragedy. But with it the Hellene had surrendered the belief in his immortality; not only the belief in an ideal past, but also the belief in an ideal future. The saying taken from the well-known epitaph, "as an old man, frivolous and capricious," applies also to aged Hellenism. The passing moment, wit, levity, and caprice, are its highest deities; the fifth class, that of the slaves, now attains to power, at least in sentiment: and if we can still speak at all of "Greek cheerfulness," it is the cheerfulness of the slave who has nothing of consequence to answer for, nothing great to strive for, and cannot value anything of the past or future higher than the present. It was this semblance of "Greek cheerfulness" which so revolted the deep-minded and formidable natures of the first four centuries of Christianity: this womanish flight from earnestness and terror, this cowardly contentedness with easy pleasure, was not only contemptible to them, but seemed to be a specifically anti-Christian sentiment. And we must ascribe it to its influence that the conception of Greek antiquity, which lived on for centuries, preserved with almost enduring persistency that peculiar hectic colour of cheerfulness—as if there had never been a Sixth Century with its birth of tragedy, its Mysteries, its Pythagoras and Heraclitus, indeed as if the art-works of that great period did not at all exist, which in fact—each by itself—can in no wise be explained as having sprung from the soil of such a decrepit and slavish love of existence and cheerfulness, and point to an altogether different conception of things as their source.

The assertion made a moment ago, that Euripides introduced the spectator on the stage to qualify him the better to pass judgment on the drama, will make it appear as if the old tragic art was always in a false relation to the spectator: and one would be tempted to extol the radical tendency of Euripides to bring about an adequate relation between art-work and public as an advance on Sophocles. But, as things are, "public" is merely a word, and not at all a homogeneous

gleichartige und in sich verharrende Größe. Woher soll dem Künstler die Verpflichtung kommen, sich einer Kraft zu akkomodieren, die ihre Stärke nur in der Zahl hat? Und wenn er sich, seiner Begabung und seinen Absichten nach, über jeden einzelnen dieser Zuschauer erhaben fühlt, wie dürfte er vor dem gemeinsamen Ausdruck aller dieser ihm untergeordneten Kapazitäten mehr Achtung empfinden als vor dem relativ am höchsten begabten einzelnen Zuschauer? In Wahrheit hat kein griechischer Künstler mit größerer Verwegenheit und Selbstgenügsamkeit sein Publikum durch ein langes Leben hindurch behandelt als gerade Euripides: er, der selbst da noch, als die Masse sich ihm zu Füßen warf, in erhabenem Trotze seiner eigenen Tendenz öffentlich ins Gesicht schlug, derselben Tendenz, mit der er über die Masse gesiegt hatte. Wenn dieser Genius die geringste Ehrfurcht vor dem Pandämonium des Publikums gehabt hätte, so wäre er unter den Keulenschlägen seiner Mißerfolge längst vor der Mitte seiner Laufbahn zusammengebrochen. Wir sehen bei dieser Erwägung, daß unser Ausdruck, Euripides habe den Zuschauer auf die Bühne gebracht, um den Zuschauer wahrhaft urteilsfähig zu machen, nur ein provisorischer war, und daß wir nach einem tieferen Verständnis seiner Tendenz zu suchen haben. Umgekehrt ist es ja allerseits bekannt, wie Äschylus und Sophokles zeit ihres Lebens, ja weit über dasselbe hinaus, im Vollbesitze der Volksgunst standen, wie also bei diesen Vorgängern des Euripides keineswegs von einem Mißverhältnis zwischen Kunstwerk und Publikum die Rede sein kann. Was trieb den reichbegabten und unablässig zum Schaffen gedrängten Künstler so gewaltsam von dem Wege ab, über dem die Sonne der größten Dichternamen und der unbewölkte Himmel der Volksgunst leuchteten? Welche sonderbare Rücksicht auf den Zuschauer führte ihn dem Zuschauer entgegen? Wie konnte er aus zu hoher Achtung vor seinem Publikum - sein Publikum mißachten?

Euripides fühlte sich - das ist die Lösung des eben dargestellten Rätsels - als Dichter wohl über die Masse, nicht aber über zwei seiner Zuschauer erhaben: die Masse brachte er auf die Bühne, jene beiden Zuschauer verehrte er als die allein urteilsfähigen Richter und Meister aller seiner Kunst: ihren Weisungen und Mahnungen folgend, übertrug er die ganze Welt von Empfindungen, Leidenschaften und Erfahrungen, die bis jetzt auf den Zuschauerbänken als unsichtbarer Chor zu jeder Festvorstellung sich einstellten, in die Seelen seiner Bühnenhelden, ihren Forderungen gab er nach, als er für diese neuen Charaktere auch das neue

and constant quantity. Why should the artist be under obligations to accommodate himself to a power whose strength is merely in numbers? And if by virtue of his endowments and aspirations he feels himself superior to every one of these spectators, how could he feel greater respect for the collective expression of all these subordinate capacities than for the relatively highest-endowed individual spectator? In truth, if ever a Greek artist treated his public throughout a long life with presumptuousness and self-sufficiency, it was Euripides, who, even when the masses threw themselves at his feet, with sublime defiance made an open assault on his own tendency, the very tendency with which he had triumphed over the masses. If this genius had had the slightest reverence for the pandemonium of the public, he would have broken down long before the middle of his career beneath the weighty blows of his own failures. These considerations here make it obvious that our formula—namely, that Euripides brought the spectator upon the stage, in order to make him truly competent to pass judgment—was but a provisional one, and that we must seek for a deeper understanding of his tendency. Conversely, it is undoubtedly well known that Aeschylus and Sophocles, during all their lives, indeed, far beyond their lives, enjoyed the full favour of the people, and that therefore in the case of these predecessors of Euripides the idea of a false relation between art-work and public was altogether excluded. What was it that thus forcibly diverted this highly gifted artist, so incessantly impelled to production, from the path over which shone the sun of the greatest names in poetry and the cloudless heaven of popular favour? What strange consideration for the spectator led him to defy, the spectator? How could he, owing to too much respect for the public—dis-respect the public?

Euripides—and this is the solution of the riddle just propounded—felt himself, as a poet, undoubtedly superior to the masses, but not to two of his spectators: he brought the masses upon the stage; these two spectators he revered as the only competent judges and masters of his art: in compliance with their directions and admonitions, he transferred the entire world of sentiments, passions, and experiences, hitherto present at every festival representation as the invisible chorus on the spectators' benches, into the souls of his stage-heroes; he yielded to their

Wort und den neuen Ton suchte, in ihren Stimmen allein hörte er die gültigen Richtersprüche seines Schaffens ebenso wie die siegverheißende Ermutigung, wenn er von der Justiz des Publikums sich wieder einmal verurteilt sah.

Von diesen beiden Zuschauern ist der eine – Euripides selbst, Euripides *als Denker*, nicht als Dichter. Von ihm könnte man sagen, daß die außerordentliche Fülle seines kritischen Talentes, ähnlich wie bei Lessing, einen produktiv künstlerischen Nebentrieb wenn nicht erzeugt, so doch fortwährend befruchtet habe. Mit dieser Begabung, mit aller Helligkeit und Behendigkeit seines kritischen Denkens hatte Euripides im Theater gesessen und sich angestrengt, an den Meisterwerken seiner großen Vorgänger wie an dunkelgewordenen Gemälden Zug um Zug, Linie um Linie wiederzuerkennen. Und hier nun war ihm begegnet, was dem in die tieferen Geheimnisse der äschyleischen Tragödie Eingeweihten nicht unerwartet sein darf: er gewahrte etwas Inkommensurables in jedem Zug und in jeder Linie, eine gewisse täuschende Bestimmtheit und zugleich eine rätselhafte Tiefe, ja Unendlichkeit des Hintergrundes. Die klarste Figur hatte immer noch einen Kometenschweif an sich, der ins Ungewisse, Unaufhellbare zu deuten schien. Dasselbe Zwielicht lag über dem Bau des Dramas, zumal über der Bedeutung des Chors. Und wie zweifelhaft blieb ihm die Lösung der ethischen Probleme! Wie fragwürdig die Behandlung der Mythen! Wie ungleichmäßig die Verteilung von Glück und Unglück! Selbst in der Sprache der älteren Tragödie war ihm vieles anstößig, mindestens rätselhaft; besonders fand er zu viel Pomp für einfache Verhältnisse, zu viel Tropen und Ungeheuerlichkeiten für die Schlichtheit der Charaktere. So saß er, unruhig grübelnd, im Theater, und er, der Zuschauer, gestand sich, daß er seine großen Vorgänger nicht verstehe. Galt ihm aber der Verstand als die eigentliche Wurzel alles Genießens und Schaffens, so mußte er fragen und um sich schauen, ob denn niemand so denke wie er und sich gleichfalls jene Inkommensurabilität eingestehe. Aber die vielen und mit ihnen die besten einzelnen hatten nur ein mißtrauisches Lächeln für ihn; erklären aber konnte ihm keiner, warum seinen Bedenken und Einwendungen gegenüber die großen Meister doch im Rechte seien. Und in diesem qualvollen Zustande fand er *den anderen Zuschauer*, der die Tragödie nicht begriff und deshalb nicht achtete. Mit diesem im Bunde durfte er es wagen, aus seiner Vereinsamung heraus den ungeheuren Kampf gegen die Kunstwerke des Äschylus und Sophokles zu beginnen – nicht mit

demands when he also sought for these new characters the new word and the new tone; in their voices alone he heard the conclusive verdict on his work, as also the cheering promise of triumph when he found himself condemned as usual by the justice of the public.

Of these two, spectators the one is—Euripides himself, Euripides *as thinker,* not as poet. It might be said of him, that his unusually large fund of critical ability, as in the case of Lessing, if it did not create, at least constantly fructified a productively artistic collateral impulse. With this faculty, with all the clearness and dexterity of his critical thought, Euripides had sat in the theatre and striven to recognise in the masterpieces of his great predecessors, as in faded paintings, feature and feature, line and line. And here had happened to him what one initiated in the deeper arcana of Aeschylean tragedy must needs have expected: he observed something incommensurable in every feature and in every line, a certain deceptive distinctness and at the same time an enigmatic profundity, yea an infinitude, of background. Even the clearest figure had always a comet's tail attached to it, which seemed to suggest the uncertain and the inexplicable. The same twilight shrouded the structure of the drama, especially the significance of the chorus. And how doubtful seemed the solution of the ethical problems to his mind! How questionable the treatment of the myths! How unequal the distribution of happiness and misfortune! Even in the language of the Old Tragedy there was much that was objectionable to him, or at least enigmatical; he found especially too much pomp for simple affairs, too many tropes and immense things for the plainness of the characters. Thus he sat restlessly pondering in the theatre, and as a spectator he acknowledged to himself that he did not understand his great predecessors. If, however, he thought the understanding the root proper of all enjoyment and productivity, he had to inquire and look about to see whether any one else thought as he did, and also acknowledged this incommensurability. But most people, and among them the best individuals, had only a distrustful smile for him, while none could explain why the great masters were still in the right in face of his scruples and objections. And in this painful condition he found *that other spectator,* who did not comprehend, and therefore did not esteem, tragedy. In alliance with him he could venture,

Streitschriften, sondern als dramatischer Dichter, der *seine* Vorstellung von der Tragödie der überlieferten entgegenstellt. –

from amid his lonesomeness, to begin the prodigious struggle against the art of Aeschylus and Sophocles—not with polemic writings, but as a dramatic poet, who opposed *his own* conception of tragedy to the traditional one.

12

Bevor wir diesen anderen Zuschauer bei Namen nennen, verharren wir hier einen Augenblick, um uns jenen früher geschilderten Eindruck des Zwiespältigen und Inkommensurablen im Wesen der äschyleischen Tragödie selbst ins Gedächtnis zurückzurufen. Denken wir an unsere eigene Befremdung dem *Chore* und dem *tragischen Helden* jener Tragödie gegenüber, die wir beide mit unseren Gewohnheiten ebensowenig wie mit der Überlieferung zu reimen wußten – bis wir jene Doppelheit selbst als Ursprung und Wesen der griechischen Tragödie wiederfanden, als den Ausdruck zweier ineinandergewobenen Kunsttriebe, *des Apollinischen und des Dionysischen.*

Before we name this other spectator, let us pause here a moment in order to recall our own impression, as previously described, of the discordant and incommensurable elements in the nature of Aeschylean tragedy. Let us think of our own astonishment at the *chorus* and the *tragic hero* of that type of tragedy, neither of which we could reconcile with our practices any more than with tradition—till we rediscovered this duplexity itself as the origin and essence of Greek tragedy, as the expression of two interwoven artistic impulses, *the* Apollonian and the Dionysian.

Jenes ursprüngliche und allmächtige dionysische Element aus der Tragödie auszuscheiden und sie rein und neu auf undionysischer Kunst, Sitte und Weltbetrachtung aufzubauen – dies ist die jetzt in heller Beleuchtung sich uns enthüllende Tendenz des Euripides.

To separate this primitive and all-powerful Dionysian element from tragedy, and to build up a new and purified form of tragedy on the basis of a non-Dionysian art, morality, and conception of things—such is the tendency of Euripides which now reveals itself to us in a clear light.

Euripides selbst hat am Abend seines Lebens die Frage nach dem Wert und der Bedeutung dieser Tendenz in einem Mythus seinen Zeitgenossen auf das nachdrücklichste vorgelegt. Darf überhaupt das Dionysische bestehn? Ist es nicht mit Gewalt aus dem hellenischen Boden auszurotten? Gewiß, sagt uns der Dichter, wenn es nur möglich wäre: aber der Gott Dionysus ist zu mächtig: der verständigste Gegner – wie Pentheus in den »Bacchen« – wird unvermutet von ihm bezaubert und läuft nachher mit dieser Verzauberung in sein Verhängnis. Das Urteil der beiden Greise Kadmus und Tiresias scheint auch das Urteil des greisen Dichters zu sein: das Nachdenken der klügsten einzelnen werfe jene alten Volkstraditionen, jene sich ewig fortpflanzende Verehrung des Dionysus nicht um, ja es gezieme sich, solchen wunderbaren Kräften gegenüber, mindestens eine diplomatisch vorsichtige Teilnahme zu zeigen: wobei es aber immer noch möglich sei, daß der Gott an einer so lauen Beteiligung Anstoß nehme und den Diplomaten – wie hier den Kadmus – schließlich in einen Drachen verwandle. Dies sagt uns der Dichter, der mit heroischer Kraft ein langes Leben hindurch

In a myth composed in the eve of his life, Euripides himself most urgently propounded to his contemporaries the question as to the value and signification of this tendency. Is the Dionysian entitled to exist at all? Should it not be forcibly rooted out of the Hellenic soil? Certainly, the poet tells us, if only it were possible: but the god Dionysus is too powerful; his most intelligent adversary—like Pentheus in the "Bacchae"—is unwittingly enchanted by him, and in this enchantment meets his fate. The judgment of the two old sages, Cadmus and Tiresias, seems to be also the judgment of the aged poet: that the reflection of the wisest individuals does not overthrow old popular traditions, nor the perpetually propagating worship of Dionysus, that in fact it behoves us to display at least a diplomatically cautious concern in the presence of such strange forces: where however it is always possible that the god may take offence at such lukewarm participation, and finally change the diplomat—in this case Cadmus—into a dragon. This is what a poet tells us, who opposed Dionysus with heroic valour throughout a long life—

dem Dionysus widerstanden hat – um am Ende desselben mit einer Glorifikation seines Gegners und einem Selbstmorde seine Laufbahn zu schließen, einem Schwindelndem gleich, der, um nur dem entsetzlichen, nicht mehr erträglichen Wirbel zu entgehen, sich vom Turme herunterstürzt. Jene Tragödie ist ein Protest gegen die Ausführbarkeit seiner Tendenz; ach, und sie war bereits ausgeführt! Das Wunderbare war geschehn: als der Dichter widerrief, hatte bereits seine Tendenz gesiegt. Dionysus war bereits von der tragischen Bühne verscheucht und zwar durch eine aus Euripides redende dämonische Macht. Auch Euripides war in gewissem Sinne nur Maske: die Gottheit, die aus ihm redete, war nicht Dionysus, auch nicht Apollo, sondern ein ganz neugeborner Dämon, genannt *Socrates*. Dies ist der neue Gegensatz: das Dionysische und das Sokratische, und das Kunstwerk der griechischen Tragödie ging an ihm zugrunde. Mag nun auch Euripides uns durch seinen Widerruf zu trösten suchen, es gelingt ihm nicht: der herrlichste Tempel liegt in Trümmern; was nützt uns die Wehklage des Zerstörers und sein Geständnis, daß es der schönste aller Tempel gewesen sei? Und selbst daß Euripides zur Strafe von den Kunstrichtern aller Zeiten in einen Drachen verwandelt worden ist – wen möchte diese erbärmliche Kompensation befriedigen?

Nähern wir uns jetzt jener *sokratischen* Tendenz, mit der Euripides die äschyleische Tragödie bekämpfte und besiegte.

Welches Ziel – so müssen wir uns jetzt fragen – konnte die euripideische Absicht, das Drama allein auf das Undionysische zu gründen, in der höchsten Idealität ihrer Durchführung überhaupt haben? Welche Form des Dramas blieb noch übrig, wenn es nicht aus dem Geburtsschoße der Musik, in jenem geheimnisvollen Zwielicht des Dionysischen geboren werden sollte? Allein *das dramatisierte Epos*: in welchem apollinischen Kunstgebiete nun freilich die *tragische* Wirkung unerreichbar ist. Es kommt hierbei nicht auf den Inhalt der dargestellten Ereignisse an; ja ich möchte behaupten, daß es Goethe in seiner projektierten »Nausikaa« unmöglich gewesen sein würde, den Selbstmord jenes idyllischen Wesens – der den fünften Akt ausfüllen sollte – tragisch ergreifend zu machen; so ungemein ist die Gewalt des Episch-Apollinischen, daß es die schreckensvollsten Dinge mit jener Lust am Scheine und der Erlösung durch den Schein vor unseren Augen verzaubert. Der Dichter des dramatischen Epos kann ebensowenig wie der epische Rhapsode mit seinen Bildern völlig verschmelzen: er

in order finally to wind up his career with a glorification of his adversary, and with suicide, like one staggering from giddiness, who, in order to escape the horrible vertigo he can no longer endure, casts himself from a tower. This tragedy—the Bacchae—is a protest against the practicability of his own tendency; alas, and it has already been put into practice! The surprising thing had happened: when the poet recanted, his tendency had already conquered. Dionysus had already been scared from the tragic stage, and in fact by a demonic power which spoke through Euripides. Even Euripides was, in a certain sense, only a mask: the deity that spoke through him was neither Dionysus nor Apollo, but an altogether new-born demon, called *Socrates*. This is the new antithesis: the Dionysian and the Socratic, and the art-work of Greek tragedy was wrecked on it. What if even Euripides now seeks to comfort us by his recantation? It is of no avail: the most magnificent temple lies in ruins. What avails the lamentation of the destroyer, and his confession that it was the most beautiful of all temples? And even that Euripides has been changed into a dragon as a punishment by the art-critics of all ages—who could be content with this wretched compensation?

Let us now approach this *Socratic* tendency with which Euripides combated and vanquished Aeschylean tragedy.

We must now ask ourselves, what could be the ulterior aim of the Euripidean design, which, in the highest ideality of its execution, would found drama exclusively on the non-Dionysian? What other form of drama could there be, if it was not to be born of the womb of music, in the mysterious twilight of the Dionysian? Only *the dramatised epos:* in which Apollonian domain of art the *tragic* effect is of course unattainable. It does not depend on the subject-matter of the events here represented; indeed, I venture to assert that it would have been impossible for Goethe in his projected “Nausikaa” to have rendered tragically effective the suicide of the idyllic being with which he intended to complete the fifth act; so extraordinary is the power of the epic-Apollonian representation, that it charms, before our eyes, the most terrible things by the joy in appearance and in redemption through appearance. The poet of the dramatised epos cannot completely blend with his pictures any more than the epic rhapsodist.

ist immer noch ruhig unbewegte, aus weiten Augen blickende Anschauung, die die Bilder *vor* sich sieht. Der Schauspieler in seinem dramatisierten Epos bleibt im tiefsten Grunde immer noch Rhapsode; die Weihe des inneren Träumens liegt auf allen seinen Aktionen, so daß er niemals ganz Schauspieler ist.

He is still just the calm, unmoved embodiment of Contemplation whose wide eyes see the picture *before* them. The actor in this dramatised epos still remains intrinsically rhapsodist: the consecration of inner dreaming is on all his actions, so that he is never wholly an actor.

Wie verhält sich nun diesem Ideal des apollinischen Dramas gegenüber das euripideische Stück? Wie zu dem feierlichen Rhapsoden der alten Zeit jener jüngere, der sein Wesen im platonischen »Jon« also beschreibt: »Wenn ich etwas Trauriges sage, füllen sich meine Augen mit Tränen; ist aber das, was ich sage, schrecklich und entsetzlich, dann stehen die Haare meines Hauptes vor Schauder zu Berge, und mein Herz klopft.« Hier merken wir nichts mehr von jenem epischen Verlorensein im Scheine, von der affektlosen Kühle des wahren Schauspielers, der, gerade in seiner höchsten Tätigkeit, ganz Schein und Lust am Scheine ist. Euripides ist der Schauspieler mit dem klopfenden Herzen, mit den zu Berge stehenden Haaren; als sokratischer Denker entwirft er den Plan, als leidenschaftlicher Schauspieler führt er ihn aus. Reiner Künstler ist er weder im Entwerfen noch im Ausführen. So ist das euripideische Drama ein zugleich kühles und feuriges Ding, zum Erstarren und zum Verbrennen gleich befähigt; es ist ihm unmöglich, die apollinische Wirkung des Epos zu erreichen, während es andererseits sich von den dionysischen Elementen möglichst gelöst hat und jetzt, um überhaupt zu wirken, neue Erregungsmittel braucht, die nun nicht mehr innerhalb der beiden einzigen Kunsttriebe, des apollinischen und des dionysischen, liegen können. Diese Erregungsmittel sind kühle paradoxe *Gedanken* – an Stelle der apollinischen Anschauungen – und feurige *Affekte* – an Stelle der dionysischen Entzückungen – und zwar höchst realistisch nachgemachte, keineswegs in den Äther der Kunst getauchte Gedanken und Affekte.

How, then, is the Euripidean play related to this ideal of the Apollonian drama? Just as the younger rhapsodist is related to the solemn rhapsodist of the old time. The former describes his own character in the Platonic *Ion* as follows: “When I am saying anything sad, my eyes fill with tears; when, however, what I am saying is awful and terrible, then my hair stands on end through fear, and my heart leaps.” Here we no longer observe anything of the epic absorption in appearance, or of the unemotional coolness of the true actor, who precisely in his highest activity is wholly appearance and joy in appearance. Euripides is the actor with leaping heart, with hair standing on end; as Socratic thinker he designs the plan, as passionate actor he executes it. Neither in the designing nor in the execution is he an artist pure and simple. And so the Euripidean drama is a thing both cool and fiery, equally capable of freezing and burning; it is impossible for it to attain the Apollonian, effect of the epos, while, on the other hand, it has severed itself as much as possible from Dionysian elements, and now, in order to act at all, it requires new stimulants, which can no longer lie within the sphere of the two unique art-impulses, the Apollonian and the Dionysian. The stimulants are cool, paradoxical *thoughts*, in place of Apollonian intuitions—and fiery *passions*—in place Dionysean ecstasies; and in fact, thoughts and passions very realistically copied, and not at all steeped in the ether of art.

Haben wir demnach so viel erkannt, daß es Euripides überhaupt nicht gelungen ist, das Drama allein auf das Apollinische zu gründen, daß sich vielmehr seine undionysische Tendenz in eine naturalistische und unkünstlerische verirrt hat, so werden wir jetzt dem Wesen des *ästhetischen Sokratismus* schon näher treten dürfen, dessen oberstes Gesetz ungefähr so lautet: »Alles muß verständig sein, um schön zu sein«; als Parallelsatz zu dem sokratischen »nur der Wissende ist tugendhaft«. Mit diesem Kanon in der Hand maß Euripides alles einzelne und rektifizierte es gemäß diesem Prinzip: die Sprache, die Charaktere, den dramaturgischen Aufbau,

Accordingly, if we have perceived this much, that Euripides did not succeed in establishing the drama exclusively on the Apollonian, but that rather his non-Dionysian inclinations deviated into a naturalistic and inartistic tendency, we shall now be able to approach nearer to the character *æsthetic Socratism.* supreme law of which reads about as follows: “to be beautiful everything must be intelligible,” as the parallel to the Socratic proposition, “only the knowing is one virtuous.” With this canon in his hands Euripides measured all the separate elements of the drama, and rectified them according to his principle: the language, the characters, the dramaturgic

die Chormusik. Was wir im Vergleich mit der sophokleischen Tragödie so häufig dem Euripides als dichterischen Mangel und Rückschritt anzurechnen pflegen, das ist zumeist das Produkt jenes eindringenden kritischen Prozesses, jener verwegenen Verständigkeit. Der euripideische *Prolog* diene uns als Beispiel für die Produktivität jener rationalistischen Methode. Nichts kann unserer Bühnentechnik widerstrebender sein als der Prolog im Drama des Euripides. Daß eine einzelne auftretende Person am Eingange des Stückes erzählt, wer sie sei, was der Handlung vorangehe, was bis jetzt geschehen, ja was im Verlaufe des Stückes geschehen werde, das würde ein moderner Theaterdichter als ein mutwilliges und nicht zu verzeihendes Verzichtleisten auf den Effekt der Spannung bezeichnen. Man weiß ja alles, was geschehen wird; wer wird abwarten wollen, daß dies wirklich geschieht? – da ja hier keinesfalls das aufregende Verhältnis eines wahrsagenden Traumes zu einer später eintretenden Wirklichkeit stattfindet. Ganz anders reflektierte Euripides. Die Wirkung der Tragödie beruhte niemals auf der epischen Spannung, auf der anreizenden Ungewißheit, was sich jetzt und nachher ereignen werde: vielmehr auf jenen großen rhetorisch-lyrischen Szenen, in denen die Leidenschaft und die Dialektik des Haupthelden zu einem breiten und mächtigen Strome anschwoll. Zum Pathos, nicht zur Handlung bereitete alles vor: und was nicht zum Pathos vorbereitete, das galt als verwerflich. Das aber, was die genußvolle Hingabe an solche Szenen am stärksten erschwert, ist ein dem Zuhörer fehlendes Glied, eine Lücke im Gewebe der Vorgeschichte; solange der Zuhörer noch ausrechnen muß, was diese und jene Person bedeute, was dieser und jener Konflikt der Neigungen und Absichten für Voraussetzungen habe, ist seine volle Versenkung in das Leiden und Tun der Hauptpersonen, ist das atemlose Mitleiden und Mitfürchten noch nicht möglich. Die äschyleisch-sophokleische Tragödie verwandte die geistreichsten Kunstmittel, um dem Zuschauer in den ersten Szenen gewissermaßen zufällig alle jene zum Verständnis notwendigen Fäden in die Hand zu geben: ein Zug, in dem sich jene edle Künstlerschaft bewährt, die das *notwendige* Formelle gleichsam maskiert und als Zufälliges erscheinen läßt. Immerhin aber glaubte Euripides zu bemerken, daß während jener ersten Szenen der Zuschauer in eigentümlicher Unruhe sei, um das Rechenexempel der Vorgeschichte auszurechnen, so daß die dichterischen Schönheiten und das Pathos der Exposition für ihn verlorenginge. Deshalb stellte er den Prolog noch vor die Exposition und legte ihn einer Person in den Mund, der man Vertrauen schenken durfte: eine Gottheit mußte

structure, and the choric music. The poetic deficiency and retrogression, which we are so often wont to impute to Euripides in comparison with Sophoclean tragedy, is for the most part the product of this penetrating critical process, this daring intelligibility. The Euripidian *prologue* may serve us as an example of the productivity of this, rationalistic method. Nothing could be more opposed to the technique of our stage than the prologue in the drama of Euripides. For a single person to appear at the outset of the play telling us who he is, what precedes the action, what has happened thus far, yea, what will happen in the course of the play, would be designated by a modern playwright as a wanton and unpardonable abandonment of the effect of suspense. Everything that is about to happen is known beforehand; who then cares to wait for it actually to happen?—considering, moreover, that here there is not by any means the exciting relation of a predicting dream to a reality taking place later on. Euripides speculated quite differently. The effect of tragedy never depended on epic suspense, on the fascinating uncertainty as to what is to happen now and afterwards: but rather on the great rhetoro-lyric scenes in which the passion and dialectics of the chief hero swelled to a broad and mighty stream. Everything was arranged for pathos, not for action: and whatever was not arranged for pathos was regarded as objectionable. But what interferes most with the hearer's pleasurable satisfaction in such scenes is a missing link, a gap in the texture of the previous history. So long as the spectator has to divine the meaning of this or that person, or the presuppositions of this or that conflict of inclinations and intentions, his complete absorption in the doings and sufferings of the chief persons is impossible, as is likewise breathless fellow-feeling and fellow-fearing. The Æschyleo-Sophoclean tragedy employed the most ingenious devices in the first scenes to place in the hands of the spectator as if by chance all the threads requisite for understanding the whole: a trait in which that noble artistry is approved, which as it were masks the *inevitably* formal, and causes it to appear as something accidental. But nevertheless Euripides thought he observed that during these first scenes the spectator was in a strange state of anxiety to make out the problem of the previous history, so that the poetic beauties and pathos of the exposition were lost to him. Accordingly he placed the prologue even before the exposition, and put it in the mouth of a person

häufig den Verlauf der Tragödie dem Publikum gewissermaßen garantieren und jeden Zweifel an der Realität des Mythus nehmen: in ähnlicher Weise, wie Descartes die Realität der empirischen Welt nur durch die Appellation an die Wahrhaftigkeit Gottes und seine Unfähigkeit zur Lüge zu beweisen vermochte. Dieselbe göttliche Wahrhaftigkeit braucht Euripides noch einmal am Schlusse seines Dramas, um die Zukunft seiner Helden dem Publikum sicherzustellen: dies ist die Aufgabe des berüchtigten *deus ex machina*. Zwischen der epischen Vorschau und Hinausschau liegt die dramatisch-lyrische Gegenwart, das eigentliche »Drama«.

So ist Euripides vor allem als Dichter der Widerhall seiner bewußten Erkenntnisse; und gerade dies verleiht ihm eine so denkwürdige Stellung in der Geschichte der griechischen Kunst. Ihm muß im Hinblick auf sein kritisch-produktives Schaffen oft zumute gewesen sein, als sollte er den Anfang der Schrift des Anaxagoras für das Drama lebendig machen, deren erste Worte lauten: »im Anfang war alles beisammen: da kam der Verstand und schuf Ordnung«. Und wenn Anaxagoras mit seinem »Nus« unter den Philosophen wie der erste Nüchterne unter lauter Trunkenen erschien, so mag auch Euripides sein Verhältnis zu den anderen Dichtern der Tragödie unter einem ähnlichen Bilde begriffen haben. Solange der einzige Ordner und Walter des Alls, der Nus, noch vom künstlerischen Schaffen ausgeschlossen war, war noch alles in einem chaotischen Urbrei beisammen; so mußte Euripides urteilen, so mußte er die »trunkenen« Dichter als der erste »Nüchterne« verurteilen. Das, was Sophokles von Äschylus gesagt hat, er tue das Rechte, obschon unbewußt, war gewiß nicht im Sinne des Euripides gesagt: der nur soviel hätte gelten lassen, daß Äschylus, *weil* er unbewußt schaffe, das Unrechte schaffe. Auch der göttliche Plato redet vom schöpferischen Vermögen des Dichters, insofern dies nicht die bewußte Einsicht ist, zu allermeist nur ironisch und stellt es der Begabung des Wahrsagers und Traumdeuters gleich; sei doch der Dichter nicht eher fähig zu dichten, als bis er bewußtlos geworden sei, und kein Verstand mehr in ihm wohne. Euripides unternahm es, wie es auch Plato unternommen hat, das Gegenstück des »unverständigen« Dichters der Welt zu zeigen, sein ästhetischer Grundsatz »alles muß bewußt sein, um schön zu sein«, ist, wie ich sagte, der Parallelsatz zu dem sokratischen »alles muß bewußt sein, um gut zu sein«. Demgemäß darf uns Euripides als der Dichter des ästhetischen Sokratismus gelten. Socrates aber war jener *zweite Zuschauer*, der die ältere Tragödie nicht begriff und deshalb nicht achtete; mit

who could be trusted: some deity had often as it were to guarantee the particulars of the tragedy to the public and remove every doubt as to the reality of the myth: as in the case of Descartes, who could only prove the reality of the empiric world by an appeal to the truthfulness of God and His inability to utter falsehood. Euripides makes use of the same divine truthfulness once more at the close of his drama, in order to ensure to the public the future of his heroes; this is the task of the notorious *deus ex machina*. Between the preliminary and the additional epic spectacle there is the dramatico-lyric present, the "drama" proper.

Thus Euripides as a poet echoes above all his own conscious knowledge; and it is precisely on this account that he occupies such a notable position in the history of Greek art. With reference to his critico-productive activity, he must often have felt that he ought to actualise in the drama the words at the beginning of the essay of Anaxagoras: "In the beginning all things were mixed together; then came the understanding and created order." And if Anaxagoras with his "νοῦς" seemed like the first sober person among nothing but drunken philosophers, Euripides may also have conceived his relation to the other tragic poets under a similar figure. As long as the sole ruler and disposer of the universe, the νοῦς, was still excluded from artistic activity, things were all mixed together in a chaotic, primitive mess;—it is thus Euripides was obliged to think, it is thus he was obliged to condemn the "drunken" poets as the first "sober" one among them. What Sophocles said of Aeschylus, that he did what was right, though unconsciously, was surely not in the mind of Euripides: who would have admitted only thus much, that Aeschylus, *because* he wrought unconsciously, did what was wrong. So also the divine Plato speaks for the most part only ironically of the creative faculty of the poet, in so far as it is not conscious insight, and places it on a par with the gift of the soothsayer and dream-interpreter; insinuating that the poet is incapable of composing until he has become unconscious and reason has deserted him. Like Plato, Euripides undertook to show to the world the reverse of the "unintelligent" poet; his æsthetic principle that "to be beautiful everything must be known" is, as I have said, the parallel to the Socratic "to be good everything must be known." Accordingly wc may regard Euripides as the poet of æsthetic Socratism. Socrates, however, was that *second*

ihm im Bunde wagte Euripides, der Herold eines neuen Kunstschaffens zu sein. Wenn an diesem die ältere Tragödie zugrunde ging, so ist also der ästhetische Sokratismus das mörderische Prinzip: insofern aber der Kampf gegen das Dionysische der älteren Kunst gerichtet war, erkennen wir in Socrates den Gegner des Dionysus, den neuen Orpheus, der sich gegen Dionysus erhebt und, obschon bestimmt, von den Mänaden des athenischen Gerichtshofes zerrissen zu werden, doch den übermächtigen Gott selbst zur Flucht nötigt: welcher, wie damals, als er vor dem Edonerkönig Lykurg floh, sich in die Tiefen des Meeres rettete, nämlich in die mystischen Fluten eines die ganze Welt allmählich überziehenden Geheimkultus.

spectator who did not comprehend and therefore did not esteem the Old Tragedy; in alliance with him Euripides ventured to be the herald of a new artistic activity. If, then, the Old Tragedy was here destroyed, it follows that æsthetic Socratism was the murderous principle; but in so far as the struggle is directed against the Dionysian element in the old art, we recognise in Socrates the opponent of Dionysus, the new Orpheus who rebels against Dionysus; and although destined to be torn to pieces by the Mænads of the Athenian court, yet puts to flight the overpowerful god himself, who, when he fled from Lycurgus, the king of Edoni, sought refuge in the depths of the ocean—namely, in the mystical flood of a secret cult which gradually overspread the earth.

13

Daß Socrates eine enge Beziehung der Tendenz zu Euripides habe, entging dem gleichzeitigen Altertume nicht; und der beredteste Ausdruck für diesen glücklichen Spürsinn ist jene in Athen umlaufende Sage, Socrates pflege dem Euripides im Dichten zu helfen. Beide Namen wurden von den Anhängern der »guten alten Zeit« in einem Atem genannt, wenn es galt, die Volksverführer der Gegenwart aufzuzählen: von deren Einflusse es herrühre, daß die alte marathonische vierschrötige Tüchtigkeit an Leib und Seele immer mehr einer zweifelhaften Aufklärung, bei fortschreitender Verkümmerung der leiblichen und seelischen Kräfte, zum Opfer falle. In dieser Tonart, halb mit Entrüstung, halb mit Verachtung, pflegt die aristophanische Komödie von jenen Männern zu reden, zum Schrecken der Neueren, welche zwar Euripides gerne preisgeben, aber sich nicht genug darüber wundern können, daß Socrates als der erste und oberste *Sophist*, als der Spiegel und Inbegriff aller sophistischen Bestrebungen bei Aristophanes erscheine: wobei es einzig einen Trost gewährt, den Aristophanes selbst als einen liederlich lügenhaften Alcibiades der Poesie an den Pranger zu stellen. Ohne an dieser Stelle die tiefen Instinkte des Aristophanes gegen solche Angriffe in Schutz zu nehmen, fahre ich fort, die enge Zusammengehörigkeit des Socrates und des Euripides aus der antiken Empfindung heraus zu erweisen; in welchem Sinne namentlich daran zu erinnern ist, daß Socrates als Gegner der tragischen Kunst sich des Besuchs der Tragödie enthielt und nur, wenn ein neues Stück des Euripides aufgeführt wurde, sich unter den Zuschauern einstellte. Am

That Socrates stood in close relationship to Euripides in the tendency of his teaching, did not escape the notice of contemporaneous antiquity; the most eloquent expression of this felicitous insight being the tale current in Athens, that Socrates was accustomed to help Euripides in poetising. Both names were mentioned in one breath by the adherents of the "good old time," whenever they came to enumerating the popular agitators of the day: to whose influence they attributed the fact that the old Marathonian stalwart capacity of body and soul was more and more being sacrificed to a dubious enlightenment, involving progressive degeneration of the physical and mental powers. It is in this tone, half indignantly and half contemptuously, that Aristophanic comedy is wont to speak of both of them—to the consternation of modern men, who would indeed be willing enough to give up Euripides, but cannot suppress their amazement that Socrates should appear in Aristophanes as the first and head *sophist,* as the mirror and epitome of all sophistical tendencies; in connection with which it offers the single consolation of putting Aristophanes himself in the pillory, as a rakish, lying Alcibiades of poetry. Without here defending the profound instincts of Aristophanes against such attacks, I shall now indicate, by means of the sentiments of the time, the close connection between Socrates and Euripides. With this purpose in view, it is especially to be remembered that Socrates, as an opponent of tragic art, did not ordinarily patronise tragedy, but only appeared

berühmtesten ist aber die nahe Zusammenstellung beider Namen in dem delphischen Orakelspruche, welcher Socrates als den Weisesten unter den Menschen bezeichnete, zugleich aber das Urteil abgab, daß dem Euripides der zweite Preis im Wettkampfe der Weisheit gebühre.

Als der dritte in dieser Stufenleiter war Sophokles genannt; er, der sich gegen Äschylus rühmen durfte, er tue das Rechte, und zwar, weil er *wisse*, was das Rechte sei. Offenbar ist gerade der Grad der Helligkeit dieses *Wissens* dasjenige, was jene drei Männer gemeinsam als die drei »Wissenden« ihrer Zeit auszeichnet.

Das schärfste Wort aber für jene neue und unerhörte Hochschätzung des Wissens und der Einsicht sprach Socrates, als er sich als den Einzigen vorfand, der sich eingestehe, *nichts zu wissen*; während er, auf seiner kritischen Wanderung durch Athen, bei den größten Staatsmännern, Rednern, Dichtern und Künstlern vorsprechend, überall die Einbildung des Wissens antraf. Mit Staunen erkannte er, daß alle jene Berühmtheiten selbst über ihren Beruf ohne richtige und sichere Einsicht seien und denselben nur aus Instinkt trieben. »Nur aus Instinkt«: mit diesem Ausdruck berühren wir Herz und Mittelpunkt der sokratischen Tendenz. Mit ihm verurteilt der Sokratismus ebenso die bestehende Kunst wie die bestehende Ethik: wohin er seine prüfenden Blicke richtet, sieht er den Mangel der Einsicht und die Macht des Wahns und schließt aus diesem Mangel auf die innerliche Verkehrtheit und Verwerflichkeit des Vorhandenen. Von diesem einen Punkte aus glaubte Socrates das Dasein korrigieren zu müssen: er, der Einzelne, tritt mit der Miene der Nichtachtung und der Überlegenheit, als der Vorläufer einer ganz anders gearteten Kultur, Kunst und Moral, in eine Welt hinein, deren Zipfel mit Ehrfurcht zu erhaschen wir uns zum größten Glücke rechnen würden.

Dies ist die ungeheure Bedenklichkeit, die uns jedesmal, angesichts des Socrates, ergreift und die uns immer und immer wieder anreizt, Sinn und Absicht dieser fragwürdigsten Erscheinung des Altertums zu erkennen. Wer ist das, der es wagen darf, als ein Einzelner das griechische Wesen zu verneinen, das als Homer, Pindar und Äschylus, als Phidias, als Perikles, als Pythia und Dionysus, als der tiefste Abgrund und die höchste Höhe unserer staunenden Anbetung gewiß ist? Welche dämonische Kraft ist es, die diesen Zaubertrank in den Staub zu schütten sich

among the spectators when a new play of Euripides was performed. The most noted thing, however, is the close juxtaposition of the two names in the Delphic oracle, which designated Socrates as the wisest of men, but at the same time decided that the second prize in the contest of wisdom was due to Euripides.

Sophocles was designated as the third in this scale of rank; he who could pride himself that, in comparison with Aeschylus, he did what was right, and did it, moreover, because he *knew* what was right. It is evidently just the degree of clearness of this *knowledge*, which distinguishes these three men in common as the three "knowing ones" of their age.

The most decisive word, however, for this new and unprecedented esteem of knowledge and insight was spoken by Socrates when he found that he was the only one who acknowledged to himself that he *knew nothing* while in his critical pilgrimage through Athens, and calling on the greatest statesmen, orators, poets, and artists, he discovered everywhere the conceit of knowledge. He perceived, to his astonishment, that all these celebrities were without a proper and accurate insight, even with regard to their own callings, and practised them only by instinct. "Only by instinct": with this phrase we touch upon the heart and core of the Socratic tendency. Socratism condemns therewith existing art as well as existing ethics; wherever Socratism turns its searching eyes it beholds the lack of insight and the power of illusion; and from this lack infers the inner perversity and objectionableness of existing conditions. From this point onwards, Socrates believed that he was called upon to, correct existence; and, with an air of disregard and superiority, as the precursor of an altogether different culture, art, and morality, he enters single-handed into a world, of which, if we reverently touched the hem, we should count it our greatest happiness.

Here is the extraordinary hesitancy which always seizes upon us with regard to Socrates, and again and again invites us to ascertain the sense and purpose of this most questionable phenomenon of antiquity. Who is it that ventures single-handed to disown the Greek character, which, as Homer, Pindar, and Aeschylus, as Phidias, as Pericles, as Pythia and Dionysus, as the deepest abyss and the

erkühnen darf? Welcher Halbgott ist es, dem der Geisterchor der Edelsten der Menschheit zurufen muß: »Weh! Weh! Du hast sie zerstört, die schöne Welt, mit mächtiger Faust; sie stürzt, sie zerfällt!«

Einen Schlüssel zu dem Wesen des Socrates bietet uns jene wunderbare Erscheinung, die als »Dämonion des Socrates« bezeichnet wird. In besonderen Lagen, in denen sein ungeheurer Verstand ins Schwanken geriet, gewann er einen festen Anhalt durch eine in solchen Momenten sich äußernde göttliche Stimme. Diese Stimme *mahnt*, wenn sie kommt, immer *ab*. Die instinktive Weisheit zeigt sich bei dieser gänzlich abnormen Natur nur, um dem bewußten Erkennen hier und da *hindernd* entgegenzutreten. Während doch bei allen produktiven Menschen der Instinkt gerade die schöpferisch-affirmative Kraft ist, und das Bewußtsein kritisch und abmahnend sich gebärdet: wird bei Socrates der Instinkt zum Kritiker, das Bewußtsein zum Schöpfer – eine wahre Monstrosität *per defectum*! Und zwar nehmen wir hier einen monströsen *defectus* jeder mystischen Anlage wahr, so daß Socrates als der spezifische *Nicht-Mystiker* zu bezeichnen wäre, in dem die logische Natur durch eine Superfötation ebenso exzessiv entwickelt ist wie im Mystiker jene instinktive Weisheit. Andrerseits aber war es jenem in Socrates erscheinenden logischen Triebe völlig versagt, sich gegen sich selbst zu kehren; in diesem fessellosen Dahinströmen zeigt er eine Naturgewalt, wie wir sie nur bei den allergrößten instinktiven Kräften zu unsrer schaudervollen Überraschung antreffen. Wer nur einen Hauch von jener göttlichen Naivität und Sicherheit der sokratischen Lebensrichtung aus den platonischen Schriften gespürt hat, der fühlt auch, wie das ungeheure Triebrad des logischen Sokratismus gleichsam *hinter* Socrates in Bewegung ist, und wie dies durch Socrates wie durch einen Schatten hindurch angeschaut werden muß. Daß er aber selbst von diesem Verhältnis eine Ahnung hatte, das drückt sich in dem würdevollen Ernste aus, mit dem er seine göttliche Berufung überall und noch vor seinen Richtern geltend machte. Ihn darin zu widerlegen war im Grunde ebenso unmöglich als seinen die Instinkte auflösenden Einfluß gutzuheißen. Bei diesem unlösbaren Konflikte war, als er einmal vor das Forum des griechischen Staates gezogen war, nur eine einzige Form der Verurteilung geboten, die Verbannung; als etwas durchaus Rätselhaftes, Unrubrizierbares, Unaufklärbares hätte man ihn über die Grenze weisen dürfen, ohne daß irgendeine Nachwelt im Recht gewesen wäre, die

highest height, is sure of our wondering admiration? What demoniac power is it which would presume to spill this magic draught in the dust? What demigod is it to whom the chorus of spirits of the noblest of mankind must call out: "Woe! Woe! You have destroyed it, the beautiful world; with powerful fist; it falls, it falls apart!"

A key to the character of Socrates is presented to us by the surprising phenomenon designated as the "daimonion" of Socrates. In special circumstances, when his gigantic intellect began to stagger, he got a secure support in the utterances of a divine voice which then spake to him. This voice, whenever it comes, always *dissuades*. In this totally abnormal nature instinctive wisdom only appears in order to hinder the progress of conscious perception here and there. While in all productive men it is instinct which is the creatively affirmative force, consciousness only comporting itself critically and dissuasively; with Socrates it is instinct which becomes critic; it is consciousness which becomes creator—a perfect monstrosity *per defectum!* And we do indeed observe here a monstrous *defectus* of all mystical aptitude, so that Socrates might be designated as the specific *non-mystic*, in whom the logical nature is developed, through a superfoetation, to the same excess as instinctive wisdom is developed in the mystic. On the other hand, however, the logical instinct which appeared in Socrates was absolutely prohibited from turning against itself; in its unchecked flow it manifests a native power such as we meet with, to our shocking surprise, only among the very greatest instinctive forces. He who has experienced even a breath of the divine naïveté and security of the Socratic course of life in the Platonic writings, will also feel that the enormous driving-wheel of logical Socratism is in motion, as it were, *behind* Socrates, and that it must be viewed through Socrates as through a shadow. And that he himself had a boding of this relation is apparent from the dignified earnestness with which he everywhere, and even before his judges, insisted on his divine calling. To refute him here was really as impossible as to approve of his instinct-disintegrating influence. In view of this indissoluble conflict, when he had at last been brought before the forum of the Greek state, there was only one punishment demanded, namely exile; he might have been sped across the borders as something thoroughly enigmatical, irrubricable and inexplicable, and so posterity would have been quite unjustified in

Athener einer schmählichen Tat zu zeihen. Daß aber der Tod und nicht nur die Verbannung über ihn ausgesprochen wurde, das scheint Socrates selbst, mit völliger Klarheit und ohne den natürlichen Schauder vor dem Tode, durchgesetzt zu haben: er ging in den Tod, mit jener Ruhe, mit der er nach Platos Schilderung als der letzte der Zecher im frühen Tagesgrauen das Symposion verläßt, um einen neuen Tag zu beginnen; indes hinter ihm, auf den Bänken und auf der Erde, die verschlafenen Tischgenossen zurückbleiben, um von Socrates, dem wahrhaften Erotiker, zu träumen. *Der sterbende Socrates* wurde das neue, noch nie sonst geschaute Ideal der edlen griechischen Jugend: vor allen hat sich der typische hellenische Jüngling, Plato, mit aller inbrünstigen Hingebung seiner Schwärmerseele vor diesem Bilde niedergeworfen.

charging the Athenians with a deed of ignominy. But that the sentence of death, and not mere exile, was pronounced upon him, seems to have been brought about by Socrates himself, with perfect knowledge of the circumstances, and without the natural fear of death: he met his death with the calmness with which, according to the description of Plato, he leaves the symposium at break of day, as the last of the revellers, to begin a new day; while the sleepy companions remain behind on the benches and the floor, to dream of Socrates, the true eroticist. *The dying Socrates* became the new ideal of the noble Greek youths—an ideal they had never yet beheld—and above all, the typical Hellenic youth, Plato, prostrated himself before this scene with all the fervent devotion of his visionary soul.

14

Denken wir uns jetzt das eine große Zyklopenauge des Socrates auf die Tragödie gewandt, jenes Auge, in dem nie der holde Wahnsinn künstlerischer Begeisterung geglüht hat – denken wir uns, wie es jenem Auge versagt war, in die dionysischen Abgründe mit Wohlgefallen zu schauen – was eigentlich mußte es in der »erhabenen und hochgepriesenen« tragischen Kunst, wie sie Plato nennt, erblicken? Etwas recht Unvernünftiges, mit Ursachen, die ohne Wirkungen, und mit Wirkungen, die ohne Ursachen zu sein schienen; dazu das ganze so bunt und mannigfaltig, daß es einer besonnenen Gemütsart widerstreben müsse, für reizbare und empfindliche Seelen aber ein gefährlicher Zunder sei. Wir wissen, welche einzige Gattung der Dichtkunst von ihm begriffen wurde, die *äsopische Fabel*: und dies geschah gewiß mit jener lächelnden Anbequemung, mit welcher der ehrliche gute Gellert in der Fabel von der Biene und der Henne das Lob der Poesie singt:

»Du siehst an mir, wozu sie nützt,
Dem, der nicht viel Verstand besitzt,
Die Wahrheit durch ein Bild zu sagen.«

Nun aber schien Socrates die tragische Kunst nicht einmal »die Wahrheit zu sagen«: abgesehen davon, daß sie sich an den wendet, der »nicht viel Verstand besitzt«, also nicht an den Philosophen: ein zweifacher Grund, von ihr fernzubleiben. Wie Plato, rechnete er sie zu den schmeichlerischen Künsten, die nur das Angenehme, nicht das Nützliche darstellen, und verlangte deshalb bei seinen Jüngern Enthaltsamkeit

Let us now imagine the one great Cyclopean eye of Socrates fixed on tragedy, that eye in which the fine frenzy of artistic enthusiasm had never glowed—let us think how it was denied to this eye to gaze with pleasure into the Dionysian abysses—what could it not but see in the "sublime and greatly lauded" tragic art, as Plato called it? Something very absurd, with causes that seemed to be without effects, and effects apparently without causes; the whole, moreover, so motley and diversified that it could not but be repugnant to a thoughtful mind, a dangerous incentive, however, to sensitive and irritable souls. We know what was the sole kind of poetry which he comprehended: the *Æsopian fable*: and he did this no doubt with that smiling complaisance with which the good honest Gellert sings the praise of poetry in the fable of the bee and the hen:—

You see from me how good it is
with someone who doesn't have a lot of sense
to tell the truth through a picture.

But then it seemed to Socrates that tragic art did not even "tell the truth": not to mention the fact that it addresses itself to him who "has but little wit"; consequently not to the philosopher: a twofold reason why it should be avoided. Like Plato, he reckoned it among the seductive arts which only represent the agreeable, not the useful, and hence he required of his disciples abstinence and strict separation from

und strenge Absonderung von solchen unphilosophischen Reizungen; mit solchem Erfolge, daß der jugendliche Tragödiendichter Plato zuallererst seine Dichtungen verbrannte, um Schüler des Socrates werden zu können. Wo aber unbesiegbare Anlagen gegen die sokratischen Maximen ankämpften, war die Kraft derselben, samt der Wucht jenes ungeheuren Charakters, immer noch groß genug, um die Poesie selbst in neue und bis dahin unbekannte Stellungen zu drängen.

Ein Beispiel dafür ist der eben genannte Plato: er, der in der Verurteilung der Tragödie und der Kunst überhaupt gewiß nicht hinter dem naiven Zynismus seines Meisters zurückgeblieben ist, hat doch aus voller künstlerischer Notwendigkeit eine Kunstform schaffen müssen, die gerade mit den vorhandenen und von ihm abgewiesenen Kunstformen innerlich verwandt ist. Der Hauptvorwurf, den Plato der älteren Kunst zu machen hatte – daß sie Nachahmung eines Scheinbildes sei, also noch einer niedrigeren Sphäre, als die empirische Welt ist, angehöre –, durfte vor allem nicht gegen das neue Kunstwerk gerichtet werden: und so sehen wir denn Plato bestrebt, über die Wirklichkeit hinauszugehn und die jener Pseudo-Wirklichkeit zugrunde liegende Idee darzustellen. Damit aber war der Denker Plato auf einem Umwege ebendahin gelangt, wo er als Dichter stets heimisch gewesen war, und von wo aus Sophokles und die ganze ältere Kunst feierlich gegen jenen Vorwurf protestierten. Wenn die Tragödie alle früheren Kunstgattungen in sich aufgesaugt hatte, so darf dasselbe wiederum in einem exzentrischen Sinne vom platonischen Dialoge gelten, der, durch Mischung aller vorhandenen Stile und Formen erzeugt, zwischen Erzählung, Lyrik, Drama, zwischen Prosa und Poesie in der Mitte schwebt und damit auch das strenge ältere Gesetz der einheitlichen sprachlichen Form durchbrochen hat; auf welchem Wege die *zynischen* Schriftsteller noch weiter gegangen sind, die in der größten Buntscheckigkeit des Stils, im Hin- und Herschwanken zwischen prosaischen und metrischen Formen, auch das literarische Bild des »rasenden Socrates«, den sie im Leben darzustellen pflegten, erreicht haben. Der platonische Dialog war gleichsam der Kahn, auf dem sich die schiffbrüchige ältere Poesie samt allen ihren Kindern rettete: auf einem engen Raum zusammengedrängt und dem einen Steuermann Socrates ängstlich untertänig, fuhren sie jetzt in eine neue Welt hinein, die an dem phantastischen Bilde dieses Aufzugs sich nie satt sehen konnte. Wirklich hat für die ganze Nachwelt Plato das Vorbild einer neuen Kunstform gegeben, das Vorbild des *Romans*: der als

such unphilosophical allurements; with such success that the youthful tragic poet Plato first of all burned his poems to be able to become a scholar of Socrates. But where unconquerable native capacities bore up against the Socratic maxims, their power, together with the momentum of his mighty character, still sufficed to force poetry itself into new and hitherto unknown channels.

An instance of this is the aforesaid Plato: he, who in the condemnation of tragedy and of art in general certainly did not fall short of the naïve cynicism of his master, was nevertheless constrained by sheer artistic necessity to create a form of art which is inwardly related even to the then existing forms of art which he repudiated. Plato's main objection to the old art—that it is the imitation of a phantom, and hence belongs to a sphere still lower than the empiric world—could not at all apply to the new art: and so we find Plato endeavouring to go beyond reality and attempting to represent the idea which underlies this pseudo-reality. But Plato, the thinker, thereby arrived by a roundabout road just at the point where he had always been at home as poet, and from which Sophocles and all the old artists had solemnly protested against that objection. If tragedy absorbed into itself all the earlier varieties of art, the same could again be said in an unusual sense of Platonic dialogue, which, engendered by a mixture of all the then existing forms and styles, hovers midway between narrative, lyric and drama, between prose and poetry, and has also thereby broken loose from the older strict law of unity of linguistic form; a movement which was carried still farther by the *cynic* writers, who in the most promiscuous style, oscillating to and fro betwixt prose and metrical forms, realised also the literary picture of the "raving Socrates" whom they were wont to represent in life. Platonic dialogue was as it were the boat in which the shipwrecked ancient poetry saved herself together with all her children: crowded into a narrow space and timidly obsequious to the one steersman, Socrates, they now launched into a new world, which never tired of looking at the fantastic spectacle of this procession. In truth, Plato has given to all posterity the prototype of a new form of art, the prototype of the *novel* which must be designated as the infinitely evolved Æsopian fable, in which poetry holds the same rank with reference to dialectic philosophy as this same

die unendlich gesteigerte äsopische Fabel zu bezeichnen ist, in der die Poesie in einer ähnlichen Rangordnung zur dialektischen Philosophie lebt, wie viele Jahrhunderte hindurch dieselbe Philosophie zur Theologie: nämlich als *ancilla*. Dies war die neue Stellung der Poesie, in die sie Plato unter dem Drucke des dämonischen Socrates drängte.

Hier überwächst der *philosophische Gedanke* die Kunst und zwingt sie zu einem engen Sich-Anklammern an den Stamm der Dialektik. In dem logischen Schematismus hat sich die *apollinische* Tendenz verpuppt: wie wir bei Euripides etwas Entsprechendes und außerdem eine Übersetzung des *Dionysischen* in den naturalistischen Affekt wahrzunehmen hatten. Socrates, der dialektische Held im platonischen Drama, erinnert uns an die verwandte Natur des euripideischen Helden, der durch Grund und Gegengrund seine Handlungen verteidigen muß und dadurch so oft in Gefahr gerät, unser tragisches Mitleiden einzubüßen: denn wer vermöchte das *optimistische* Element im Wesen der Dialektik zu verkennen, das in jedem Schlusse sein Jubelfest feiert und allein in kühler Helle und Bewußtheit atmen kann: das optimistische Element, das, einmal in die Tragödie eingedrungen, ihre dionysischen Regionen allmählich überwuchern und sie notwendig zur Selbstvernichtung treiben muß – bis zum Todessprunge ins bürgerliche Schauspiel. Man vergegenwärtige sich nur die Konsequenzen der sokratischen Sätze: »Tugend ist Wissen; es wird nur gesündigt aus Unwissenheit; der Tugendhafte ist der Glückliche«; in diesen drei Grundformen des Optimismus liegt der Tod der Tragödie. Denn jetzt muß der tugendhafte Held Dialektiker sein, jetzt muß zwischen Tugend und Wissen, Glaube und Moral ein notwendiger sichtbarer Verband sein, jetzt ist die transzendentale Gerechtigkeitslösung des Äschylus zu dem flachen und frechen Prinzip der »poetischen Gerechtigkeit« mit seinem üblichen *deus ex machina* erniedrigt.

Wie erscheint dieser neuen sokratisch-optimistischen Bühnenwelt gegenüber jetzt der *Chor* und überhaupt der ganze musikalisch-dionysische Untergrund der Tragödie? Als etwas Zufälliges, als eine auch wohl zu missende Reminiszenz an den Ursprung der Tragödie; während wir doch eingesehen haben, daß der Chor nur als *Ursache* der Tragödie und des Tragischen überhaupt verstanden werden kann. Schon bei Sophokles zeigt sich jene Verlegenheit in betreff des Chors – ein wichtiges Zeichen, daß schon bei ihm der dionysische Boden der Tragödie zu

philosophy held for many centuries with reference to theology: namely, the rank of *ancilla*. This was the new position of poetry into which Plato forced it under the pressure of the demon-inspired Socrates.

Here *philosophic thought* overgrows art and compels it to cling close to the trunk of dialectics. The *Apollonian* tendency has chrysalised in the logical schematism; just as something analogous in the case of Euripides (and moreover a translation of the *Dionysian* into the naturalistic emotion) was forced upon our attention. Socrates, the dialectical hero in Platonic drama, reminds us of the kindred nature of the Euripidean hero, who has to defend his actions by arguments and counter-arguments, and thereby so often runs the risk of forfeiting our tragic pity; for who could mistake the *optimistic* element in the essence of dialectics, which celebrates a jubilee in every conclusion, and can breathe only in cool clearness and consciousness: the optimistic element, which, having once forced its way into tragedy, must gradually overgrow its Dionysian regions, and necessarily impel it to self-destruction—even to the death-leap into the bourgeois drama. Let us but realise the consequences of the Socratic maxims: "Virtue is knowledge; man only sins from ignorance; he who is virtuous is happy": these three fundamental forms of optimism involve the death of tragedy. For the virtuous hero must now be a dialectician; there must now be a necessary, visible connection between virtue and knowledge, between belief and morality; the transcendental justice of the plot in Aeschylus is now degraded to the superficial and audacious principle of poetic justice with its usual *deus ex machina*.

How does the *chorus*, and, in general, the entire Dionyso-musical substratum of tragedy, now appear in the light of this new Socrato-optimistic stage-world? As something accidental, as a readily dispensable reminiscence of the origin of tragedy; while we have in fact seen that the chorus can be understood only as the cause of tragedy, and of the tragic generally. This perplexity with respect to the chorus first manifests itself in Sophocles—an important sign that the Dionysian basis of tragedy already begins to disintegrate with him. He no longer ventures to entrust to the chorus the main share of the effect, but limits its sphere to such an extent that it now appears almost co-

zerbröckeln beginnt. Er wagt es nicht mehr, dem Chor den Hauptanteil der Wirkung anzuvertrauen, sondern schränkt sein Bereich dermaßen ein, daß er jetzt fast den Schauspielern koordiniert erscheint, gleich als ob er aus der Orchestra in die Szene hineingehoben würde: womit freilich sein Wesen völlig zerstört ist, mag auch Aristoteles gerade dieser Auffassung des Chors seine Beistimmung geben. Jene Verrückung der Chorposition, welche Sophokles jedenfalls durch seine Praxis und, der Überlieferung nach, sogar durch eine Schrift anempfohlen hat, ist der erste Schritt zur *Vernichtung* des Chors, deren Phasen in Euripides, Agathon und der neueren Komödie mit erschreckender Schnelligkeit aufeinanderfolgen. Die optimistische Dialektik treibt mit der Geißel ihrer Syllogismen die *Musik* aus der Tragödie: d.h. sie zerstört das Wesen der Tragödie, welches sich einzig als eine Manifestation und Verbildlichung dionysischer Zustände, als sichtbare Symbolisierung der Musik, als die Traumwelt eines dionysischen Rausches interpretieren läßt.

Haben wir also sogar eine schon vor Socrates wirkende antidionysische Tendenz anzunehmen, die nur in ihm einen unerhört großartigen Ausdruck gewinnt: so müssen wir nicht vor der Frage zurückschrecken, wohin denn eine solche Erscheinung wie die des Socrates deute: die wir doch nicht imstande sind, angesichts der platonischen Dialoge, als eine nur auflösende negative Macht zu begreifen. Und so gewiß die allernächste Wirkung des sokratischen Triebes auf eine Zersetzung der dionysischen Tragödie ausging, so zwingt uns eine tiefsinnige Lebenserfahrung des Socrates selbst zu der Frage, ob denn zwischen dem Sokratismus und der Kunst *notwendig* nur ein antipodisches Verhältnis bestehe und ob die Geburt eines »künstlerischen Socrates« überhaupt etwas in sich Widerspruchsvolles sei.

Jener despotische Logiker hatte nämlich hier und da der Kunst gegenüber das Gefühl einer Lücke, einer Leere, eines halben Vorwurfs, einer vielleicht versäumten Pflicht. Öfters kam ihm, wie er im Gefängnis seinen Freunden erzählt, ein und dieselbe Traumerscheinung, die immer dasselbe sagte: »Socrates, treibe Musik!« Er beruhigt sich bis zu seinen letzten Tagen mit der Meinung, sein Philosophieren sei die höchste Musenkunst, und glaubt nicht recht, daß eine Gottheit ihn an jene »gemeine, populäre Musik« erinnern werde. Endlich im Gefängnis versteht er sich, um sein Gewissen gänzlich zu entlasten, auch dazu, jene von ihm gering geachtete Musik zu treiben. Und in dieser Gesinnung dichtet er ein Proömium auf

ordinate with the actors, just as if it were elevated from the orchestra into the scene: whereby of course its character is completely destroyed, notwithstanding that Aristotle countenances this very theory of the chorus. This alteration of the position of the chorus, which Sophocles at any rate recommended by his practice, and, according to tradition, even by a treatise, is the first step towards the *annihilation* of the chorus, the phases of which follow one another with alarming rapidity in Euripides, Agathon, and the New Comedy. Optimistic dialectics drives, *music* out of tragedy with the scourge of its syllogisms: that is, it destroys the essence of tragedy, which can be explained only as a manifestation and illustration of Dionysian states, as the visible symbolisation of music, as the dream-world of Dionysian ecstasy.

If, therefore, we are to assume an anti-Dionysian tendency operating even before Socrates, which received in him only an unprecedentedly grand expression, we must not shrink from the question as to what a phenomenon like that of Socrates indicates: whom in view of the Platonic dialogues we are certainly not entitled to regard as a purely disintegrating, negative power. And though there can be no doubt whatever that the most immediate effect of the Socratic impulse tended to the dissolution of Dionysian tragedy, yet a profound experience of Socrates' own life compels us to ask whether there is *necessarily* only an antipodal relation between Socratism and art, and whether the birth of an "artistic Socrates" is in general something contradictory in itself.

For that despotic logician had now and then the feeling of a gap, or void, a sentiment of semi-reproach, as of a possibly neglected duty with respect to art. There often came to him, as he tells his friends in prison, one and the same dream-apparition, which kept constantly repeating to him: "Socrates, practise music." Up to his very last days he solaces himself with the opinion that his philosophising is the highest form of poetry, and finds it hard to believe that a deity will remind him of the "common, popular music." Finally, when in prison, he consents to practise also this despised music, in order thoroughly to unburden his conscience. And in this frame of mind he composes a poem on Apollo and turns a few Æsopian fables into verse. It was something similar to the demonian warning voice which

Apollo und bringt einige äsopische Fabeln in Verse. Das war etwas der dämonischen warnenden Stimme Ähnliches, was ihn zu diesen Übungen drängte, es war seine apollinische Einsicht, daß er wie ein Barbarenkönig ein edles Götterbild nicht verstehe und in der Gefahr sei, sich an seiner Gottheit zu versündigen - durch sein Nichtverstehn. Jenes Wort der sokratischen Traumerscheinung ist das einzige Zeichen einer Bedenklichkeit über die Grenzen der logischen Natur: vielleicht - so mußte er sich fragen - ist das mir Nichtverständliche doch nicht auch sofort das Unverständige? Vielleicht gibt es ein Reich der Weisheit, aus dem der Logiker verbannt ist? Vielleicht ist die Kunst sogar ein notwendiges Korrelativum und Supplement der Wissenschaft?

urged him to these practices; it was because of his Apollonian insight that, like a barbaric king, he did not understand the noble image of a god and was in danger of sinning against a deity—through ignorance. The prompting voice of the Socratic dream-vision is the only sign of doubtfulness as to the limits of logical nature. "Perhaps "—thus he had to ask himself—"what is not intelligible to me is not therefore unreasonable? Perhaps there is a realm of wisdom from which the logician is banished? Perhaps art is even a necessary correlative of and supplement to science?"

15

Im Sinne dieser letzten ahnungsvollen Fragen muß nun ausgesprochen werden, wie der Einfluß des Socrates, bis auf diesen Moment hin, ja in alle Zukunft hinaus, sich, gleich einem in der Abendsonne immer größer werdenden Schatten, über die Nachwelt hin ausgebreitet hat, wie derselbe zur Neuschaffung der *Kunst* - und zwar der Kunst im bereits metaphysischen, weitesten und tiefsten Sinne - immer wieder nötigt und, bei seiner eignen Unendlichkeit, auch deren Unendlichkeit verbürgt.

Bevor dies erkannt werden konnte, bevor die innerste Abhängigkeit jeder Kunst von den Griechen, den Griechen von Homer bis auf Socrates, überzeugend dargetan war, mußte es uns mit diesen Griechen ergehen wie den Athenern mit Socrates. Fast jede Zeit und Bildungsstufe hat einmal sich mit tiefem Mißmute von den Griechen zu befreien gesucht, weil angesichts derselben alles Selbstgeleistete, scheinbar völlig Originelle und recht aufrichtig Bewunderte plötzlich Farbe und Leben zu verlieren schien und zur mißlungenen Kopie, ja zur Karikatur zusammenschrumpfte. Und so bricht immer von neuem einmal der herzliche Ingrimm gegen jenes anmaßliche Völkchen hervor, das sich erkühnte, alles Nichteinheimische für alle Zeiten als »barbarisch« zu bezeichnen: wer sind jene, fragt man sich, die, obschon sie nur einen ephemeren historischen Glanz, nur lächerlich engbegrenzte Institutionen, nur eine zweifelhafte Tüchtigkeit der Sitte aufzuweisen haben und sogar mit häßlichen Lastern gekennzeichnet sind, doch die Würde und Sonderstellung unter den Völkern in Anspruch nehmen, die dem Genius unter der Masse zukommt? Leider war man nicht so glücklich, den

In the sense of these last portentous questions it must now be indicated how the influence of Socrates (extending to the present moment, indeed, to all futurity) has spread over posterity like an ever-increasing shadow in the evening sun, and how this influence again and again necessitates a regeneration of *art*—yea, of art already with metaphysical, broadest and profoundest sense—and its own eternity guarantees also the eternity of art.

Before this could be perceived, before the intrinsic dependence of every art on the Greeks, the Greeks from Homer to Socrates, was conclusively demonstrated, it had to happen to us with regard to these Greeks as it happened to the Athenians with regard to Socrates. Nearly every age and stage of culture has at some time or other sought with deep displeasure to free itself from the Greeks, because in their presence everything self-achieved, sincerely admired and apparently quite original, seemed all of a sudden to lose life and colour and shrink to an abortive copy, even to caricature. And so hearty indignation breaks forth time after time against this presumptuous little nation, which dared to designate as "barbaric" for all time everything not native: who are they, one asks one's self, who, though they possessed only an ephemeral historical splendour, ridiculously restricted institutions, a dubious excellence in their customs, and were even branded with ugly vices, yet lay claim to the dignity and singular position among the peoples to which genius is entitled among the masses.

Schierlingsbecher zu finden, mit dem ein solches Wesen einfach abgetan werden konnte: denn alles Gift, das Neid, Verleumdung und Ingrimm in sich erzeugten, reichte nicht hin, jene selbstgenugsame Herrlichkeit zu vernichten. Und so schämt und fürchtet man sich vor den Griechen; es sei denn, daß einer die Wahrheit über alles achte und so sich auch diese Wahrheit einzugestehen wage, daß die Griechen unsere und jegliche Kultur als Wagenlenker in den Händen haben, daß aber fast immer Wagen und Pferde von zu geringem Stoffe und der Glorie ihrer Führer unangemessen sind, die dann es für einen Scherz erachten, ein solches Gespann in den Abgrund zu jagen: über den sie selbst, mit dem Sprunge des Achilles, hinwegsetzen.

Um die Würde einer solchen Führerstellung auch für Socrates zu erweisen, genügt es, in ihm den Typus einer vor ihm unerhörten Daseinsform zu erkennen, den Typus des *theoretischen Menschen*, über dessen Bedeutung und Ziel zur Einsicht zu kommen, unsere nächste Aufgabe ist. Auch der theoretische Mensch hat ein unendliches Vergnügen am Vorhandenen, wie der Künstler, und ist wie jener vor der praktischen Ethik des Pessimismus und vor seinen nur im Finsteren leuchtenden Lynkeusaugen durch jenes Genügen geschützt. Wenn nämlich der Künstler bei jeder Enthüllung der Wahrheit immer nur mit verzückten Blicken an dem hängen bleibt, was auch jetzt, nach der Enthüllung, noch Hülle bleibt, genießt und befriedigt sich der theoretische Mensch an der abgeworfenen Hülle und hat sein höchstes Lustziel in dem Prozeß einer immer glücklichen, durch eigene Kraft gelingenden Enthüllung. Es gäbe keine Wissenschaft, wenn ihr nur um jene *eine* nackte Göttin und um nichts anderes zu tun wäre. Denn dann müßte es ihren Jüngern zumute sein, wie solchen, die ein Loch gerade durch die Erde graben wollten: von denen ein jeder einsieht, daß er, bei größter und lebenslänglicher Anstrengung, nur ein ganz kleines Stück der ungeheuren Tiefe zu durchgraben imstande sei, welches vor seinen Augen durch die Arbeit des nächsten wieder überschüttet wird, so daß ein dritter wohl daran zu tun scheint, wenn er auf eigne Faust eine neue Stelle für seine Bohrversuche wählt. Wenn jetzt nun einer zur Überzeugung beweist, daß auf diesem direkten Wege das Antipodenziel nicht zu erreichen sei, wer wird noch in den alten Tiefen weiterarbeiten wollen, es sei denn, daß er sich nicht inzwischen genügen lasse, edles Gestein zu finden oder Naturgesetze zu entdecken. Darum hat Lessing, der ehrlichste theoretische Mensch, es auszusprechen gewagt, daß ihm mehr am Suchen der Wahrheit als an

What a pity one has not been so fortunate as to find the cup of hemlock with which such an affair could be disposed of without ado: for all the poison which envy, calumny, and rankling resentment engendered within themselves have not sufficed to destroy that self-sufficient grandeur! And so one feels ashamed and afraid in the presence of the Greeks: unless one prize truth above all things, and dare also to acknowledge to one's self this truth, that the Greeks, as charioteers, hold in their hands the reins of our own and of every culture, but that almost always chariot and horses are of too poor material and incommensurate with the glory of their guides, who then will deem it sport to run such a team into an abyss: which they themselves clear with the leap of Achilles.

In order to assign also to Socrates the dignity of such a leading position, it will suffice to recognise in him the type of an unheard-of form of existence, the type of the *theoretical man*, with regard to whose meaning and purpose it will be our next task to attain an insight. Like the artist, the theorist also finds an infinite satisfaction in what *is* and, like the former, he is shielded by this satisfaction from the practical ethics of pessimism with its lynx eyes which shine only in the dark. For if the artist in every unveiling of truth always cleaves with raptured eyes only to that which still remains veiled after the unveiling, the theoretical man, on the other hand, enjoys and contents himself with the cast-off veil, and finds the consummation of his pleasure in the process of a continuously successful unveiling through his own unaided efforts. There would have been no science if it had only been concerned about that *one* naked goddess and nothing else. For then its disciples would have been obliged to feel like those who purposed to dig a hole straight through the earth: each one of whom perceives that with the utmost lifelong exertion he is able to excavate only a very little of the enormous depth, which is again filled up before his eyes by the labours of his successor, so that a third man seems to do well when on his own account he selects a new spot for his attempts at tunnelling. If now some one proves conclusively that the antipodal goal cannot be attained in this direct way, who will still care to toil on in the old depths, unless he has learned to content himself in the meantime with finding precious stones or discovering natural laws? For that reason Lessing, the most honest theoretical

ihr selbst gelegen sei: womit das Grundgeheimnis der Wissenschaft, zum Erstaunen, ja Ärger der Wissenschaftlichen, aufgedeckt worden ist. Nun steht freilich neben dieser vereinzelten Erkenntnis, als einem Exzeß der Ehrlichkeit, wenn nicht des Übermutes, eine tiefsinnige *Wahnvorstellung*, welche zuerst in der Person des Socrates zur Welt kam, – jener unerschütterliche Glaube, daß das Denken, an dem Leitfaden der Kausalität, bis in die tiefsten Abgründe des Seins reiche, und daß das Denken das Sein nicht nur zu erkennen, sondern sogar zu *korrigieren* imstande sei. Dieser erhabene metaphysische Wahn ist als Instinkt der Wissenschaft beigegeben und führt sie immer und immer wieder zu ihren Grenzen, an denen sie in *Kunst* umschlagen muß: *auf welche es eigentlich, bei diesem Mechanismus, abgesehen ist.*

Schauen wir jetzt, mit der Fackel dieses Gedankens, auf Socrates hin: so erscheint er uns als der erste, der an der Hand jenes Instinktes der Wissenschaft nicht nur leben, sondern – was bei weitem mehr ist – auch sterben konnte; und deshalb ist das Bild des *sterbenden Socrates* als des durch Wissen und Gründe der Todesfurcht enthobenen Menschen das Wappenschild, das über dem Eingangstor der Wissenschaft einen jeden an deren Bestimmung erinnert, nämlich das Dasein als begreiflich und damit als gerechtfertigt erscheinen zu machen: wozu freilich, wenn die Gründe nicht reichen, schließlich auch der *Mythus* dienen muß, den ich sogar als notwendige Konsequenz, ja als Absicht der Wissenschaft soeben bezeichnete.

Wer sich einmal anschaulich macht, wie nach Socrates, dem Mystagogen der Wissenschaft, eine Philosophenschule nach der anderen wie Welle auf Welle sich ablöst, wie eine nie geahnte Universalität der Wissensgier in dem weitesten Bereich der gebildeten Welt und als eigentliche Aufgabe für jeden höher Befähigten die Wissenschaft auf die hohe See führte, von der sie niemals seitdem wieder völlig vertrieben werden konnte, wie durch diese Universalität erst ein gemeinsames Netz des Gedankens über den gesamten Erdball, ja mit Ausblicken über die Gesetzlichkeit eines ganzen Sonnensystems, gespannt wurde; wer dies alles, samt der erstaunlich hohen Wissenspyramide der Gegenwart, sich vergegenwärtigt, der kann sich nicht entbrechen, in Socrates den einen Wendepunkt und Wirbel der sogenannten Weltgeschichte zu sehen. Denn dächte man sich einmal diese ganze unbezifferbare Summe von Kraft, die für jene Welttendenz verbraucht worden ist, *nicht* im Dienste des Erkennens, sondern auf die praktischen, d.h.

man, ventured to say that he cared more for the search after truth than for truth itself: in saying which he revealed the fundamental secret of science, to the astonishment, and indeed, to the vexation of scientific men. Well, to be sure, there stands alongside of this detached perception, as an excess of honesty, if not of presumption, a profound *illusion* which first came to the world in the person of Socrates, the imperturbable belief that, by means of the clue of causality, thinking reaches to the deepest abysses of being, and that thinking is able not only to perceive being but even to *correct* it. This sublime metaphysical illusion is added as an instinct to science and again and again leads the latter to its limits, where it must change into art; which is really the end, to be attained by this mechanism.

If we now look at Socrates in the light of this thought, he appears to us as the first who could not only live, but—what is far more—also die under the guidance of this instinct of science: and hence the picture of the *dying, Socrates*, as the man delivered from the fear of death by knowledge and argument, is the escutcheon, above the entrance to science which reminds every one of its mission, namely, to make existence appear to be comprehensible, and therefore to be justified: for which purpose, if arguments do not suffice, *myth* also must be used, which I just now designated even as the necessary consequence, yea, as the end of science.

He who once makes intelligible to himself how, after the death of Socrates, the mystagogue of science, one philosophical school succeeds another, like wave upon wave—how an entirely unfore-shadowed universal development of the thirst for knowledge in the widest compass of the cultured world (and as the specific task for every one highly gifted) led science on to the high sea from which since then it has never again been able to be completely ousted; how through the universality of this movement a common net of thought was first stretched over the entire globe, with prospects, moreover, of conformity to law in an entire solar system;—he who realises all this, together with the amazingly high pyramid of our present-day knowledge, cannot fail to see in Socrates the turning-point and vortex of so-called universal history. For if one were to imagine the whole incalculable sum of energy which has been used up by that universal tendency—

egoistischen Ziele der Individuen und Völker verwendet, so wäre wahrscheinlich in allgemeinen Vernichtungskämpfen und fortdauernden Völkerwanderungen die instinktive Lust zum Leben so abgeschwächt, daß, bei der Gewohnheit des Selbstmordes, der einzelne vielleicht den letzten Rest von Pflichtgefühl empfinden müßte, wenn er, wie der Bewohner der Fidschi-Inseln, als Sohn seine Eltern, als Freund seinen Freund erdrosselt: ein praktischer Pessimismus, der selbst eine grausenhafte Ethik des Völkermordes aus Mitleid erzeugen könnte – der übrigens überall in der Welt vorhanden ist und vorhanden war, wo nicht die Kunst in irgendwelchen Formen, besonders als Religion und Wissenschaft, zum Heilmittel und zur Abwehr jenes Pesthauchs erschienen ist.

Angesichts dieses praktischen Pessimismus ist Socrates das Urbild des theoretischen Optimisten, der in dem bezeichneten Glauben an die Ergründlichkeit der Natur der Dinge dem Wissen und der Erkenntnis die Kraft einer Universalmedizin beilegt und im Irrtum das Übel an sich begreift. In jene Gründe einzudringen und die wahre Erkenntnis vom Schein und vom Irrtum zu sondern, dünkte dem sokratischen Menschen der edelste, selbst der einzige wahrhaft menschliche Beruf zu sein: so wie jener Mechanismus der Begriffe, Urteile und Schlüsse von Socrates ab als höchste Betätigung und bewunderungswürdigste Gabe der Natur über alle anderen Fähigkeiten geschätzt wurde. Selbst die erhabensten sittlichen Taten, die Regungen des Mitleids, der Aufopferung, des Heroismus und jene schwer zu erringende Meeresstille der Seele, die der apollinische Grieche Sophrosyne nannte, wurden von Socrates und seinen gleichgesinnten Nachfolgern bis auf die Gegenwart hin aus der Dialektik des Wissens abgeleitet und demgemäß als lehrbar bezeichnet. Wer die Lust einer sokratischen Erkenntnis an sich erfahren hat und spürt, wie diese, in immer weiteren Ringen, die ganze Welt der Erscheinungen zu umfassen sucht, der wird von da an keinen Stachel, der zum Dasein drängen könnte, heftiger empfinden als die Begierde, jene Eroberung zu vollenden und das Netz undurchdringbar fest zu spinnen. Einem so Gestimmten erscheint dann der platonische Socrates als der Lehrer einer ganz neuen Form der »griechischen Heiterkeit« und Daseinsseligkeit, welche sich in Handlungen zu entladen sucht und diese Entladungen zumeist in mäeutischen und erziehenden Einwirkungen auf edle Jünglinge, zum Zweck der endlichen Erzeugung des Genius, finden wird.

employed, *not* in the service of knowledge, but for the practical, *i.e.*, egoistical ends of individuals and peoples—then probably the instinctive love of life would be so much weakened in universal wars of destruction and incessant migrations of peoples, that, owing to the practice of suicide, the individual would perhaps feel the last remnant of a sense of duty, when, like the native of the Fiji Islands, as son he strangles his parents and, as friend, his friend: a practical pessimism which might even give rise to a horrible ethics of general slaughter out of pity—which, for the rest, exists and has existed wherever art in one form or another, especially as science and religion, has not appeared as a remedy and preventive of that pestilential breath.

In view of this practical pessimism, Socrates is the archetype of the theoretical optimist, who in the above-indicated belief in the fathomableness of the nature of things, attributes to knowledge and perception the power of a universal medicine, and sees in error and evil. To penetrate into the depths of the nature of things, and to separate true perception from error and illusion, appeared to the Socratic man the noblest and even the only truly human calling: just as from the time of Socrates onwards the mechanism of concepts, judgments, and inferences was prized above all other capacities as the highest activity and the most admirable gift of nature. Even the sublimest moral acts, the stirrings of pity, of self-sacrifice, of heroism, and that tranquillity of soul, so difficult of attainment, which the Apollonian Greek called Sophrosyne, were derived by Socrates, and his like-minded successors up to the present day, from the dialectics of knowledge, and were accordingly designated as teachable. He who has experienced in himself the joy of a Socratic perception, and felt how it seeks to embrace, in constantly widening circles, the entire world of phenomena, will thenceforth find no stimulus which could urge him to existence more forcible than the desire to complete that conquest and to knit the net impenetrably close. To a person thus minded the Platonic Socrates then appears as the teacher of an entirely new form of "Greek cheerfulness" and felicity of existence, which seeks to discharge itself in actions, and will find its discharge for the most part in maieutic and pedagogic influences on noble youths, with a view to the ultimate production of genius.

Nun aber eilt die Wissenschaft, von ihrem kräftigen Wahne angespornt, unaufhaltsam bis zu ihren Grenzen, an denen ihr im Wesen der Logik verborgener Optimismus scheitert. Denn die Peripherie des Kreises der Wissenschaft hat unendlich viele Punkte, und während noch gar nicht abzusehen ist, wie jemals der Kreis völlig ausgemessen werden könnte, so trifft doch der edle und begabte Mensch, noch vor der Mitte seines Daseins und unvermeidlich, auf solche Grenzpunkte der Peripherie, wo er in das Unaufhellbare starrt. Wenn er hier zu seinem Schrecken sieht, wie die Logik sich an diesen Grenzen um sich selbst ringelt und endlich sich in den Schwanz beißt – da bricht die neue Form der Erkenntnis durch, *die tragische Erkenntnis*, die, um nur ertragen zu werden, als Schutz und Heilmittel die Kunst braucht.

But now science, spurred on by its powerful illusion, hastens irresistibly to its limits, on which its optimism, hidden in the essence of logic, is wrecked. For the periphery of the circle of science has an infinite number of points, and while there is still no telling how this circle can ever be completely measured, yet the noble and gifted man, even before the middle of his career, inevitably comes into contact with those extreme points of the periphery where he stares at the inexplicable. When he here sees to his dismay how logic coils round itself at these limits and finally bites its own tail—then the new form of perception discloses itself, namely *tragic perception,* which, in order even to be endured, requires art as a safeguard and remedy.

Schauen wir, mit gestärkten und an den Griechen erlabten Augen, auf die höchsten Sphären derjenigen Welt, die uns umflutet, so gewahren wir die in Socrates vorbildlich erscheinende Gier der unersättlichen optimistischen Erkenntnis in tragische Resignation und Kunstbedürftigkeit umgeschlagen: während allerdings dieselbe Gier, auf ihren niederen Stufen, sich kunstfeindlich äußern und vornehmlich die dionysisch-tragische Kunst innerlich verabscheuen muß, wie dies an der Bekämpfung der äschyleischen Tragödie durch den Sokratismus beispielsweise dargestellt wurde.

If, with eyes strengthened and refreshed at the sight of the Greeks, we look upon the highest spheres of the world that surrounds us, we behold the avidity of the insatiate optimistic knowledge, of which Socrates is the typical representative, transformed into tragic resignation and the need of art: while, to be sure, this same avidity, in its lower stages, has to exhibit itself as antagonistic to art, and must especially have an inward detestation of Dionyso-tragic art, as was exemplified in the opposition of Socratism to Aeschylean tragedy.

Hier nun klopfen wir, bewegten Gemütes, an die Pforten der Gegenwart und Zukunft: wird jenes »Umschlagen« zu immer neuen Konfigurationen des Genius und gerade des *musiktreibenden Socrates* führen? Wird das über das Dasein gebreitete Netz der Kunst, sei es auch unter dem Namen der Religion oder der Wissenschaft, immer fester und zarter geflochten werden, oder ist ihm bestimmt, unter dem ruhelos barbarischen Treiben und Wirbeln, das sich jetzt »die Gegenwart« nennt, in Fetzen zu reißen? – Besorgt, doch nicht trostlos stehen wir eine kleine Weile beiseite, als die Beschaulichen, denen es erlaubt ist, Zeugen jener ungeheuren Kämpfe und Übergänge zu sein. Ach! Es ist der Zauber dieser Kämpfe, daß, wer sie schaut, sie auch kämpfen muß!

Here then with agitated spirit we knock at the gates of the present and the future: will that "transforming" lead to ever new configurations of genius, and especially of the *music-practising Socrates*? Will the net of art which is spread over existence, whether under the name of religion or of science, be knit always more closely and delicately, or is it destined to be torn to shreds under the restlessly barbaric activity and whirl which is called "the present day"?—Anxious, yet not disconsolate, we stand aloof for a little while, as the spectators who are permitted to be witnesses of these tremendous struggles and transitions. Alas! It is the charm of these struggles that he who beholds them must also fight them!

16

An diesem ausgeführten historischen Beispiel haben wir klarzumachen gesucht, wie die Tragödie an dem Entschwinden des Geistes der Musik ebenso gewiß zugrunde geht, wie sie aus diesem Geiste allein geboren werden kann. Das Ungewöhnliche dieser Behauptung zu mildern und andererseits den Ursprung dieser unserer Erkenntnis aufzuzeigen, müssen wir uns jetzt freien Blicks den analogen Erscheinungen der Gegenwart gegenüberstellen; wir müssen mitten hinein in jene Kämpfe treten, welche, wie ich eben sagte, zwischen der unersättlichen optimistischen Erkenntnis und der tragischen Kunstbedürftigkeit in den höchsten Sphären unserer jetzigen Welt gekämpft werden. Ich will hierbei von allen den anderen gegnerischen Trieben absehen, die zu jeder Zeit der Kunst und gerade der Tragödie entgegenarbeiten und die auch in der Gegenwart in dem Maße siegesgewiß um sich greifen, daß von den theatralischen Künsten z.B. allein die Posse und das Ballett in einem einigermaßen üppigen Wuchern ihre vielleicht nicht für jedermann wohlriechenden Blüten treiben. Ich will nur von der *erlauchtesten Gegnerschaft* der tragischen Weltbetrachtung reden und meine damit die in ihrem tiefsten Wesen optimistische Wissenschaft, mit ihrem Ahnherrn Socrates an der Spitze. Alsbald sollen auch die Mächte bei Namen genannt werden, welche mir *eine Wiedergeburt der Tragödie* – und welche andere selige Hoffnungen für das deutsche Wesen! – zu verbürgen scheinen.

Bevor wir uns mitten in jene Kämpfe hineinstürzen, hüllen wir uns in die Rüstung unserer bisher eroberten Erkenntnisse. Im Gegensatz zu allen denen, welche beflissen sind, die Künste aus einem einzigen Prinzip, als dem notwendigen Lebensquell jedes Kunstwerks, abzuleiten, halte ich den Blick auf jene beiden künstlerischen Gottheiten der Griechen, Apollo und Dionysus, geheftet und erkenne in ihnen die lebendigen und anschaulichen Repräsentanten *zweier* in ihrem tiefsten Wesen und ihren höchsten Zielen verschiedenen Kunstwelten. Apollo steht vor mir als der verklärende Genius des *principii individuationis*, durch den allein die Erlösung im Scheine wahrhaft zu erlangen ist: während unter dem mystischen Jubelruf des Dionysus der Bann der Individuation zersprengt wird und der Weg zu den Müttern des Seins, zu dem innersten Kern der Dinge offenliegt. Dieser ungeheure Gegensatz, der sich zwischen der plastischen Kunst als der apollinischen und der Musik als der dionysischen Kunst klaffend

By this elaborate historical example we have endeavoured to make it clear that tragedy perishes as surely by evanescence of the spirit of music as it can be born only out of this spirit. In order to qualify the singularity of this assertion, and, on the other hand, to disclose the source of this insight of ours, we must now confront with clear vision the analogous phenomena of the present time; we must enter into the midst of these struggles, which, as I said just now, are being carried on in the highest spheres of our present world between the insatiate optimistic perception and the tragic need of art. In so doing I shall leave out of consideration all other antagonistic tendencies which at all times oppose art, especially tragedy, and which at present again extend their sway triumphantly, to such an extent that of the theatrical arts only the farce and the ballet, for example, put forth their blossoms, which perhaps not every one cares to smell, in tolerably rich luxuriance. I will speak only of the *Most Illustrious Opposition* to the tragic conception of things—and by this I mean essentially optimistic science, with its ancestor Socrates at the head of it. Presently also the forces will be designated which seem to me to guarantee *a re-birth of tragedy*—and who knows what other blessed hopes for the German genius!

Before we plunge into the midst of these struggles, let us array ourselves in the armour of our hitherto acquired knowledge. In contrast to all those who are intent on deriving the arts from one exclusive principle, as the necessary vital source of every work of art, I keep my eyes fixed on the two artistic deities of the Greeks, Apollo and Dionysus, and recognise in them the living and conspicuous representatives of *two* worlds of art which differ in their intrinsic essence and in their highest aims. Apollo stands before me as the transfiguring genius of the *principium individuationis* through which alone the redemption in appearance is to be truly attained, while by the mystical cheer of Dionysus the spell of individuation is broken, and the way lies open to the Mothers of Being, to the innermost heart of things. This extraordinary antithesis, which opens up yawningly between physical art as the Apollonian and music as the Dionysian art, has become manifest to only one of the great thinkers, to such an extent that, even without this key to the symbolism of the Hellenic divinities, he allowed to music a different

auftut, ist einem einzigen der großen Denker in dem Maße offenbar geworden, daß er, selbst ohne jene Anleitung der hellenischen Göttersymbolik, der Musik einen verschiedenen Charakter und Ursprung vor allen anderen Künsten zuerkannte, weil sie nicht, wie jene alle, Abbild der Erscheinung, sondern unmittelbar Abbild des Willens selbst sei und also zu *allem Physischen der Welt das Metaphysische*, zu aller Erscheinung das Ding an sich darstelle. (Schopenhauer, Welt als Wille und Vorstellung I, S. 310.) Auf diese wichtigste Erkenntnis aller Ästhetik, mit der, in einem ernsteren Sinne genommen, die Ästhetik erst beginnt, hat Richard Wagner, zur Bekräftigung ihrer ewigen Wahrheit seinen Stempel gedrückt, wenn er im »Beethoven« feststellt, daß die Musik nach ganz anderen ästhetischen Prinzipien als alle bildenden Künste und überhaupt nicht nach der Kategorie der Schönheit zu bemessen sei: obgleich eine irrige Ästhetik, an der Hand einer mißleiteten und entarteten Kunst, von jenem in der bildnerischen Welt geltenden Begriff der Schönheit aus sich gewöhnt habe, von der Musik eine ähnliche Wirkung wie von den Werken der bildenden Kunst zu fordern, nämlich die Erregung *des Gefallens an schönen Formen*. Nach der Erkenntnis jenes ungeheuren Gegensatzes fühlte ich eine starke Nötigung, mich dem Wesen der griechischen Tragödie und damit der tiefsten Offenbarung des hellenischen Genius zu nahen: denn erst jetzt glaubte ich des Zaubers mächtig zu sein, über die Phraseologie unserer üblichen Ästhetik hinaus, das Urproblem der Tragödie mir leibhaft vor die Seele stellen zu können: wodurch mir ein so befremdlich eigentümlicher Blick in das Hellenische vergönnt war, daß es mir scheinen mußte, als ob unsre so stolz sich gebärdende klassisch-hellenische Wissenschaft in der Hauptsache bis jetzt nur an Schattenspielen und Äußerlichkeiten sich zu weiden gewußt habe.

Jenes Urproblem möchten wir vielleicht mit dieser Frage berühren: welche ästhetische Wirkung entsteht, wenn jene an sich getrennten Kunstmächte des Apollinischen und des Dionysischen nebeneinander in Tätigkeit geraten? Oder in kürzerer Form: wie verhält sich die Musik zu Bild und Begriff? – Schopenhauer, dem Richard Wagner gerade für diesen Punkt eine nicht zu überbietende Deutlichkeit und Durchsichtigkeit der Darstellung nachrühmt, äußert sich hierüber am ausführlichsten in der folgenden Stelle, die ich hier in ihrer ganzen Länge wiedergeben werde. Welt als Wille und Vorstellung I, S. 309: »Diesem allen zufolge können wir die erscheinende Welt, oder die Natur, und die Musik als

character and origin in advance of all the other arts, because, unlike them, it is not a copy of the phenomenon, but a direct copy of the will itself, and therefore represents the metaphysical of everything physical in the *world*, the thing-in-itself of every phenomenon. (Schopenhauer, *Welt als Wille und Vorstellung*, I. 310.) To this most important perception of æsthetics (with which, taken in a serious sense, æsthetics properly commences), Richard Wagner, by way of confirmation of its eternal truth, affixed his seal, when he asserted in his *Beethoven* that music must be judged according to æsthetic principles quite different from those which apply to the physical arts, and not, in general, according to the category of beauty: although an erroneous æsthetics, inspired by a misled and degenerate art, has by virtue of the concept of beauty prevailing in the plastic domain accustomed itself to demand of music an effect analogous to that of the works of plastic art, namely the suscitating *delight in beautiful forms*. Upon perceiving this extraordinary antithesis, I felt a strong inducement to approach the essence of Greek tragedy, and, by means of it, the profoundest revelation of Hellenic genius: for I at last thought myself to be in possession of a charm to enable me—far beyond the phraseology of our usual æsthetics—to represent vividly to my mind the primitive problem of tragedy: whereby such an astounding insight into the Hellenic character was afforded me that it necessarily seemed as if our proudly comporting classico-Hellenic science had thus far contrived to subsist almost exclusively on phantasmagoria and externalities.

Perhaps we may lead up to this primitive problem with the question: what æsthetic effect results when the intrinsically separate art-powers, the Apollonian and the Dionysian, enter into concurrent actions? Or, in briefer form: how is music related to image and concept?—Schopenhauer, whom Richard Wagner, with especial reference to this point, accredits with an unsurpassable clearness and perspicuity of exposition, expresses himself most copiously on the subject in the following passage which I shall cite here at full length (*World and Will as Idea*): "According to all this, we may regard the phenomenal world, or nature, and music as two different expressions of the same thing, which is therefore itself the only medium of the analogy between these two expressions, so that a

zwei verschiedene Ausdrücke derselben Sache ansehen, welche selbst daher das allein Vermittelnde der Analogie beider ist, dessen Erkenntnis erfordert wird, um jene Analogie einzusehen. Die Musik ist demnach, wenn als Ausdruck der Welt angesehen, eine im höchsten Grad allgemeine Sprache, die sich sogar zur Allgemeinheit der Begriffe ungefähr verhält wie diese zu den einzelnen Dingen. Ihre Allgemeinheit ist aber keineswegs jene leere Allgemeinheit der Abstraktion, sondern ganz anderer Art, und ist verbunden mit durchgängiger deutlicher Bestimmtheit. Sie gleicht hierin den geometrischen Figuren und den Zahlen, welche als die allgemeinen Formen aller möglichen Objekte der Erfahrung und auf alle *a priori* anwendbar, doch nicht abstrakt, sondern anschaulich und durchgängig bestimmt sind. Alle möglichen Bestrebungen, Erregungen und Äußerungen des Willens, alle jene Vorgänge im Innern des Menschen, welche die Vernunft in den weiten negativen Begriff Gefühl wirft, sind durch die unendlich vielen möglichen Melodien auszudrücken, aber immer in der Allgemeinheit bloßer Form, ohne den Stoff, immer nur nach dem An-sich, nicht nach der Erscheinung, gleichsam die innerste Seele derselben, ohne Körper. Aus diesem innigen Verhältnis, welches die Musik zum wahren Wesen aller Dinge hat, ist auch dies zu erklären, daß, wenn zu irgendeiner Szene, Handlung, Vorgang, Umgebung eine passende Musik ertönt, diese uns den geheimsten Sinn derselben aufzuschließen scheint und als der richtigste und deutlichste Kommentar dazu auftritt: ingleichen, daß es dem, der sich dem Eindruck einer Symphonie ganz hingibt, ist, als sähe er alle möglichen Vorgänge des Lebens und der Welt an sich vorüberziehen: dennoch kann er, wenn er sich besinnt, keine Ähnlichkeit angeben zwischen jenem Tonspiel und den Dingen, die ihm vorschwebten. Denn die Musik ist, wie gesagt, darin von allen anderen Künsten verschieden, daß sie nicht Abbild der Erscheinung, oder richtiger, der adäquaten Objektität des Willens, sondern unmittelbar Abbild des Willens selbst ist und also zu allem Physischen der Welt das Metaphysische, zu aller Erscheinung das Ding an sich darstellt. Man könnte demnach die Welt ebensowohl verkörperte Musik, als verkörperten Willen nennen: daraus also ist es erklärlich, warum Musik jedes Gemälde, ja jede Szene des wirklichen Lebens und der Welt, sogleich in erhöhter Bedeutsamkeit hervortreten läßt; freilich um so mehr, je analoger ihre Melodie dem innern Geiste der gegebenen Erscheinung ist. Hierauf beruht es, daß man ein Gedicht als Gesang, oder eine anschauliche Darstellung als Pantomime, oder beides als Oper der Musik unterlegen kann. Solche einzelne Bilder des

knowledge of this medium is required in order to understand that analogy. Music, therefore, if regarded as an expression of the world, is in the highest degree a universal language, which is related indeed to the universality of concepts, much as these are related to the particular things. Its universality, however, is by no means the empty universality of abstraction, but of quite a different kind, and is united with thorough and distinct definiteness. In this respect it resembles geometrical figures and numbers, which are the universal forms of all possible objects of experience and applicable to them all *a priori*, and yet are not abstract but perceptiple and thoroughly determinate. All possible efforts, excitements and manifestations of will, all that goes on in the heart of man and that reason includes in the wide, negative concept of feeling, may be expressed by the infinite number of possible melodies, but always in the universality of mere form, without the material, always according to the thing-in-itself, not the phenomenon—of which they reproduce the very soul and essence as it were, without the body. This deep relation which music bears to the true nature of all things also explains the fact that suitable music played to any scene, action, event, or surrounding seems to disclose to us its most secret meaning, and appears as the most accurate and distinct commentary upon it; as also the fact that whoever gives himself up entirely to the impression of a symphony seems to see all the possible events of life and the world take place in himself: nevertheless upon reflection he can find no likeness between the music and the things that passed before his mind. For, as we have said, music is distinguished from all the other arts by the fact that it is not a copy of the phenomenon, or, more accurately, the adequate objectivity of the will, but the direct copy of the will itself, and therefore represents the metaphysical of everything physical in the world, and the thing-in-itself of every phenomenon. We might, therefore, just as well call the world embodied music as embodied will: and this is the reason why music makes every picture, and indeed every scene of real life and of the world, at once appear with higher significance; all the more so, to be sure, in proportion as its melody is analogous to the inner spirit of the given phenomenon. It rests upon this that we are able to set a poem to music as a song, or a perceptible representation as a pantomime, or both as an opera. Such particular pictures of human life, set to the universal language of music, are never bound to it or correspond to it with

Menschenlebens, der allgemeinen Sprache der Musik untergelegt, sind nie mit durchgängiger Notwendigkeit ihr verbunden oder entsprechend; sondern sie stehen zu ihr nur im Verhältnis eines beliebigen Beispiels zu einem allgemeinen Begriff: sie stellen in der Bestimmtheit der Wirklichkeit dasjenige dar, was die Musik in der Allgemeinheit bloßer Form aussagt. Denn die Melodien sind gewissermaßen, gleich den allgemeinen Begriffen, ein Abstraktum der Wirklichkeit. Diese nämlich, also die Welt der einzelnen Dinge, liefert das Anschauliche, das Besondere und Individuelle, den einzelnen Fall, sowohl zur Allgemeinheit der Begriffe, als zur Allgemeinheit der Melodien, welche beide Allgemeinheiten einander aber in gewisser Hinsicht entgegengesetzt sind; indem die Begriffe nur die allererst aus der Anschauung abstrahierten Formen, gleichsam die abgezogene äußere Schale der Dinge enthalten, also ganz eigentlich Abstrakta sind; die Musik hingegen den innersten aller Gestaltung vorhergängigen Kern, oder das Herz der Dinge gibt. Dies Verhältnis ließe sich recht gut in der Sprache der Scholastiker ausdrücken, indem man sagte: die Begriffe sind die *universalia post rem*, die Musik aber gibt die *universalia ante rem*, und die Wirklichkeit die *universalia in re*. – Daß aber überhaupt eine Beziehung zwischen einer Komposition und einer anschaulichen Darstellung möglich ist, beruht, wie gesagt, darauf, daß beide nur ganz verschiedene Ausdrücke des selben innern Wesens der Welt sind. Wann nun im einzelnen Fall eine solche Beziehung wirklich vorhanden ist, also der Komponist die Willensregungen, welche den Kern einer Begebenheit ausmachen, in der allgemeinen Sprache der Musik auszusprechen gewußt hat: dann ist die Melodie des Liedes, die Melodie der Oper ausdrucksvoll. Die vom Komponisten aufgefundene Analogie zwischen jenen beiden muß aber aus der unmittelbaren Erkenntnis des Wesens der Welt, seiner Vernunft unbewußt, hervorgegangen und darf nicht, mit bewußter Absichtlichkeit, durch Begriffe vermittelte Nachahmung sein: sonst spricht die Musik nicht das innere Wesen, den Willen selbst aus; sondern ahmt nur seine Erscheinung ungenügend nach; wie dies alle eigentlich nachbildende Musik tut.« –

Wir verstehen also, nach der Lehre Schopenhauers, die Musik als die Sprache des Willens unmittelbar und fühlen unsere Phantasie angeregt, jene zu uns redende, unsichtbare und doch so lebhaft bewegte Geisterwelt zu gestalten und sie in einem analogen Beispiel uns zu verkörpern. Andrerseits kommt Bild und Begriff, unter der Einwirkung einer wahrhaft

stringent necessity, but stand to it only in the relation of an example chosen at will to a general concept. In the determinateness of the real they represent that which music expresses in the universality of mere form. For melodies are to a certain extent, like general concepts, an abstraction from the actual. This actual world, then, the world of particular things, affords the object of perception, the special and the individual, the particular case, both to the universality of concepts and to the universality of the melodies. But these two universalities are in a certain respect opposed to each other; for the concepts contain only the forms, which are first of all abstracted from perception—the separated outward shell of things, as it were—and hence they are, in the strictest sense of the term, *abstracta*; music, on the other hand, gives the inmost kernel which precedes all forms, or the heart of things. This relation may be very well expressed in the language of the schoolmen, by saying: the concepts are the *universalia post rem*, but music gives the universalia ante rem, and the real world the universalia in *re*.—But that in general a relation is possible between a composition and a perceptible representation rests, as we have said, upon the fact that both are simply different expressions of the same inner being of the world. When now, in the particular case, such a relation is actually given, that is to say, when the composer has been able to express in the universal language of music the emotions of will which constitute the heart of an event, then the melody of the song, the music of the opera, is expressive. But the analogy discovered by the composer between the two must have proceeded from the direct knowledge of the nature of the world unknown to his reason, and must not be an imitation produced with conscious intention by means of conceptions; otherwise the music does not express the inner nature of the will itself, but merely gives an inadequate imitation of its phenomenon: all specially imitative music does this."

We have therefore, according to the doctrine of Schopenhauer, an immediate understanding of music as the language of the will, and feel our imagination stimulated to give form to this invisible and yet so actively stirred spirit-world which speaks to us, and prompted to embody it in an analogous example. On the other hand, image and concept, under the influence of a truly conformable music, acquire a higher significance.

entsprechenden Musik, zu einer erhöhten Bedeutsamkeit. Zweierlei Wirkungen pflegt also die dionysische Kunst auf das apollinische Kunstvermögen auszuüben: die Musik reizt zum *gleichnisartigen Anschauen* der dionysischen Allgemeinheit, die Musik läßt sodann das gleichnisartige Bild *in höchster Bedeutsamkeit* hervortreten. Aus diesen an sich verständlichen und keiner tieferen Beobachtung unzugänglichen Tatsachen erschließe ich die Befähigung der Musik, *den Mythus*, d.h. das bedeutsamste Exempel zu gebären und gerade den *tragischen* Mythus: den Mythus, der von der dionysischen Erkenntnis in Gleichnissen redet. An dem Phänomen des Lyrikers habe ich dargestellt, wie die Musik im Lyriker darnach ringt, in apollinischen Bildern über ihr Wesen sich kund zu geben: denken wir uns jetzt, daß die Musik in ihrer höchsten Steigerung auch zu einer höchsten Verbildlichung zu kommen suchen muß, so müssen wir für möglich halten, daß sie auch den symbolischen Ausdruck für ihre eigentliche dionysische Weisheit zu finden wisse; und wo anders werden wir diesen Ausdruck zu suchen haben, wenn nicht in der Tragödie und überhaupt im Begriff *des Tragischen*?

Aus dem Wesen der Kunst, wie sie gemeinhin nach der einzigen Kategorie des Scheines und der Schönheit begriffen wird, ist das Tragische in ehrlicher Weise gar nicht abzuleiten; erst aus dem Geiste der Musik heraus verstehen wir eine Freude an der Vernichtung des Individuums. Denn an den einzelnen Beispielen einer solchen Vernichtung wird uns nur das ewige Phänomen der dionysischen Kunst deutlich gemacht, die den Willen in seiner Allmacht gleichsam hinter dem *principio individuationis*, das ewige Leben jenseits aller Erscheinung und trotz aller Vernichtung zum Ausdruck bringt. Die metaphysische Freude am Tragischen ist eine Übersetzung der instinktiv unbewußten dionysischen Weisheit in die Sprache des Bildes: der Held, die höchste Willenserscheinung, wird zu unserer Lust verneint, weil er doch nur Erscheinung ist, und das ewige Leben des Willens durch seine Vernichtung nicht berührt wird. »Wir glauben an das ewige Leben«, so ruft die Tragödie; während die Musik die unmittelbare Idee dieses Lebens ist. Ein ganz verschiedenes Ziel hat die Kunst des Plastikers: hier überwindet Apollo das Leiden des Individuums durch die leuchtende Verherrlichung der *Ewigkeit der Erscheinung*, hier siegt die Schönheit über das dem Leben inhärierende Leiden, der Schmerz wird in einem gewissen Sinne aus den Zügen der Natur hinweggelogen. In der dionysischen Kunst und in

Dionysian art therefore is wont to exercise—two kinds of influences, on the Apollonian art-faculty: music firstly incites to the *symbolic intuition* of Dionysian universality, and, secondly, it causes the symbolic image to stand forth *in its fullest significance.* From these facts, intelligible in themselves and not inaccessible to profounder observation, I infer the capacity of music to give birth to *myth,* that is to say, the most significant exemplar, and precisely *tragic* myth: the myth which speaks of Dionysian knowledge in symbols. In the phenomenon of the lyrist, I have set forth that in him music strives to express itself with regard to its nature in Apollonian images. If now we reflect that music in its highest potency must seek to attain also to its highest symbolisation, we must deem it possible that it also knows how to find the symbolic expression of its inherent Dionysian wisdom; and where shall we have to seek for this expression if not in tragedy and, in general, in the conception of the tragic?

From the nature of art, as it is ordinarily conceived according to the single category of appearance and beauty, the tragic cannot be honestly deduced at all; it is only through the spirit of music that we understand the joy in the annihilation of the individual. For in the particular examples of such annihilation only is the eternal phenomenon of Dionysian art made clear to us, which gives expression to the will in its omnipotence, as it were, behind the *principium individuationis,* the eternal life beyond all phenomena, and in spite of all annihilation. The metaphysical delight in the tragic is a translation of the instinctively unconscious Dionysian wisdom into the language of the scene: the hero, the highest manifestation of the will, is disavowed for our pleasure, because he is only phenomenon, and because the eternal life of the will is not affected by his annihilation. "We believe in eternal life," tragedy exclaims; while music is the proximate idea of this life. Plastic art has an altogether different object: here Apollo vanquishes the suffering of the individual by the radiant glorification of the *eternity of the phenomenon*; here beauty triumphs over the suffering inherent in life; pain is in a manner surreptitiously obliterated from the features of nature. In Dionysian art and its tragic symbolism the same nature speaks to us with its true undissembled voice: "Be as I am! Amidst the ceaseless change of phenomena, eternally impelling all into existence,

deren tragischer Symbolik redet uns dieselbe Natur mit ihrer wahren, unverstellten Stimme an: »Seid wie ich bin! Unter dem unaufhörlichen Wechsel der Erscheinungen die ewig schöpferische, ewig zum Dasein zwingende, an diesem Erscheinungswechsel sich ewig befriedigende Urmutter!«

eternally self-satisfying in this changing of phenomena, I am the eternally creating primordial mother!"

17

Auch die dionysische Kunst will uns von der ewigen Lust des Daseins überzeugen: nur sollen wir diese Lust nicht in den Erscheinungen, sondern hinter den Erscheinungen suchen. Wir sollen erkennen, wie alles, was entsteht, zum leidvollen Untergange bereit sein muß, wir werden gezwungen, in die Schrecken der Individualexistenz hineinzublicken – und sollen doch nicht erstarren: ein metaphysischer Trost reißt uns momentan aus dem Getriebe der Wandelgestalten heraus. Wir sind wirklich in kurzen Augenblicken das Urwesen selbst und fühlen dessen unbändige Daseinsgier und Daseinslust; der Kampf, die Qual, die Vernichtung der Erscheinungen dünkt uns jetzt wie notwendig, bei dem Übermaß von unzähligen, sich ins Leben drängenden und stoßenden Daseinsformen, bei der überschwänglichen Fruchtbarkeit des Weltwillens; wir werden von dem wütenden Stachel dieser Qualen in demselben Augenblicke durchbohrt, wo wir gleichsam mit der unermeßlichen Urlust am Dasein eins geworden sind und wo wir die Unzerstörbarkeit und Ewigkeit dieser Lust in dionysischer Entzückung ahnen. Trotz Furcht und Mitleid sind wir die Glücklich- Lebendigen, nicht als Individuen, sondern als das *eine* Lebendige, mit dessen Zeugungslust wir verschmolzen sind.

Die Entstehungsgeschichte der griechischen Tragödie sagt uns jetzt mit lichtvoller Bestimmtheit, wie das tragische Kunstwerk der Griechen wirklich aus dem Geiste der Musik herausgeboren ist: durch welchen Gedanken wir zum ersten Male dem ursprünglichen und so erstaunlichen Sinne des Chors gerecht geworden zu sein glauben. Zugleich aber müssen wir zugeben, daß die vorhin aufgestellte Bedeutung des tragischen Mythus den griechischen Dichtern, geschweige den griechischen Philosophen, niemals in begrifflicher Deutlichkeit durchsichtig geworden ist; ihre Helden sprechen gewissermaßen oberflächlicher, als sie handeln; der Mythus findet in dem gesprochnen Wort durchaus nicht seine adäquate Objektivation. Das Gefüge der Szenen und die anschaulichen Bilder offenbaren eine tiefere Weisheit, als der Dichter selbst in Worte und Begriffe fassen

Dionysian art, too, seeks to convince us of the eternal joy of existence: only we are to seek this joy not in phenomena, but behind phenomena. We are to perceive how all that comes into being must be ready for a sorrowful end; we are compelled to look into the terrors of individual existence—yet we are not to become torpid: a metaphysical comfort tears us momentarily from the bustle of the transforming figures. We are really for brief moments Primordial Being itself, and feel its indomitable desire for being and joy in existence; the struggle, the pain, the destruction of phenomena, now appear to us as something necessary, considering the surplus of innumerable forms of existence which throng and push one another into life, considering the exuberant fertility of the universal will. We are pierced by the maddening sting of these pains at the very moment when we have become, as it were, one with the immeasurable primordial joy in existence, and when we anticipate, in Dionysian ecstasy, the indestructibility and eternity of this joy. In spite of fear and pity, we are the happy living beings, not as individuals, but as the *one* living being, with whose procreative joy we are blended.

The history of the rise of Greek tragedy now tells us with luminous precision that the tragic art of the Greeks was really born of the spirit of music: with which conception we believe we have done justice for the first time to the original and most astonishing significance of the chorus. At the same time, however, we must admit that the import of tragic myth as set forth above never became transparent with sufficient lucidity to the Greek poets, let alone the Greek philosophers; their heroes speak, as it were, more superficially than they act; the myth does not at all find its adequate objectification in the spoken word. The structure of the scenes and the conspicuous images reveal a deeper wisdom than the poet himself can put into words and concepts: the

kann: wie das gleiche auch bei Shakespeare beobachtet wird, dessen Hamlet z.B. in einem ähnlichen Sinne oberflächlicher redet, als er handelt, so daß nicht aus den Worten heraus, sondern aus dem vertieften Anschauen und Überschauen des Ganzen jene früher erwähnte Hamletlehre zu entnehmen ist. In betreff der griechischen Tragödie, die uns freilich nur als Wortdrama entgegentritt, habe ich sogar angedeutet, daß jene Inkongruenz zwischen Mythus und Wort uns leicht verführen könnte, sie für flacher und bedeutungsloser zu halten, als sie ist, und demnach auch eine oberflächlichere Wirkung für sie vorauszusetzen, als sie nach den Zeugnissen der Alten gehabt haben muß: denn wie leicht vergißt man, daß, was dem Wortdichter nicht gelungen war, die höchste Vergeistigung und Idealität des Mythus zu erreichen, ihm als schöpferischer Musiker in jedem Augenblick gelingen konnte! Wir freilich müssen uns die Übermacht der musikalischen Wirkung fast auf gelehrtem Wege rekonstruieren, um etwas von jenem unvergleichlichen Troste zu empfangen, der der wahren Tragödie zu eigen sein muß. Selbst diese musikalische Übermacht aber würden wir nur, wenn wir Griechen wären, als solche empfunden haben: während wir in der ganzen Entfaltung der griechischen Musik – der uns bekannten und vertrauten, so unendlich reicheren gegenüber – nur das in schüchternem Kraftgefühle angestimmte Jünglingslied des musikalischen Genius zu hören glauben. Die Griechen sind, wie die ägyptischen Priester sagen, die ewigen Kinder, und auch in der tragischen Kunst nur die Kinder, welche nicht wissen, welches erhabene Spielzeug unter ihren Händen entstanden ist und – zertrümmert wird.

Jenes Ringen des Geistes der Musik nach bildlicher und mythischer Offenbarung, welches von den Anfängen der Lyrik bis zur attischen Tragödie sich steigert, bricht plötzlich, nach eben erst errungener üppiger Entfaltung, ab und verschwindet gleichsam von der Oberfläche der hellenischen Kunst: während die aus diesem Ringen geborene dionysische Weltbetrachtung in den Mysterien weiterlebt und in den wunderbarsten Metamorphosen und Entartungen nicht aufhört, ernstere Naturen an sich zu ziehen. Ob sie nicht aus ihrer mystischen Tiefe einst wieder als Kunst emporsteigen wird?

Hier beschäftigt uns die Frage, ob die Macht, an deren Entgegenwirken die Tragödie sich brach, für alle Zeit genug Stärke hat, um das künstlerische Wiedererwachen der Tragödie und der tragischen Weltbetrachtung zu verhindern. Wenn die alte

same being also observed in Shakespeare, whose Hamlet, for instance, in an analogous manner talks more superficially than he acts, so that the previously mentioned lesson of Hamlet is to be gathered not from his words, but from a more profound contemplation and survey of the whole. With respect to Greek tragedy, which of course presents itself to us only as word-drama, I have even intimated that the incongruence between myth and expression might easily tempt us to regard it as shallower and less significant than it really is, and accordingly to postulate for it a more superficial effect than it must have had according to the testimony of the ancients: for how easily one forgets that what the word-poet did not succeed in doing, namely realising the highest spiritualisation and ideality of myth, he might succeed in doing every moment as creative musician! We require, to be sure, almost by philological method to reconstruct for ourselves the ascendency of musical influence in order to receive something of the incomparable comfort which must be characteristic of true tragedy. Even this musical ascendency, however, would only have been felt by us as such had we been Greeks: while in the entire development of Greek music—as compared with the infinitely richer music known and familiar to us—we imagine we hear only the youthful song of the musical genius intoned with a feeling of diffidence. The Greeks are, as the Egyptian priests say, eternal children, and in tragic art also they are only children who do not know what a sublime play-thing has originated under their hands and—is being demolished.

That striving of the spirit of music for symbolic and mythical manifestation, which increases from the beginnings of lyric poetry to Attic tragedy, breaks off all of a sudden immediately after attaining luxuriant development, and disappears, as it were, from the surface of Hellenic art: while the Dionysian view of things born of this striving lives on in Mysteries and, in its strangest metamorphoses and debasements, does not cease to attract earnest natures. Will it not one day rise again as art out of its mystic depth?

Here the question occupies us, whether the power by the counteracting influence of which tragedy perished, has for all time strength enough to prevent the artistic reawaking of tragedy and of the tragic view of things. If ancient tragedy was

Tragödie durch den dialektischen Trieb zum Wissen und zum Optimismus der Wissenschaft aus ihrem Gleise gedrängt wurde, so wäre aus dieser Tatsache auf einen ewigen Kampf zwischen *der theoretischen* und *der tragischen Weltbetrachtung* zu schließen; und erst nachdem der Geist der Wissenschaft bis an seine Grenze geführt ist, und sein Anspruch auf universale Gültigkeit durch den Nachweis jener Grenzen vernichtet ist, dürfte auf eine Wiedergeburt der Tragödie zu hoffen sein: für welche Kulturform wir das Symbol *des musiktreibenden Socrates*, in dem früher erörterten Sinne, hinzustellen hätten. Bei dieser Gegenüberstellung verstehe ich unter dem Geiste der Wissenschaft jenen zuerst in der Person des Socrates ans Licht gekommenen Glauben an die Ergründlichkeit der Natur und an die Universalheilkraft des Wissens.

Wer sich an die nächsten Folgen dieses rastlos vorwärtsdringenden Geistes der Wissenschaft erinnert, wird sich sofort vergegenwärtigen, wie durch ihn der *Mythus* vernichtet wurde und wie durch diese Vernichtung die Poesie aus ihrem natürlichen idealen Boden als eine nunmehr heimatlose, verdrängt war. Haben wir mit Recht der Musik die Kraft zugesprochen, den Mythus wieder aus sich gebären zu können, so werden wir den Geist der Wissenschaft auch auf der Bahn zu suchen haben, wo er dieser mythenschaffenden Kraft der Musik feindlich entgegentritt. Dies geschieht in der Entfaltung des *neueren attischen Dithyrambus*, dessen Musik nicht mehr das innere Wesen, den Willen selbst aussprach, sondern nur die Erscheinung ungenügend, in einer durch Begriffe vermittelten Nachahmung wiedergab: von welcher innerlich entarteten Musik sich die wahrhaft musikalischen Naturen mit demselben Widerwillen abwandten, den sie vor der kunstmörderischen Tendenz des Socrates hatten. Der sicher zugreifende Instinkt des Aristophanes hat gewiß das Rechte erfaßt, wenn er Socrates selbst, die Tragödie des Euripides und die Musik der neueren Dithyrambiker in dem gleichen Gefühle des Hasses zusammenfaßte und in allen drei Phänomenen die Merkmale einer degenerierten Kultur witterte. Durch jenen neueren Dithyrambus ist die Musik in frevelhafter Weise zum imitatorischen Konterfei der Erscheinung z.B. einer Schlacht, eines Seesturmes gemacht und damit allerdings ihrer mythenschaffenden Kraft gänzlich beraubt worden. Denn wenn sie unsere Ergötzung nur dadurch zu erregen sucht, daß sie uns zwingt, äußerliche Analogien zwischen einem Vorgange des Lebens und der Natur und gewissen rhythmischen Figuren und

driven from its course by the dialectical desire for knowledge and the optimism of science, it might be inferred that there is an eternal conflict between *the theoretic* and *the tragic view of things*, and only after the spirit of science has been led to its boundaries, and its claim to universal validity has been destroyed by the evidence of these boundaries, can we hope for a re-birth of tragedy: for which form of culture we should have to use the symbol *of the music-practising Socrates* in the sense spoken of above. In this contrast, I understand by the spirit of science the belief which first came to light in the person of Socrates—the belief in the fathomableness of nature and in knowledge as a panacea.

He who recalls the immediate consequences of this restlessly onward-pressing spirit of science will realise at once that *myth* was annihilated by it, and that, in consequence of this annihilation, poetry was driven as a homeless being from her natural ideal soil. If we have rightly assigned to music the capacity to reproduce myth from itself, we may in turn expect to find the spirit of science on the path where it inimically opposes this mythopoeic power of music. This takes place in the development of the *New Attic Dithyramb*, the music of which no longer expressed the inner essence, the will itself, but only rendered the phenomenon insufficiently, in an imitation by means of concepts; from which intrinsically degenerate music the truly musical natures turned away with the same repugnance that they felt for the art-destroying tendency of Socrates. The unerring instinct of Aristophanes surely did the proper thing when it comprised Socrates himself, the tragedy of Euripides, and the music of the new Dithyrambic poets in the same feeling of hatred, and perceived in all three phenomena the symptoms of a degenerate culture. By this New Dithyramb, music has in an outrageous manner been made the imitative portrait of phenomena, for instance, of a battle or a storm at sea, and has thus, of course, been entirely deprived of its mythopoeic power. For if it endeavours to excite our delight only by compelling us to seek external analogies between a vital or natural process and certain rhythmical figures and characteristic sounds of music; if our understanding is expected to satisfy itself with the perception of these analogies, we are reduced to a frame of mind in which the reception of the mythical is impossible; for the myth as a unique

charakteristischen Klängen der Musik zu suchen, wenn sich unser Verstand an der Erkenntnis dieser Analogien befriedigen soll, so sind wir in eine Stimmung herabgezogen, in der eine Empfängnis des Mythischen unmöglich ist; denn der Mythus will als ein einziges Exempel einer ins Unendliche hinein starrenden Allgemeinheit und Wahrheit anschaulich empfunden werden. Die wahrhaft dionysische Musik tritt uns als ein solcher allgemeiner Spiegel des Weltwillens gegenüber: jenes anschauliche Ereignis, das sich in diesem Spiegel bricht, erweitert sich sofort für unser Gefühl zum Abbilde einer ewigen Wahrheit. Umgekehrt wird ein solches anschauliches Ereignis durch die Tonmalerei des neueren Dithyrambus sofort jedes mythischen Charakters entkleidet; jetzt ist die Musik zum dürftigen Abbilde der Erscheinung geworden und darum unendlich ärmer als die Erscheinung selbst: durch welche Armut sie für unsere Empfindung die Erscheinung selbst noch herabzieht, so daß jetzt z.B. eine derartig musikalisch imitierte Schlacht sich in Marschlärm, Signalklängen usw. erschöpft, und unsere Phantasie gerade bei diesen Oberflächlichkeiten festgehalten wird. Die Tonmalerei ist also in jeder Beziehung das Gegenstück zu der mythenschaffenden Kraft der wahren Musik: durch sie wird die Erscheinung noch ärmer, als sie ist, während durch die dionysische Musik die einzelne Erscheinung sich zum Weltbilde bereichert und erweitert. Es war ein mächtiger Sieg des undionysischen Geistes, als er, in der Entfaltung des neueren Dithyrambus, die Musik sich selbst entfremdet und sie zur Sklavin der Erscheinung herabgedrückt hatte. Euripides, der in einem höheren Sinne eine durchaus unmusikalische Natur genannt werden muß, ist aus eben diesem Grunde leidenschaftlicher Anhänger der neueren dithyrambischen Musik und verwendet mit der Freigebigkeit eines Räubers alle ihre Effektstücke und Manieren.

Nach einer anderen Seite sehen wir die Kraft dieses undionysischen, gegen den Mythus gerichteten Geistes in Tätigkeit, wenn wir unsere Blicke auf das Überhandnehmen der *Charakterdarstellung* und des psychologischen Raffinements in der Tragödie von Sophokles abrichten. Der Charakter soll sich nicht mehr zum ewigen Typus erweitern lassen, sondern im Gegenteil so durch künstliche Nebenzüge und Schattierungen, durch feinste Bestimmtheit aller Linien individuell wirken, daß der Zuschauer überhaupt nicht mehr den Mythus, sondern die mächtige Naturwahrheit und die Imitationskraft des Künstlers empfindet. Auch hier gewahren wir den Sieg der Erscheinung über das Allgemeine und die Lust an

exemplar of generality and truth towering into the infinite, desires to be conspicuously perceived. The truly Dionysean music presents itself to us as such a general mirror of the universal will: the conspicuous event which is refracted in this mirror expands at once for our consciousness to the copy of an eternal truth. Conversely, such a conspicious event is at once divested of every mythical character by the tone-painting of the New Dithyramb; music has here become a wretched copy of the phenomenon, and therefore infinitely poorer than the phenomenon itself: through which poverty it still further reduces even the phenomenon for our consciousness, so that now, for instance, a musically imitated battle of this sort exhausts itself in marches, signal-sounds, etc., and our imagination is arrested precisely by these superficialities. Tone-painting is therefore in every respect the counterpart of true music with its mythopoeic power: through it the phenomenon, poor in itself, is made still poorer, while through an isolated Dionysian music the phenomenon is evolved and expanded into a picture of the world. It was an immense triumph of the non-Dionysian spirit, when, in the development of the New Dithyramb, it had estranged music from itself and reduced it to be the slave of phenomena. Euripides, who, albeit in a higher sense, must be designated as a thoroughly unmusical nature, is for this very reason a passionate adherent of the New Dithyrambic Music, and with the liberality of a freebooter employs all its effective turns and mannerisms.

In another direction also we see at work the power of this un-Dionysian, myth-opposing spirit, when we turn our eyes to the prevalence of *character representation* and psychological refinement from Sophocles onwards. The character must no longer be expanded into an eternal type, but, on the contrary, must operate individually through artistic by-traits and shadings, through the nicest precision of all lines, in such a manner that the spectator is in general no longer conscious of the myth, but of the mighty nature-myth and the imitative power of the artist. Here also we observe the victory of the phenomenon over the Universal, and the delight in the particular quasi-anatomical preparation; we actually breathe the air of a theoretical world, in which scientific knowledge is valued more

dem einzelnen gleichsam anatomischen Präparat, wir atmen bereits die Luft einer theoretischen Welt, welcher die wissenschaftliche Erkenntnis höher gilt als die künstlerische Wiederspiegelung einer Weltregel. Die Bewegung auf der Linie des Charakteristischen geht schnell weiter: während noch Sophokles ganze Charaktere malt und zu ihrer raffinierten Entfaltung den Mythus ins Joch spannt, malt Euripides bereits nur noch große einzelne Charakterzüge, die sich in heftigen Leidenschaften zu äußern wissen; in der neuern attischen Komödie gibt es nur noch Masken mit *einem* Ausdruck, leichtsinnige Alte, geprellte Kuppler, verschmitzte Sklaven in unermüdlicher Wiederholung. Wohin ist jetzt der mythenbildende Geist der Musik? Was jetzt noch von Musik übrig ist, das ist entweder Aufregungs- oder Erinnerungsmusik, d.h. entweder ein Stimulanzmittel für stumpfe und verbrauchte Nerven oder Tonmalerei. Für die erstere kommt es auf den untergelegten Text kaum noch an: schon bei Euripides geht es, wenn seine Helden oder Chöre erst zu singen anfangen, recht liederlich zu; wohin mag es bei seinen frechen Nachfolgern gekommen sein?

Am allerdeutlichsten aber offenbart sich der neue undionysische Geist in den *Schlüssen* der neueren Dramen. In der alten Tragödie war der metaphysische Trost am Ende zu spüren gewesen, ohne den die Lust an der Tragödie überhaupt nicht zu erklären ist: am reinsten tönt vielleicht im Ödipus auf Kolonos der versöhnende Klang aus einer anderen Welt. Jetzt, als der Genius der Musik aus der Tragödie entflohen war, ist, im strengen Sinne, die Tragödie tot: denn woher sollte man jetzt jenen metaphysischen Trost schöpfen können? Man suchte daher nach einer irdischen Lösung der tragischen Dissonanz; der Held, nachdem er durch das Schicksal hinreichend gemartert war, erntete in einer stattlichen Heirat, in göttlichen Ehrenbezeugungen einen wohlverdienten Lohn. Der Held war zum Gladiator geworden, dem man, nachdem er tüchtig geschunden und mit Wunden überdeckt war, gelegentlich die Freiheit schenkte. Der *deus ex machina* ist an Stelle des metaphysischen Trostes getreten. Ich will nicht sagen, daß die tragische Weltbetrachtung überall und völlig durch den andrängenden Geist des Undionysischen zerstört wurde: wir wissen nur, daß sie sich aus der Kunst gleichsam in die Unterwelt, in einer Entartung zum Geheimkult, flüchten mußte. Aber auf dem weitesten Gebiete der Oberfläche des hellenischen Wesens wütete der verzehrende Hauch jenes Geistes, welcher sich in jener Form der »griechischen Heiterkeit« kundgibt, von der bereits früher, als von einer

highly than the artistic reflection of a universal law. The movement along the line of the representation of character proceeds rapidly: while Sophocles still delineates complete characters and employs myth for their refined development, Euripides already delineates only prominent individual traits of character, which can express themselves in violent bursts of passion; in the New Attic Comedy, however, there are only masks with *one* expression: frivolous old men, duped panders, and cunning slaves in untiring repetition. Where now is the mythopoeic spirit of music? What is still left now of music is either excitatory music or souvenir music, that is, either a stimulant for dull and used-up nerves, or tone-painting. As regards the former, it hardly matters about the text set to it: the heroes and choruses of Euripides are already dissolute enough when once they begin to sing; to what pass must things have come with his brazen successors?

The new un-Dionysian spirit, however, manifests itself most clearly in the *dénouements* of the new dramas. In the Old Tragedy one could feel at the close the metaphysical comfort, without which the delight in tragedy cannot be explained at all; the conciliating tones from another world sound purest, perhaps, in the Oedipus at Colonus. Now that the genius of music has fled from tragedy, tragedy is, strictly speaking, dead: for from whence could one now draw the metaphysical comfort? One sought, therefore, for an earthly unravelment of the tragic dissonance; the hero, after he had been sufficiently tortured by fate, reaped a well-deserved reward through a superb marriage or divine tokens of favour. The hero had turned gladiator, on whom, after being liberally battered about and covered with wounds, freedom was occasionally bestowed. The *deus ex machina* took the place of metaphysical comfort. I will not say that the tragic view of things was everywhere completely destroyed by the intruding spirit of the un-Dionysian: we only know that it was compelled to flee from art into the under-world as it were, in the degenerate form of a secret cult. Over the widest extent of the Hellenic character, however, there raged the consuming blast of this spirit, which manifests itself in the form of "Greek cheerfulness," which we have already spoken of as a senile, unproductive love of existence; this cheerfulness is the counterpart of the splendid

greisenhaft unproduktiven Daseinslust, die Rede war; diese Heiterkeit ist ein Gegenstück zu der herrlichen »Naivität« der älteren Griechen, wie sie, nach der gegebenen Charakteristik, zu fassen ist als die aus einem düsteren Abgrunde hervorwachsende Blüte der apollinischen Kultur, als der Sieg, den der hellenische Wille durch seine Schönheitsspiegelung über das Leiden und die Weisheit des Leidens davonträgt. Die edelste Form jener anderen Form der »griechischen Heiterkeit«, der alexandrinischen, ist die Heiterkeit des *theoretischen Menschen*: sie zeigt dieselben charakteristischen Merkmale, die ich soeben aus dem Geiste des Undionysischen ableitete, – daß sie die dionysische Weisheit und Kunst bekämpft, daß sie den Mythus aufzulösen trachtet, daß sie an Stelle eines metaphysischen Trostes eine irdische Konsonanz, ja einen eigenen *deus ex machina* setzt, nämlich den Gott der Maschinen und Schmelztiegel, d.h. die im Dienste des höheren Egoismus erkannten und verwendeten Kräfte der Naturgeister, daß sie an eine Korrektur der Welt durch das Wissen, an ein durch die Wissenschaft geleitetes Leben glaubt und auch wirklich imstande ist, den einzelnen Menschen in einen allerengsten Kreis von lösbaren Aufgaben zu bannen, innerhalb dessen er heiter zum Leben sagt: »Ich will dich: du bist wert erkannt zu werden.«

"naïveté" of the earlier Greeks, which, according to the characteristic indicated above, must be conceived as the blossom of the Apollonian culture growing out of a dark abyss, as the victory which the Hellenic will, through its mirroring of beauty, obtains over suffering and the wisdom of suffering. The noblest manifestation of that other form of "Greek cheerfulness," the Alexandrine, is the cheerfulness of the *theoretical man*: it exhibits the same symptomatic characteristics as I have just inferred concerning the spirit of the un-Dionysian:—it combats Dionysian wisdom and art, it seeks to dissolve myth, it substitutes for metaphysical comfort an earthly consonance, in fact, a *deus ex machina* of its own, namely the god of machines and crucibles, that is, the powers of the genii of nature recognised and employed in the service of higher egoism; it believes in amending the world by knowledge, in guiding life by science, and that it can really confine the individual within a narrow sphere of solvable problems, where he cheerfully says to life: "You I want: you are worth knowing."

18

Es ist ein ewiges Phänomen: immer findet der gierige Wille ein Mittel, durch eine über die Dinge gebreitete Illusion seine Geschöpfe im Leben festzuhalten und zum Weiterleben zu zwingen. Diesen fesselt die sokratische Lust des Erkennens und der Wahn, durch dasselbe die ewige Wunde des Daseins heilen zu können, jenen umstrickt der vor seinen Augen wehende verführerische Schönheitsschleier der Kunst, jenen wiederum der metaphysische Trost, daß unter dem Wirbel der Erscheinungen das ewige Leben unzerstörbar weiterfließt: um von den gemeineren und fast noch kräftigeren Illusionen, die der Wille in jedem Augenblick bereithält, zu schweigen. Jene drei Illusionsstufen sind überhaupt nur für die edler ausgestatteten Naturen, von denen die Last und Schwere des Daseins überhaupt mit tieferer Unlust empfunden wird, und die durch ausgesuchte Reizmittel über diese Unlust hinwegzutäuschen sind. Aus diesen Reizmitteln besteht alles, was wir Kultur nennen: je nach der Proportion der Mischungen haben wir eine vorzugsweise *sokratische* oder *künstlerische* oder *tragische* Kultur; oder wenn man historische Exemplifikationen erlauben will: es gibt entweder eine

IT IS an eternal phenomenon: the avidious will can always, by means of an illusion spread over things, detain its creatures in life and compel them to live on. One is chained by the Socratic love of knowledge and the vain hope of being able thereby to heal the eternal wound of existence; another is ensnared by art's seductive veil of beauty fluttering before his eyes; still another by the metaphysical comfort that eternal life flows on indestructibly beneath the whirl of phenomena: to say nothing of the more ordinary and almost more powerful illusions which the will has always at hand. These three specimens of illusion are on the whole designed only for the more nobly endowed natures, who in general feel profoundly the weight and burden of existence, and must be deluded into forgetfulness of their displeasure by exquisite stimulants. All that we call culture is made up of these stimulants; and, according to the proportion of the ingredients, we have either a specially *Socratic* or *artistic* or *tragic culture*: or, if historical exemplifications are wanted, there is either an

alexandrinische oder eine hellenische oder eine buddhaistische Kultur.

Unsere ganze moderne Welt ist in dem Netz der alexandrinischen Kultur befangen und kennt als Ideal den mit höchsten Erkenntniskräften ausgerüsteten, im Dienste der Wissenschaft arbeitenden *theoretischen Menschen*, dessen Urbild und Stammvater Socrates ist. Alle unsere Erziehungsmittel haben ursprünglich dieses Ideal im Auge: jede andere Existenz hat sich mühsam nebenbei emporzuringen, als erlaubte, nicht als beabsichtigte Existenz. In einem fast erschreckenden Sinne ist hier eine lange Zeit der Gebildete allein in der Form des Gelehrten gefunden worden; selbst unsere dichterischen Künste haben sich aus gelehrten Imitationen entwickeln müssen, und in dem Haupteffekt des Reimes erkennen wir noch die Entstehung unserer poetischen Form aus künstlichen Experimenten mit einer nicht heimischen, recht eigentlich gelehrten Sprache. Wie unverständlich müßte einem echten Griechen der an sich verständliche moderne Kulturmensch *Faust* erscheinen, der durch alle Fakultäten unbefriedigt stürmende, aus Wissenstrieb da Magie und dem Teufel ergebene Faust, den wir nur zur Vergleichung neben Socrates zu stellen haben, um zu erkennen, daß der moderne Mensch die Grenzen jener sokratischen Erkenntnislust zu ahnen beginnt und aus dem weiten wüsten Wissensmeere nach einer Küste verlangt. Wenn Goethe einmal zu Eckermann, mit Bezug auf Napoleon, äußert: »Ja mein Guter, es gibt auch eine Produktivität der Taten«, so hat er, in anmutig naiver Weise, daran erinnert, daß der nicht theoretische Mensch für den modernen Menschen etwas Unglaubwürdiges und Staunenerregendes ist, so daß es wieder der Weisheit eines Goethe bedarf, um auch eine so befremdende Existenzform begreiflich, ja verzeihlich zu finden.

Und nun soll man sich nicht verbergen, was im Schoße dieser sokratischen Kultur verborgen liegt! Der unumschränkt sich wähnende Optimismus! Nun soll man nicht erschrecken, wenn die Früchte dieses Optimismus reifen, wenn die von einer derartigen Kultur bis in die niedrigsten Schichten hinein durchsäuerte Gesellschaft allmählich unter üppigen Wallungen und Begehrungen erzittert, wenn der Glaube an das Erdenglück aller, wenn der Glaube an die Möglichkeit einer solchen allgemeinen Wissenskultur allmählich in die drohende Forderung eines solchen alexandrinischen Erdenglückes, in die Beschwörung eines euripideischen *deus ex machina* umschlägt! Man soll es merken: die alexandrinische

Alexandrine or a Hellenic or a Buddhistic culture.

Our whole modern world is entangled in the meshes of Alexandrine culture, and recognises as its ideal the *theorist* equipped with the most potent means of knowledge, and labouring in the service of science, of whom the archetype and progenitor is Socrates. All our educational methods have originally this ideal in view: every other form of existence must struggle onwards wearisomely beside it, as something tolerated, but not intended. In an almost alarming manner the cultured man was here found for a long time only in the form of the scholar: even our poetical arts have been forced to evolve from learned imitations, and in the main effect of the rhyme we still recognise the origin of our poetic form from artistic experiments with a non-native and thoroughly learned language. How unintelligible must *Faust*, the modern cultured man, who is in himself intelligible, have appeared to a true Greek—Faust, storming discontentedly through all the faculties, devoted to magic and the devil from a desire for knowledge, whom we have only to place alongside of Socrates for the purpose of comparison, in order to see that modern man begins to divine the boundaries of this Socratic love of perception and longs for a coast in the wide waste of the ocean of knowledge. When Goethe on one occasion said to Eckermann with reference to Napoleon: "Yes, my good friend, there is also a productiveness of deeds," he reminded us in a charmingly naïve manner that the non-theorist is something incredible and astounding to modern man; so that the wisdom of Goethe is needed once more in order to discover that such a surprising form of existence is comprehensible, nay even pardonable.

Now, we must not hide from ourselves what is concealed in the heart of this Socratic culture: Optimism, deeming itself absolute! Well, we must not be alarmed if the fruits of this optimism ripen—if society, leavened to the very lowest strata by this kind of culture, gradually begins to tremble through wanton agitations and desires, if the belief in the earthly happiness of all, if the belief in the possibility of such a general intellectual culture is gradually transformed into the threatening demand for such an Alexandrine earthly happiness, into the conjuring of a Euripidean *deus ex machina*. Let us mark this well: the Alexandrine culture requires a slave

Kultur braucht einen Sklavenstand, um auf die Dauer existieren zu können: aber sie leugnet, in ihrer optimistischen Betrachtung des Daseins, die Notwendigkeit eines solchen Standes und geht deshalb, wenn der Effekt ihrer schönen Verführungs- und Beruhigungsworte von der »Würde des Menschen« und der »Würde der Arbeit« verbraucht ist, allmählich einer grauenvollen Vernichtung entgegen. Es gibt nichts Furchtbareres als einen barbarischen Sklavenstand, der seine Existenz als ein Unrecht zu betrachten gelernt hat und sich anschickt, nicht nur für sich, sondern für alle Generationen Rache zu nehmen. Wer wagt es, solchen drohenden Stürmen entgegen, sicheren Mutes an unsere blassen und ermüdeten Religionen zu appelieren, die selbst in ihren Fundamenten zu Gelehrtenreligionen entartet sind: so daß der Mythus, die notwendige Voraussetzung jeder Religion, bereits überall gelähmt ist, und selbst auf diesem Bereich jener optimistische Geist zur Herrschaft gekommen ist, den wir als den Vernichtungskeim unserer Gesellschaft eben bezeichnet haben.

Während das im Schoße der theoretischen Kultur schlummernde Unheil allmählich den modernen Menschen zu ängstigen beginnt, und er, unruhig, aus dem Schatze seiner Erfahrungen nach Mitteln greift, um die Gefahr abzuwenden, ohne selbst an diese Mittel recht zu glauben; während er also seine eigenen Konsequenzen zu ahnen beginnt: haben große allgemein angelegte Naturen, mit einer unglaublichen Besonnenheit, das Rüstzeug der Wissenschaft selbst zu benützen gewußt, um die Grenzen und die Bedingtheit des Erkennens überhaupt darzulegen und damit den Anspruch der Wissenschaft auf universale Geltung und universale Zwecke entscheidend zu leugnen: bei welchem Nachweise zum ersten Male jene Wahnvorstellung als solche erkannt wurde, welche, an der Hand der Kausalität, sich anmaßt, das innerste Wesen der Dinge ergründen zu können. Der ungeheuren Tapferkeit und Weisheit *Kants* und *Schopenhauers* ist der schwerste Sieg gelungen, der Sieg über den im Wesen der Logik verborgen liegenden Optimismus, der wiederum der Untergrund unserer Kultur ist. Wenn dieser an die Erkennbarkeit und Ergründlichkeit aller Welträtsel, gestützt auf die ihm unbedenklichen *aeternae veritates*, geglaubt und Raum, Zeit und Kausalität als gänzlich unbedingte Gesetze von allgemeinster Gültigkeit behandelt hatte, offenbarte Kant, wie diese eigentlich nur dazu dienten, die bloße Erscheinung, das Werk der Maja, zur einzigen und höchsten Realität zu erheben und sie an die Stelle des innersten und wahren Wesens der Dinge

class, to be able to exist permanently: but, in its optimistic view of life, it denies the necessity of such a class, and consequently, when the effect of its beautifully seductive and tranquillising utterances about the "dignity of man" and the "dignity of labour" is spent, it gradually drifts towards a dreadful destination. There is nothing more terrible than a barbaric slave class, who have learned to regard their existence as an injustice, and now prepare to take vengeance, not only for themselves, but for all generations. In the face of such threatening storms, who dares to appeal with confident spirit to our pale and exhausted religions, which even in their foundations have degenerated into scholastic religions?—so that myth, the necessary prerequisite of every religion, is already paralysed everywhere, and even in this domain the optimistic spirit—which we have just designated as the annihilating germ of society—has attained the mastery.

While the evil slumbering in the heart of theoretical culture gradually begins to disquiet modern man, and makes him anxiously ransack the stores of his experience for means to avert the danger, though not believing very much in these means; while he, therefore, begins to divine the consequences his position involves: great, universally gifted natures have contrived, with an incredible amount of thought, to make use of the apparatus of science itself, in order to point out the limits and the relativity of knowledge generally, and thus definitely to deny the claim of science to universal validity and universal ends: with which demonstration the illusory notion was for the first time recognised as such, which pretends, with the aid of causality, to be able to fathom the innermost essence of things. The extraordinary courage and wisdom of *Kant* and *Schopenhauer* have succeeded in gaining the most, difficult, victory, the victory over the optimism hidden in the essence of logic, which optimism in turn is the basis of our culture. While this optimism, resting on apparently unobjectionable *æterna veritates,* believed in the intelligibility and solvability of all the riddles of the world, and treated space, time, and causality as totally unconditioned laws of the most universal validity, Kant, on the other hand, showed that these served in reality only to elevate the mere phenomenon, the work of Mâyâ, to the sole and highest reality, putting it in place of the innermost and true essence of things, thus

zu setzen und die wirkliche Erkenntnis von diesem dadurch unmöglich zu machen, d.h., nach einem Schopenhauerschen Ausspruche, den Träumer noch fester einzuschläfern (W. a. W. u. V. I, S. 498). Mit dieser Erkenntnis ist eine Kultur eingeleitet, welche ich als eine tragische zu bezeichnen wage: deren wichtigstes Merkmal ist, daß an die Stelle der Wissenschaft als höchstes Ziel die Weisheit gerückt wird, die sich, ungetäuscht durch die verführerischen Ablenkungen der Wissenschaften, mit unbewegtem Blicke dem Gesamtbilde der Welt zuwendet und in diesem das ewige Leiden mit sympathischer Liebesempfindung als das eigne Leiden zu ergreifen sucht. Denken wir uns eine heranwachsende Generation mit dieser Unerschrockenheit des Blicks, mit diesem heroischen Zug ins Ungeheure, denken wir uns den kühnen Schritt dieser Drachentöter, die stolze Verwegenheit, mit der sie allen den Schwächlichkeitsdoktrinen jenes Optimismus den Rücken kehren, um im Ganzen und Vollen »resolut zu leben«: sollte es nicht nötig sein, daß der tragische Mensch dieser Kultur, bei seiner Selbsterziehung zum Ernst und zum Schrecken, eine neue Kunst, die Kunst des metaphysischen Trostes, die Tragödie als die ihm zugehörige Helena begehren und mit Faust ausrufen muß:

Und sollt ich nicht, sehnsüchtigster Gewalt,
Ins Leben ziehn die einzigste Gestalt?

Nachdem aber die sokratische Kultur von zwei Seiten aus erschüttert ist und das Szepter ihrer Unfehlbarkeit nur noch mit zitternden Händen zu halten vermag, einmal aus Furcht vor ihren eigenen Konsequenzen, die sie nachgerade zu ahnen beginnt, sodann weil sie selbst von der ewigen Gültigkeit ihres Fundamentes nicht mehr mit dem früheren naiven Zutrauen überzeugt ist: so ist es ein trauriges Schauspiel, wie sich der Tanz ihres Denkens sehnsüchtig immer auf neue Gestalten stürzt, um sie zu umarmen, und sie dann plötzlich wieder, wie Mephistopheles die verführerischen Lamien, schaudernd fahren läßt. Das ist ja das Merkmal jenes »Bruches«, von dem jedermann als von dem Urleiden der modernen Kultur zu reden pflegt, daß der theoretische Mensch vor seinen Konsequenzen erschrickt und unbefriedigt es nicht mehr wagt, sich dem furchtbaren Eisstrome des Daseins anzuvertrauen: ängstlich läuft er am Ufer auf und ab. Er will nichts mehr ganz haben, ganz auch mit aller der natürlichen Grausamkeit der Dinge. Soweit hat ihn das optimistische Betrachten verzärtelt. Dazu fühlt er, wie eine Kultur, die auf dem Prinzip der Wissenschaft

making the actual knowledge of this essence impossible, that is, according to the expression of Schopenhauer, to lull the dreamer still more soundly asleep (*Welt als Wille und Vorstellung,* I. 498). With this knowledge a culture is inaugurated which I venture to designate as a tragic culture; the most important characteristic of which is that wisdom takes the place of science as the highest end—wisdom, which, uninfluenced by the seductive distractions of the sciences, turns with unmoved eye to the comprehensive view of the world, and seeks to apprehend therein the eternal suffering as its own with sympathetic feelings of love. Let us imagine a rising generation with this undauntedness of vision, with this heroic desire for the prodigious, let us imagine the bold step of these dragon-slayers, the proud and daring spirit with which they turn their backs on all the effeminate doctrines of optimism in order "to live resolutely" in the Whole and in the Full: would it not be necessary for the tragic man of this culture, with his self-discipline to earnestness and terror, to desire a new art, the art of metaphysical comfort—namely, tragedy, as the Helen belonging to him, and that he should exclaim with Faust:

And shall I not, most powerful desire,
draw this unique form into life?

But now that the Socratic culture has been shaken from two directions, and is only able to hold the sceptre of its infallibility with trembling hands—once by the fear of its own conclusions which it at length begins to surmise, and again, because it is no longer convinced with its former naïve trust of the eternal validity of its foundation, —it is a sad spectacle to behold how the dance of its thought always rushes longingly on new forms, to embrace them, and then, shuddering, lets them go of a sudden, as Mephistopheles does the seductive Lamiæ. It is certainly the symptom of the "breach" which all are wont to speak of as the primordial suffering of modern culture that the theoretical man, alarmed and dissatisfied at his own conclusions, no longer dares to entrust himself to the terrible ice-stream of existence: he runs timidly up and down the bank. He no longer wants to have anything entire, with all the natural cruelty of things, so thoroughly has he been spoiled by his optimistic contemplation. Besides, he feels that a culture built up on the principles of science must perish when it begins to grow

aufgebaut ist, zugrunde gehen muß, wenn sie anfängt, *unlogisch* zu werden, d.h. vor ihren Konsequenzen zurückzufliehen. Unsere Kunst offenbart diese allgemeine Not: umsonst, daß man sich an alle großen produktiven Perioden und Naturen imitatorisch anlehnt, umsonst, daß man die ganze »Weltliteratur« zum Troste des modernen Menschen um ihn versammelt und ihn mitten unter die Kunststile und Künstler aller Zeiten hinstellt, damit er ihnen, wie Adam den Tieren, einen Namen gebe: er bleibt doch der ewig Hungernde, der »Kritiker« ohne Lust und Kraft, der alexandrinische Mensch, der im Grunde Bibliothekar und Korrektor ist und an Bücherstaub und Druckfehlern elend erblindet.

illogical, that is, to avoid its own conclusions. Our art reveals this universal trouble: in vain does one seek help by imitating all the great productive periods and natures, in vain does one accumulate the entire "world-literature" around modern man for his comfort, in vain does one place one's self in the midst of the art-styles and artists of all ages, so that one may give names to them as Adam did to the beasts: one still continues the eternal hungerer, the "critic" without joy and energy, the Alexandrine man, who is in the main a librarian and corrector of proofs, and who, pitiable wretch goes blind from the dust of books and printers' errors.

19

Man kann den innersten Gehalt dieser sokratischen Kultur nicht schärfer bezeichnen, als wenn man sie *die Kultur der Oper* nennt: denn auf diesem Gebiete hat sich die Kultur mit eigener Naivität über ihr Wollen und Erkennen ausgesprochen, zu unserer Verwunderung, wenn wir die Genesis der Oper und die Tatsache der Opernentwicklung mit den ewigen Wahrheiten des Apollinischen und des Dionysischen zusammenhalten. Ich erinnere zunächst an die Entstehung des *stilo rappresentativo* und des Rezitativs. Ist es glaublich, daß diese gänzlich veräußerlichte, der Andacht unfähige Musik der Oper von einer Zeit mit schwärmerischer Gunst, gleichsam als die Wiedergeburt aller wahren Musik, empfangen und gehegt werden konnte, aus der sich soeben die unaussprechbar erhabene und heilige Musik Palestrinas erhoben hatte? Und wer möchte andrerseits nur die zerstreuungssüchtige Üppigkeit jener Florentiner Kreise und die Eitelkeit ihrer dramatischen Sänger für die so ungestüm sich verbreitende Lust an der Oper verantwortlich machen? Daß in derselben Zeit, ja in demselben Volke neben dem Gewölbebau Palestrinascher Harmonien, an dem das gesamte christliche Mittelalter gebaut hatte, jene Leidenschaft für eine halbmusikalische Sprechart erwachte, vermag ich mir nur aus einer im Wesen des Rezitativs mitwirkenden *außerkünstlerischen Tendenz* zu erklären.

Dem Zuhörer, der das Wort unter dem Gesange deutlich vernehmen will, entspricht der Sänger dadurch, daß er mehr spricht als singt und daß er den pathetischen Wortausdruck in diesem Halbgesange verschärft: durch diese Verschärfung des Pathos erleichtert er das Verständnis des Wortes und

We cannot designate the intrinsic substance of Socratic culture more distinctly than by calling it *the culture of the opera*: for it is in this department that culture has expressed itself with special naïveté concerning its aims and perceptions, which is sufficiently surprising when we compare the genesis of the opera and the facts of operatic development with the eternal truths of the Apollonian and Dionysian. I call to mind first of all the origin of the *stilo rappresentativo* and the recitative. Is it credible that this thoroughly externalised operatic music, incapable of devotion, could be received and cherished with enthusiastic favour, as a re-birth, as it were, of all true music, by the very age in which the ineffably sublime and sacred music of Palestrina had originated? And who, on the other hand, would think of making only the diversion-craving luxuriousness of those Florentine circles and the vanity of their dramatic singers responsible for the love of the opera which spread with such rapidity? That in the same age, even among the same people, this passion for a half-musical mode of speech should awaken alongside of the vaulted structure of Palestrine harmonies which the entire Christian Middle Age had been building up, I can explain to myself only by a co-operating *extra-artistic tendency* in the essence of the recitative.

The listener, who insists on distinctly hearing the words under the music, has his wishes met by the singer in that he speaks rather than sings, and intensifies the pathetic expression of the words in this half-song: by this intensification of the pathos he facilitates the understanding of the words and

überwindet jene übrig gebliebene Hälfte der Musik. Die eigentliche Gefahr, die ihm jetzt droht, ist die, daß er der Musik einmal zur Unzeit das Übergewicht erteilt, wodurch sofort Pathos der Rede und Deutlichkeit des Wortes zugrunde gehen müßte: während er andrerseits immer den Trieb zu musikalischer Entladung und zu virtuosenhafter Präsentation seiner Stimme fühlt. Hier kommt ihm der »Dichter« zu Hilfe, der ihm genug Gelegenheit zu lyrischen Interjektionen, Wort- und Sentenzenwiederholungen usw. zu bieten weiß: an welchen Stellen der Sänger jetzt in dem rein musikalischen Elemente, ohne Rücksicht auf das Wort, ausruhen kann. Dieser Wechsel affektvoll eindringlicher, doch nur halb gesungener Rede und ganz gesungener Interjektion, der im Wesen des *stilo rappresentativo* liegt, dies rasch wechselnde Bemühen, bald auf den Begriff und die Vorstellung, bald auf den musikalischen Grund des Zuhörers zu wirken, ist etwas so gänzlich Unnatürliches und den Kunsttrieben des Dionysischen und des Apollinischen in gleicher Weise so innerlich Widersprechendes, daß man auf einen Ursprung des Rezitativs zu schließen hat, der außerhalb aller künstlerischen Instinkte liegt. Das Rezitativ ist nach dieser Schilderung zu definieren als die Vermischung des epischen und des lyrischen Vortrags und zwar keinesfalls die innerlich beständige Mischung, die bei so gänzlich disparaten Dingen nicht erreicht werden konnte, sondern die äußerlichste mosaikartige Konglutination, wie etwas derartiges im Bereich der Natur und der Erfahrung gänzlich vorbildlos ist. *Dies war aber nicht die Meinung jener Erfinder des Rezitativs*: vielmehr glauben sie selbst und mit ihnen ihr Zeitalter, daß durch jenen *stilo rappresentativo* das Geheimnis der antiken Musik gelöst sei, aus dem sich allein die ungeheure Wirkung eines Orpheus, Amphion, ja auch der griechischen Tragödie erklären lasse. Der neue Stil galt als die Wiedererweckung der wirkungsvollsten Musik, der altgriechischen: ja man durfte sich, bei der allgemeinen und ganz volkstümlichen Auffassung der homerischen Welt *als der Urwelt*, dem Traume überlassen, jetzt wieder in die paradiesischen Anfänge der Menschheit hinabgestiegen zu sein, in der notwendig auch die Musik jene unübertroffne Reinheit, Macht und Unschuld gehabt haben müßte, von der die Dichter in ihren Schäferspielen so rührend zu erzählen wußten. Hier sehen wir in das innerlichste Werden dieser recht eigentlich modernen Kunstgattung, der Oper: ein mächtiges Bedürfnis erzwingt sich hier eine Kunst, aber ein Bedürfnis unästhetischer Art: die Sehnsucht zum Idyll, der Glaube an eine urvorzeitliche Existenz des

surmounts the remaining half of the music. The specific danger which now threatens him is that in some unguarded moment he may give undue importance to music, which would forthwith result in the destruction of the pathos of the speech and the distinctness of the words: while, on the other hand, he always feels himself impelled to musical delivery and to virtuose exhibition of vocal talent. Here the "poet" comes to his aid, who knows how to provide him with abundant opportunities for lyrical interjections, repetitions of words and sentences, etc.—at which places the singer, now in the purely musical element, can rest himself without minding the words. This alternation of emotionally impressive, yet only half-sung speech and wholly sung interjections, which is characteristic of the *stilo rappresentativo,* this rapidly changing endeavour to operate now on the conceptional and representative faculty of the hearer, now on his musical sense, is something so thoroughly unnatural and withal so intrinsically contradictory both to the Apollonian and Dionysian artistic impulses, that one has to infer an origin of the recitative foreign to all artistic instincts. The recitative must be defined, according to this description, as the combination of epic and lyric delivery, not indeed as an intrinsically stable combination which could not be attained in the case of such totally disparate elements, but an entirely superficial mosaic conglutination, such as is totally unprecedented in the domain of nature and experience. *But this was* not the opinion of the inventors of the recitative: they themselves, and their age with them, believed rather that the mystery of antique music had been solved by this *stilo rappresentativo,* in which, as they thought, the only explanation of the enormous influence of an Orpheus, an Amphion, and even of Greek tragedy was to be found. The new style was regarded by them as the re-awakening of the most effective music, the Old Greek music: indeed, with the universal and popular conception of the Homeric world *as the primitive world,* they could abandon themselves to the dream of having descended once more into the paradisiac beginnings of mankind, wherein music also must needs have had the unsurpassed purity, power, and innocence of which the poets could give such touching accounts in their pastoral plays. Here we see into the internal process of development of this thoroughly modern variety of art, the opera: a powerful need here acquires an art, but it is a need of an unæsthetic kind: the

künstlerischen und guten Menschen. Das Rezitativ galt als die wiederentdeckte Sprache jenes Urmenschen; die Oper als das wiederaufgefundene Land jenes idyllisch oder heroisch guten Wesens, das zugleich in allen seinen Handlungen einem natürlichen Kunsttriebe folgt, das bei allem, was es zu sagen hat, wenigstens etwas singt, um, bei der leisesten Gefühlserregung, sofort mit voller Stimme zu singen. Es ist für uns jetzt gleichgültig, daß mit diesem neugeschaffenen Bilde des paradiesischen Künstlers die damaligen Humanisten gegen die alte kirchliche Vorstellung vom an sich verderbten und verlornen Menschen ankämpften: so daß die Oper als das Oppositionsdogma vom guten Menschen zu verstehen ist, mit dem aber zugleich ein Trostmittel gegen jenen Pessimismus gefunden war, zu dem gerade die Ernstgesinnten jener Zeit, bei der grauenhaften Unsicherheit aller Zustände, am stärksten gereizt waren. Genug, wenn wir erkannt haben, wie der eigentliche Zauber und damit die Genesis dieser neuen Kunstform in der Befriedigung eines gänzlich unästhetischen Bedürfnisses liegt, in der optimistischen Verherrlichung des Menschen an sich, in der Auffassung des Urmenschen als des von Natur guten und künstlerischen Menschen: welches Prinzip der Oper sich allmählich in eine drohende und entsetzliche *Forderung* umgewandelt hat, die wir, im Angesicht der sozialistischen Bewegungen der Gegenwart, nicht mehr überhören können. Der »gute Urmensch« will seine Rechte: welche paradiesischen Aussichten!

Ich stelle daneben noch eine ebenso deutliche Bestätigung meiner Ansicht, daß die Oper auf den gleichen Prinzipien mit unserer alexandrinischen Kultur aufgebaut ist. Die Oper ist die Geburt des theoretischen Menschen, des kritischen Laien, nicht des Künstlers: eine der befremdlichsten Tatsachen in der Geschichte aller Künste. Es war die Forderung recht eigentlich unmusikalischer Zuhörer, daß man vor allem das Wort verstehen müsse: so daß eine Wiedergeburt der Tonkunst nur zu erwarten sei, wenn man irgendeine Gesangsweise entdecken werde, bei welcher das Textwort über den Kontrapunkt wie der Herr über den Diener herrsche. Denn die Worte seien um so viel edler als das begleitende harmonische System, um wieviel die Seele edler als der Körper sei. Mit der laienhaft unmusikalischen Rohheit dieser Ansichten wurde in den Anfängen der Oper die Verbindung von Musik, Bild und Wort behandelt; im Sinne dieser Ästhetik kam es auch in den vornehmen Laienkreisen von Florenz, durch hier patronisierte Dichter und Sänger, zu den ersten Experimenten. Der

yearning for the idyll, the belief in the prehistoric existence of the artistic, good man. The recitative was regarded as the rediscovered language of this primitive man; the opera as the recovered land of this idyllically or heroically good creature, who in every action follows at the same time a natural artistic impulse, who sings a little along with all he has to say, in order to sing immediately with full voice on the slightest emotional excitement. It is now a matter of indifference to us that the humanists of those days combated the old ecclesiastical representation of man as naturally corrupt and lost, with this new-created picture of the paradisiac artist: so that opera may be understood as the oppositional dogma of the good man, whereby however a solace was at the same time found for the pessimism to which precisely the seriously-disposed men of that time were most strongly incited, owing to the frightful uncertainty of all conditions of life. It is enough to have perceived that the intrinsic charm, and therefore the genesis, of this new form of art lies in the gratification of an altogether unæsthetic need, in the optimistic glorification of man as such, in the conception of the primitive man as the man naturally good and artistic: a principle of the opera which has gradually changed into a threatening and terrible *demand,* which, in face of the socialistic movements of the present time, we can no longer ignore. The "good primitive man" wants his rights: what paradisiac prospects!

I here place by way of parallel still another equally obvious confirmation of my view that opera is built up on the same principles as our Alexandrine culture. Opera is the birth of the theoretical man, of the critical layman, not of the artist: one of the most surprising facts in the whole history of art. It was the demand of thoroughly unmusical hearers that the words must above all be understood, so that according to them a re-birth of music is only to be expected when some mode of singing has been discovered in which the text-word lords over the counterpoint as the master over the servant. For the words, it is argued, are as much nobler than the accompanying harmonic system as the soul is nobler than the body. It was in accordance with the laically unmusical crudeness of these views that the combination of music, picture and expression was effected in the beginnings of the opera: in the spirit of this æsthetics the first experiments were also made in the leading laic

kunstohnmächtige Mensch erzeugt sich eine Art von Kunst, gerade dadurch, daß er der unkünstlerische Mensch an sich ist. Weil er die dionysische Tiefe der Musik nicht ahnt, verwandelt er sich den Musikgenuß zur verstandesmäßigen Wort- und Tonrhetorik der Leidenschaft im *stilo rappresentativo* und zur Wollust der Gesangeskünste; weil er keine Vision zu schauen vermag, zwingt er den Maschinisten und Dekorationskünstler in seinen Dienst; weil er das wahre Wesen des Künstlers nicht zu erfassen weiß, zaubert er vor sich den »künstlerischen Urmenschen« nach seinem Geschmack hin, d.h. den Menschen, der in der Leidenschaft singt und Verse spricht. Er träumt sich in eine Zeit hinein, in der die Leidenschaft ausreicht, um Gesänge und Dichtungen zu erzeugen: als ob je der Affekt imstande gewesen sei, etwas Künstlerisches zu schaffen. Die Voraussetzung der Oper ist ein falscher Glaube über den künstlerischen Prozeß, und zwar jener idyllische Glaube, daß eigentlich jeder empfindende Mensch Künstler sei. Im Sinne dieses Glaubens ist die Oper der Ausdruck des Laientums in der Kunst, das seine Gesetze mit dem heitern Optimismus des theoretischen Menschen diktiert.

Sollten wir wünschen, die beiden eben geschilderten, bei der Entstehung der Oper wirksamen Vorstellungen unter einen Begriff zu vereinigen, so würde uns nur übrig bleiben, von einer *idyllischen Tendenz der Oper* zu sprechen: wobei wir uns allein der Ausdrucksweise und Erklärung Schillers zu bedienen hätten. Entweder, sagt dieser, ist die Natur und das Ideal ein Gegenstand der Trauer, wenn jene als verloren, dieses als unerreicht dargestellt wird. Oder beide sind ein Gegenstand der Freude, indem sie als wirklich vorgestellt werden. Das erste gibt die Elegie in engerer, das andere die Idylle in weitester Bedeutung. Hier ist nun sofort auf das gemeinsame Merkmal jener beiden Vorstellungen in der Operngenesis aufmerksam zu machen, daß in ihnen das Ideal nicht als unerreicht, die Natur nicht als verloren empfunden wird. Es gab nach dieser Empfindung eine Urzeit des Menschen, in der er am Herzen der Natur lag und bei dieser Natürlichkeit zugleich das Ideal der Menschheit, in einer paradiesischen Güte und Künstlerschaft, erreicht hatte: von welchem vollkommnen Urmenschen wir alle abstammen sollten, ja dessen getreues Ebenbild wir noch wären: nur müßten wir einiges von uns werfen, um uns selbst wieder als diesen Urmenschen zu erkennen, vermöge einer freiwilligen Entäußerung von überflüssiger Gelehrsamkeit, von überreicher Kultur. Der Bildungsmensch der Renaissance ließ sich

circles of Florence by the poets and singers patronised there. The man incapable of art creates for himself a species of art precisely because he is the inartistic man as such. Because he does not divine the Dionysian depth of music, he changes his musical taste into appreciation of the understandable word-and-tone-rhetoric of the passions in the *stilo rappresentativo,* and into the voluptuousness of the arts of song; because he is unable to behold a vision, he forces the machinist and the decorative artist into his service; because he cannot apprehend the true nature of the artist, he conjures up the "artistic primitive man" to suit his taste, that is, the man who sings and recites verses under the influence of passion. He dreams himself into a time when passion suffices to generate songs and poems: as if emotion had ever been able to create anything artistic. The postulate of the opera is a false belief concerning the artistic process, in fact, the idyllic belief that every sentient man is an artist. In the sense of this belief, opera is the expression of the taste of the laity in art, who dictate their laws with the cheerful optimism of the theorist.

Should we desire to unite in one the two conceptions just set forth as influential in the origin of opera, it would only remain for us to speak of an *idyllic tendency of the opera*: in which connection we may avail ourselves exclusively of the phraseology and illustration of Schiller. "Nature and the ideal," he says, "are either objects of grief, when the former is represented as lost, the latter unattained; or both are objects of joy, in that they are represented as real. The first case furnishes the elegy in its narrower signification, the second the idyll in its widest sense." Here we must at once call attention to the common characteristic of these two conceptions in operatic genesis, namely, that in them the ideal is not regarded as unattained or nature as lost Agreeably to this sentiment, there was a primitive age of man when he lay close to the heart of nature, and, owing to this naturalness, had attained the ideal of mankind in a paradisiac goodness and artist-organisation: from which perfect primitive man all of us were supposed to be descended; whose faithful copy we were in fact still said to be: only we had to cast off some few things in order to recognise ourselves once more as this primitive man, on the strength of a voluntary renunciation of superfluous learnedness, of super-abundant culture. It was to

durch seine opernhafte Imitation der griechischen Tragödie zu einem solchen Zusammenklang von Natur und Ideal, zu einer idyllischen Wirklichkeit zurückgeleiten, er benutzte diese Tragödie, wie Dante den Virgil benutzte, um bis an die Pforten des Paradieses geführt zu werden: während er von hier aus selbständig noch weiter schritt und von einer Imitation der höchsten griechischen Kunstform zu einer »Wiederbringung aller Dinge«, zu einer Nachbildung der ursprünglichen Kunstwelt des Menschen überging. Welche zuversichtliche Gutmütigkeit dieser verwegenen Bestrebungen, mitten im Schoße der theoretischen Kultur! – einzig nur aus dem tröstenden Glauben zu erklären, daß »der Mensch an sich« der ewig tugendhafte Opernheld, der ewig flötende oder singende Schäfer sei, der sich endlich immer als solchen wiederfinden müsse, falls er sich selbst irgendwann einmal wirklich auf einige Zeit verloren habe, einzig die Frucht jenes Optimismus, der aus der Tiefe der sokratischen Weltbetrachtung hier wie eine süßlich verführerische Duftsäule emporsteigt.

Es liegt also auf den Zügen der Oper keinesfalls jener elegische Schmerz eines ewigen Verlustes, vielmehr die Heiterkeit des ewigen Wiederfindens, die bequeme Lust an einer idyllischen Wirklichkeit, die man wenigstens sich als wirklich in jedem Augenblicke vorstellen kann: wobei man vielleicht einmal ahnt, daß diese vermeinte Wirklichkeit nichts als ein phantastisch läppisches Getändel ist, dem jeder, der es an dem furchtbaren Ernst der wahren Natur zu messen und mit den eigentlichen Urszenen der Menschheitsanfänge zu vergleichen vermöchte, mit Ekel zurufen müßte: Weg mit dem Phantom! Trotzdem würde man sich täuschen, wenn man glaubte, ein solches tändelndes Wesen, wie die Oper ist, einfach durch einen kräftigen Anruf, wie ein Gespenst, verscheuchen zu können. Wer die Oper vernichten will, muß den Kampf gegen jene alexandrinische Heiterkeit aufnehmen, die sich in ihr so naiv über ihre Lieblingsvorstellung ausspricht, ja deren eigentliche Kunstform sie ist. Was ist aber für die Kunst selbst von dem Wirken einer Kunstform zu erwarten, deren Ursprünge überhaupt nicht im ästhetischen Bereiche liegen, die sich vielmehr aus einer halb moralischen Sphäre auf das künstlerische Gebiet hinübergestohlen hat und über diese hybride Entstehung nur hier und da einmal hinwegzutäuschen vermochte? Von welchen Säften nährt sich dieses parasitische Opernwesen, wenn nicht von denen der wahren Kunst? Wird nicht zu mutmaßen sein, daß, unter seinen idyllischen Verführungen, unter seinen

such a concord of nature and the ideal, to an idyllic reality, that the cultured man of the Renaissance suffered himself to be led back by his operatic imitation of Greek tragedy; he made use of this tragedy, as Dante made use of Vergil, in order to be led up to the gates of paradise: while from this point he went on without assistance and passed over from an imitation of the highest form of Greek art to a "restoration of all things," to an imitation of man's original art-world. What delightfully naïve hopefulness of these daring endeavours, in the very heart of theoretical culture!—solely to be explained by the comforting belief, that "man-in-himself" is the eternally virtuous hero of the opera, the eternally fluting or singing shepherd, who must always in the end rediscover himself as such, if he has at any time really lost himself; solely the fruit of the optimism, which here rises like a sweetishly seductive column of vapour out of the depth of the Socratic conception of the world.

The features of the opera therefore do not by any means exhibit the elegiac sorrow of an eternal loss, but rather the cheerfulness of eternal rediscovery, the indolent delight in an idyllic reality which one can at least represent to one's self each moment as real: and in so doing one will perhaps surmise some day that this supposed reality is nothing but a fantastically silly dawdling, concerning which every one, who could judge it by the terrible earnestness of true nature and compare it with the actual primitive scenes of the beginnings of mankind, would have to call out with loathing: Away with the phantom! Nevertheless one would err if one thought it possible to frighten away merely by a vigorous shout such a dawdling thing as the opera, as if it were a spectre. He who would destroy the opera must join issue with Alexandrine cheerfulness, which expresses itself so naïvely therein concerning its favourite representation; of which in fact it is the specific form of art. But what is to be expected for art itself from the operation of a form of art, the beginnings of which do not at all lie in the æsthetic province; which has rather stolen over from a half-moral sphere into the artistic domain, and has been able only now and then to delude us concerning this hybrid origin? By what sap is this parasitic opera-concern nourished, if not by that of true art? Must we not suppose that the highest and indeed the truly serious task of art—to free the eye from its glance

alexandrinischen Schmeichelkünsten, die höchste und wahrhaftig ernst zu nennende Aufgabe der Kunst – das Auge vom Blick ins Grauen der Nacht zu erlösen und das Subjekt durch den heilenden Balsam des Scheins aus dem Krampfe der Willensregungen zu retten – zu einer leeren und zerstreuenden Ergötzlichkeitstendenz entarten werde? Was wird aus den ewigen Wahrheiten des Dionysischen und des Apollinischen, bei einer solchen Stilvermischung, wie ich sie am Wesen des *stilo rappresentativo* dargelegt habe? wo die Musik als Diener, das Textwort als Herr betrachtet, die Musik mit dem Körper, das Textwort mit der Seele verglichen wird? wo das höchste Ziel bestenfalls auf eine umschreibende Tonmalerei gerichtet sein wird, ähnlich wie ehedem im neuen attischen Dithyrambus? wo der Musik ihre wahre Würde, dionysischer Weltspiegel zu sein, völlig entfremdet ist, so daß ihr nur übrig bleibt, als Sklavin der Erscheinung, das Formenwesen der Erscheinung nachzuahmen und in dem Spiele der Linien und Proportionen eine äußerliche Ergötzung zu erregen. Einer strengen Betrachtung fällt dieser verhängnisvolle Einfluß der Oper auf die Musik geradezu mit der gesamten modernen Musikentwicklung zusammen; dem in der Genesis der Oper und im Wesen der durch sie repräsentierten Kultur lauernden Optimismus ist es in beängstigender Schnelligkeit gelungen, die Musik ihrer dionysischen Weltbestimmung zu entkleiden und ihr einen formenspielerischen, vergnüglichen Charakter aufzuprägen: mit welcher Veränderung nur etwa die Metamorphose des äschyleischen Menschen in den alexandrinischen Heiterkeitsmenschen verglichen werden dürfte.

Wenn wir aber mit Recht in der hiermit angedeuteten Exemplifikation das Entschwinden des dionysischen Geistes mit einer höchstauffälligen, aber bisher unerklärten Umwandlung und Degeneration des griechischen Menschen in Zusammenhang gebracht haben – welche Hoffnungen müssen in uns aufleben, wenn uns die allersichersten Auspizien *den umgekehrten Prozeß, das allmähliche Erwachen des dionysischen Geistes* in unserer gegenwärtigen Welt, verbürgen! Es ist nicht möglich, daß die göttliche Kraft des Herakles ewig im üppigen Frondienste der Omphale erschlafft. Aus dem dionysischen Grunde des deutschen Geistes ist eine Macht emporgestiegen, die mit den Urbedingungen der sokratischen Kultur nichts gemein hat und aus ihnen weder zu erklären noch zu entschuldigen ist, vielmehr von dieser Kultur als das Schrecklich-Unerklärliche, als das Übermächtig-Feindselige empfunden wird, *die*

into the horrors of night and to deliver the "subject" by the healing balm of appearance from the spasms of volitional agitations—will degenerate under the influence of its idyllic seductions and Alexandrine adulation to an empty dissipating tendency, to pastime? What will become of the eternal truths of the Dionysian and Apollonian in such an amalgamation of styles as I have exhibited in the character of the *stilo rappresentativo*? where music is regarded as the servant, the text as the master, where music is compared with the body, the text with the soul? where at best the highest aim will be the realisation of a paraphrastic tone-painting, just as formerly in the New Attic Dithyramb? where music is completely alienated from its true dignity of being, the Dionysian mirror of the world, so that the only thing left to it is, as a slave of phenomena, to imitate the formal character thereof, and to excite an external pleasure in the play of lines and proportions. On close observation, this fatal influence of the opera on music is seen to coincide absolutely with the universal development of modern music; the optimism lurking in the genesis of the opera and in the essence of culture represented thereby, has, with alarming rapidity, succeeded in divesting music of its Dionyso-cosmic mission and in impressing on it a playfully formal and pleasurable character: a change with which perhaps only the metamorphosis of the Aeschylean man into the cheerful Alexandrine man could be compared.

If, however, in the exemplification herewith indicated we have rightly associated the evanescence of the Dionysian spirit with a most striking, but hitherto unexplained transformation and degeneration of the Hellene—what hopes must revive in us when the most trustworthy auspices guarantee the reverse process, the gradual awakening of *the Dionysian spirit* in our modern world! It is impossible for the divine strength of Herakles to languish for ever in voluptuous bondage to Omphale. Out of the Dionysian root of the German spirit a power has arisen which has nothing in common with the primitive conditions of Socratic culture, and can neither be explained nor excused thereby, but is rather regarded by this culture as something terribly inexplicable and overwhelmingly hostile—namely, *German music* as we have to understand it, especially in its vast solar orbit from Bach to Beethoven, from Beethoven to Wagner. What even under the most

deutsche Musik, wie wir sie vornehmlich in ihrem mächtigen Sonnenlaufe von Bach zu Beethoven, von Beethoven zu Wagner zu verstehen haben. Was vermag die erkenntnislüsterne Sokratik unserer Tage günstigenfalls mit diesem aus unerschöpflichen Tiefen emporsteigenden Dämon zu beginnen? Weder von dem Zacken- und Arabeskenwerk der Opernmelodie aus, noch mit Hilfe des arithmetischen Rechenbretts der Fuge und der kontrapunktischen Dialektik will sich die Formel finden lassen, in deren dreimal gewaltigem Licht man jenen Dämon sich unterwürfig zu machen und zum Reden zu zwingen vermöchte. Welches Schauspiel, wenn jetzt unsere Ästhetiker, mit dem Fangnetz einer ihnen eignen »Schönheit«, nach dem vor ihnen mit unbegreiflichem Leben sich tummelnden Musikgenius schlagen und haschen, unter Bewegungen, die nach der ewigen Schönheit ebensowenig als nach dem Erhabenen beurteilt werden wollen. Man mag sich nur diese Musikgönner einmal leibhaft und in der Nähe besehen, wenn sie so unermüdlich Schönheit! Schönheit! rufen, ob sie sich dabei wie die im Schoße des Schönen gebildeten und verwöhnten Lieblingskinder der Natur ausnehmen oder ob sie nicht vielmehr für die eigne Rohheit eine lügnerisch verhüllende Form, für die eigne empfindungsarme Nüchternheit einen ästhetischen Vorwand suchen: wobei ich z.B. an Otto Jahn denke. Vor der deutschen Musik aber mag sich der Lügner und Heuchler in acht nehmen: denn gerade sie ist, inmitten aller unserer Kultur, der einzig reine, lautere und läuternde Feuergeist, von dem aus und zu dem hin, wie in der Lehre des großen Heraklit von Ephesus, sich alle Dinge in doppelter Kreisbahn bewegen: alles, was wir jetzt Kultur, Bildung, Zivilisation nennen, wird einmal vor dem untrüglichen Richter Dionysus erscheinen müssen.

Erinnern wir uns sodann, wie dem aus gleichen Quellen strömenden Geiste *der deutschen Philosophie*, durch Kant und Schopenhauer, es ermöglicht war, die zufriedne Daseinslust der wissenschaftlichen Sokratik, durch den Nachweis ihrer Grenzen, zu vernichten, wie durch diesen Nachweis eine unendlich tiefere und ernstere Betrachtung der ethischen Fragen und der Kunst eingeleitet wurde, die wir geradezu als die in Begriffe gefaßte *dionysische Weisheit* bezeichnen können: wohin weist uns das Mysterium dieser Einheit zwischen der deutschen Musik und der deutschen Philosophie, wenn nicht auf eine neue Daseinsform, über deren Inhalt wir uns nur aus hellenischen Analogien ahnend unterrichten können? Denn diesen unausmeßbaren Wert behält für uns, die wir an der Grenzscheide zweier verschiedener

favourable circumstances can the knowledge-craving Socratism of our days do with this demon rising from unfathomable depths? Neither by means of the zig-zag and arabesque work of operatic melody, nor with the aid of the arithmetical counting board of fugue and contrapuntal dialectics is the formula to be found, in the trebly powerful light of which one could subdue this demon and compel it to speak. What a spectacle, when our æsthetes, with a net of "beauty" peculiar to themselves, now pursue and clutch at the genius of music romping about before them with incomprehensible life, and in so doing display activities which are not to be judged by the standard of eternal beauty any more than by the standard of the sublime. Let us but observe these patrons of music as they are, at close range, when they call out so indefatigably "beauty! beauty!" to discover whether they have the marks of nature's darling children who are fostered and fondled in the lap of the beautiful, or whether they do not rather seek a disguise for their own rudeness, an æsthetical pretext for their own unemotional insipidity: I am thinking here, for instance, of Otto Jahn. But let the liar and the hypocrite beware of our German music: for in the midst of all our culture it is really the only genuine, pure and purifying fire-spirit from which and towards which, as in the teaching of the great Heraclitus of Ephesus, all things move in a double orbit-all that we now call culture, education, civilisation, must appear some day before the unerring judge, Dionysus.

Let us recollect furthermore how Kant and Schopenhauer made it possible for the spirit of *German philosophy* streaming from the same sources to annihilate the satisfied delight in existence of scientific Socratism by the delimitation of the boundaries thereof; how through this delimitation an infinitely profounder and more serious view of ethical problems and of art was inaugurated, which we may unhesitatingly designate as *Dionysian* wisdom comprised in concepts. To what then does the mystery of this oneness of German music and philosophy point, if not to a new form of existence, concerning the substance of which we can only inform ourselves presentiently from Hellenic analogies? For to us who stand on the boundary line between two different forms of existence, the Hellenic prototype retains the immeasurable value, that therein all these transitions and struggles are

Daseinsformen stehen, das hellenische Vorbild, daß in ihm auch alle jene Übergänge und Kämpfe zu einer klassisch-belehrenden Form ausgeprägt sind: nur daß wir gleichsam in *umgekehrter* Ordnung die großen Hauptepochen des hellenischen Wesens analogisch durcherleben und zum Beispiel jetzt aus dem alexandrinischen Zeitalter rückwärts zur Periode der Tragödie zu schreiten scheinen. Dabei lebt in uns die Empfindung, als ob die Geburt eines tragischen Zeitalters für den deutschen Geist nur eine Rückkehr zu sich selbst, ein seliges Sichwiederfinden zu bedeuten habe, nachdem für eine lange Zeit ungeheure von außen her eindringende Mächte den in hilfloser Barbarei der Form Dahinlebenden zu einer Knechtschaft unter ihrer Form gezwungen hatten. Jetzt endlich darf er, nach seiner Heimkehr zum Urquell seines Wesens, vor allen Völkern kühn und frei, ohne das Gängelband einer romanischen Zivilisation, einherzuschreiten wagen: wenn er nur von einem Volke unentwegt zu lernen versteht, von dem überhaupt lernen zu können schon ein hoher Ruhm und eine auszeichnende Seltenheit ist, von den Griechen. Und wann brauchten wir diese allerhöchsten Lehrmeister mehr als jetzt, wo wir *die Wiedergeburt der Tragödie* erleben und in Gefahr sind, weder zu wissen, woher sie kommt, noch uns deuten zu können, wohin sie will?

imprinted in a classically instructive form: except that we, as it were, experience analogically in *reverse* order the chief epochs of the Hellenic genius, and seem now, for instance, to pass backwards from the Alexandrine age to the period of tragedy. At the same time we have the feeling that the birth of a tragic age betokens only a return to itself of the German spirit, a blessed self-rediscovering after excessive and urgent external influences have for a long time compelled it, living as it did in helpless barbaric formlessness, to servitude under their form. It may at last, after returning to the primitive source of its being, venture to stalk along boldly and freely before all nations without hugging the leading-strings of a Romanic civilisation: if only it can learn implicitly of one people—the Greeks, of whom to learn at all is itself a high honour and a rare distinction. And when did we require these highest of all teachers more than at present, when we experience *a re-birth of tragedy* and are in danger alike of not knowing whence it comes, and of being unable to make clear to ourselves whither it tends.

20

Es möchte einmal, unter den Augen eines unbestochenen Richters, abgewogen werden, in welcher Zeit und in welchen Männern bisher der deutsche Geist von den Griechen zu lernen am kräftigsten gerungen hat; und wenn wir mit Zuversicht annehmen, daß dem edelsten Bildungskampfe Goethes, Schillers und Winckelmanns dieses einzige Lob zugesprochen werden müßte, so wäre jedenfalls hinzuzufügen, daß seit jener Zeit und den nächsten Einwirkungen jenes Kampfes das Streben, auf einer gleichen Bahn zur Bildung und zu den Griechen zu kommen, in unbegreiflicher Weise schwächer und schwächer geworden ist. Sollten wir, um nicht ganz an dem deutschen Geist verzweifeln zu müssen, nicht daraus den Schluß ziehen dürfen, daß in irgendwelchem Hauptpunkte es auch jenen Kämpfern nicht gelungen sein möchte, in den Kern des hellenischen Wesens einzudringen und einen dauernden Liebesbund zwischen der deutschen und der griechischen Kultur herzustellen? – so daß vielleicht ein unbewußtes Erkennen jenes Mangels auch in den ernsteren Naturen den verzagten Zweifel

It may be weighed some day before an impartial judge, in what time and in what men the German spirit has thus far striven most resolutely to learn of the Greeks: and if we confidently assume that this unique praise must be accorded to the noblest intellectual efforts of Goethe, Schiller, and Winkelmann, it will certainly have to be added that since their time, and subsequently to the more immediate influences of these efforts, the endeavour to attain to culture and to the Greeks by this path has in an incomprehensible manner grown feebler and feebler. In order not to despair altogether of the German spirit, must we not infer therefrom that possibly, in some essential matter, even these champions could not penetrate into the core of the Hellenic nature, and were unable to establish a permanent friendly alliance between German and Greek culture? So that perhaps an unconscious perception of this shortcoming might raise also in more serious minds the disheartening doubt as to whether after such predecessors they could advance still farther on

erregte, ob sie, nach solchen Vorgängern, auf diesem Bildungswege noch weiter wie jene und überhaupt zum Ziele kommen würden. Deshalb sehen wir seit jener Zeit das Urteil über den Wert der Griechen für die Bildung in der bedenklichsten Weise entarten; der Ausdruck mitleidiger Überlegenheit ist in den verschiedensten Feldlagern des Geistes und des Ungeistes zu hören; anderwärts tändelt eine gänzlich wirkungslose Schönrednerei mit der »griechischen Harmonie«, der »griechischen Schönheit«, der »griechischen Heiterkeit«. Und gerade in den Kreisen, deren Würde es sein könnte, aus dem griechischen Strombett unermüdet, zum Heile deutscher Bildung, zu schöpfen, in den Kreisen der Lehrer an den höheren Bildungsanstalten, hat man am besten gelernt, sich mit den Griechen zeitig und in bequemer Weise abzufinden, nicht selten bis zu einem skeptischen Preisgeben des hellenischen Ideals und bis zu einer gänzlichen Verkehrung der wahren Absicht aller Altertumsstudien. Wer überhaupt in jenen Kreisen sich nicht völlig in dem Bemühen, ein zuverlässiger Korrektor von alten Texten oder ein naturhistorischer Sprachmikroskopiker zu sein, erschöpft hat, der sucht vielleicht auch das griechische Altertum, neben anderen Altertümern, sich »historisch« anzueignen, aber jedenfalls nach der Methode und mit den überlegenen Mienen unserer jetzigen gebildeten Geschichtsschreibung. Wenn demnach die eigentliche Bildungskraft der höheren Lehranstalten wohl noch niemals niedriger und schwächlicher gewesen ist wie in der Gegenwart, wenn der »Journalist«, der papierne Sklave des Tages, in jeder Rücksicht auf Bildung den Sieg über den höheren Lehrer davongetragen hat, und letzterem nur noch die bereits oft erlebte Metamorphose übrigbleibt, sich jetzt nun auch in der Sprechweise des Journalisten, mit der »leichten Eleganz« dieser Sphäre, als heiterer gebildeter Schmetterling zu bewegen – in welcher peinlichen Verwirrung müssen die derartig Gebildeten einer solchen Gegenwart jenes Phänomen anstarren, das nur etwa aus dem tiefsten Grunde des bisher unbegriffnen hellenischen Genius analogisch zu begreifen wäre, das Wiedererwachen des dionysischen Geistes und die Wiedergeburt der Tragödie? Es gibt keine andere Kunstperiode, in der sich die sogenannte Bildung und die eigentliche Kunst so befremdet und abgeneigt gegenübergestanden hätten, als wir das in der Gegenwart mit Augen sehn. Wir verstehen es, warum eine so schwächliche Bildung die wahre Kunst haßt; denn sie fürchtet durch sie ihren Untergang. Aber sollte nicht eine ganze Art der Kultur, nämlich jene sokratisch-alexandrinische, sich ausgelebt haben, nachdem sie in eine so zierlich-schmächtige Spitze, wie die gegenwärtige Bildung ist, auslaufen konnte! Wenn

this path of culture, or could reach the goal at all. Accordingly, we see the opinions concerning the value of Greek contribution to culture degenerate since that time in the most alarming manner; the expression of compassionate superiority may be heard in the most heterogeneous intellectual and non-intellectual camps, and elsewhere a totally ineffective declamation dallies with "Greek harmony," "Greek beauty," "Greek cheerfulness." And in the very circles whose dignity it might be to draw indefatigably from the Greek channel for the good of German culture, in the circles of the teachers in the higher educational institutions, they have learned best to compromise with the Greeks in good time and on easy terms, to the extent often of a sceptical abandonment of the Hellenic ideal and a total perversion of the true purpose of antiquarian studies. If there be any one at all in these circles who has not completely exhausted himself in the endeavour to be a trustworthy corrector of old texts or a natural-history microscopist of language, he perhaps seeks also to appropriate Grecian antiquity "historically" along with other antiquities, and in any case according to the method and with the supercilious air of our present cultured historiography. When, therefore, the intrinsic efficiency of the higher educational institutions has never perhaps been lower or feebler than at present, when the "journalist," the paper slave of the day, has triumphed over the academic teacher in all matters pertaining to culture, and there only remains to the latter the often previously experienced metamorphosis of now fluttering also, as a cheerful cultured butterfly, in the idiom of the journalist, with the "light elegance" peculiar thereto—with what painful confusion must the cultured persons of a period like the present gaze at the phenomenon (which can perhaps be comprehended analogically only by means of the profoundest principle of the hitherto unintelligible Hellenic genius) of the reawakening of the Dionysian spirit and the re-birth of tragedy? Never has there been another art-period in which so-called culture and true art have been so estranged and opposed, as is so obviously the case at present. We understand why so feeble a culture hates true art; it fears destruction thereby. But must not an entire domain of culture, namely the Socratic-Alexandrine, have exhausted its powers after contriving to culminate in such a daintily-tapering point as our present culture? When it was not permitted to heroes like Goethe and Schiller to break open the enchanted gate

es solchen Helden, wie Schiller und Goethe, nicht gelingen durfte, jene verzauberte Pforte zu erbrechen, die in den hellenischen Zauberberg führt, wenn es bei ihrem mutigsten Ringen nicht weiter gekommen ist als bis zu jenem sehnsüchtigen Blick, den die Goethesche Iphigenie vom barbarischen Tauris aus nach der Heimat über das Meer hin sendet, was bliebe den Epigonen solcher Helden zu hoffen, wenn sich ihnen nicht plötzlich, an einer ganz anderen, von allen Bemühungen der bisherigen Kultur unberührten Seite die Pforte von selbst auftäte – unter dem mystischen Klange der wiedererweckten Tragödienmusik.

Möge uns niemand unsern Glauben an eine noch bevorstehende Wiedergeburt des hellenischen Altertums zu verkümmern suchen; denn in ihm finden wir allein unsere Hoffnung für eine Erneuerung und Läuterung des deutschen Geistes durch den Feuerzauber der Musik. Was wüßten wir sonst zu nennen, was in der Verödung und Ermattung der jetzigen Kultur irgendwelche tröstliche Erwartung für die Zukunft erwecken könnte? Vergebens spähen wir nach einer einzigen kräftig geästeten Wurzel, nach einem Fleck fruchtbaren und gesunden Erdbodens: überall Staub, Sand, Erstarrung, Verschmachten. Da möchte sich ein trostlos Vereinsamter kein besseres Symbol wählen können, als den Ritter mit Tod und Teufel, wie ihn uns Dürer gezeichnet hat, den geharnischten Ritter mit dem erzenen, harten Blicke, der seinen Schreckensweg, unbeirrt durch seine grausen Gefährten, und doch hoffnungslos, allein mit Roß und Hund zu nehmen weiß. Ein solcher Dürerscher Ritter war unser Schopenhauer: ihm fehlte jede Hoffnung, aber er wollte die Wahrheit. Es gibt nicht seinesgleichen. –

Aber wie verändert sich plötzlich jene eben so düster geschilderte Wildnis unserer ermüdeten Kultur, wenn sie der dionysische Zauber berührt! Ein Sturmwind packt alles Abgelebte, Morsche, Zerbrochne, Verkümmerte, hüllt es wirbelnd in eine rote Staubwolke und trägt es wie ein Geier in die Lüfte. Verwirrt suchen unsere Blicke nach dem Entschwundenen: denn was sie sehen, ist wie aus einer Versenkung ans goldne Licht gestiegen, so voll und grün, so üppig lebendig, so sehnsuchtsvoll unermeßlich. Die Tragödie sitzt inmitten dieses Überflusses an Leben, Leid und Lust, in erhabener Entzückung, sie horcht einem fernen schwermütigen Gesange – er erzählt von den Müttern des Seins, deren Namen lauten: Wahn, Wille, Wehe. – Ja, meine Freunde, glaubt mit mir an das dionysische Leben und an die Wiedergeburt der Tragödie. Die Zeit des

which leads into the Hellenic magic mountain, when with their most dauntless striving they did not get beyond the longing gaze which the Goethean Iphigenia cast from barbaric Tauris to her home across the ocean, what could the epigones of such heroes hope for, if the gate should not open to them suddenly of its own accord, in an entirely different position, quite overlooked in all endeavours of culture hitherto—amidst the mystic tones of reawakened tragic music.

Let no one attempt to weaken our faith in an impending re-birth of Hellenic antiquity; for in it alone we find our hope of a renovation and purification of the German spirit through the fire-magic of music. What else do we know of amidst the present desolation and languor of culture, which could awaken any comforting expectation for the future? We look in vain for one single vigorously-branching root, for a speck of fertile and healthy soil: there is dust, sand, torpidness and languishing everywhere! Under such circumstances a cheerless solitary wanderer could choose for himself no better symbol than the Knight with Death and the Devil, as Dürer has sketched him for us, the mail-clad knight, grim and stern of visage, who is able, unperturbed by his gruesome companions, and yet hopelessly, to pursue his terrible path with horse and hound alone. Our Schopenhauer was such a Dürerian knight: he was destitute of all hope, but he sought the truth. There is not his equal.

But how suddenly this gloomily depicted wilderness of our exhausted culture changes when the Dionysian magic touches it! A hurricane seizes everything decrepit, decaying, collapsed, and stunted; wraps it whirlingly into a red cloud of dust; and carries it like a vulture into the air. Confused thereby, our glances seek for what has vanished: for what they see is something risen to the golden light as from a depression, so full and green, so luxuriantly alive, so ardently infinite. Tragedy sits in the midst of this exuberance of life, sorrow and joy, in sublime ecstasy; she listens to a distant doleful song—it tells of the Mothers of Being, whose names are: *Wahn, Wille, Wehe*—Yes, my friends, believe with me in Dionysian life and in the re-birth of tragedy. The time of the Socratic man is past: crown yourselves with ivy, take in your hands the thyrsus, and do not marvel if tigers and panthers lie down fawning at your

sokratischen Menschen ist vorüber: kränzt euch mit Epheu, nehmt den Thyrsusstab zur Hand und wundert euch nicht, wenn Tiger und Panther sich schmeichelnd zu euren Knien niederlegen. Jetzt wagt es nur, tragische Menschen zu sein: denn ihr sollt erlöst werden. Ihr sollt den dionysischen Festzug von Indien nach Griechenland geleiten! Rüstet euch zu hartem Streite, aber glaubt an die Wunder eures Gottes!

feet. Dare now to be tragic men, for ye are to be redeemed! Ye are to accompany the Dionysian festive procession from India to Greece! Equip yourselves for severe conflict, but believe in the wonders of your god!

21

Von diesen exhortativen Tönen in die Stimmung zurückgleitend, die dem Beschaulichen geziemt, wiederhole ich, daß nur von den Griechen gelernt werden kann, was ein solches wundergleiches plötzliches Aufwachen der Tragödie für den innersten Lebensgrund eines Volkes zu bedeuten hat. Es ist das Volk der tragischen Mysterien, das die Perserschlachten schlägt: und wiederum braucht das Volk, das jene Kriege geführt hat, die Tragödie als notwendigen Genesungstrank. Wer würde gerade bei diesem Volke, nachdem es durch mehrere Generationen von den stärksten Zuckungen des dionysischen Dämon bis ins Innerste erregt wurde, noch einen so gleichmäßig kräftigen Erguß des einfachsten politischen Gefühls, der natürlichsten Heimatsinstinkte, der ursprünglichen männlichen Kampflust vermuten? Ist es doch bei jedem bedeutenden Umsichgreifen dionysischer Erregungen immer zu spüren, wie die dionysische Lösung von den Fesseln des Individuums sich am allerersten in einer bis zur Gleichgültigkeit, ja Feindseligkeit gesteigerten Beeinträchtigung der politischen Instinkte fühlbar macht, so gewiß andererseits der staatenbildende Apollo auch der Genius des *principii individuationis* ist, und Staat und Heimatsinn nicht ohne Bejahung der individuellen Persönlichkeit leben können. Von dem Orgiasmus aus führt für ein Volk nur ein Weg, der Weg zum indischen Buddhaismus, der, um überhaupt mit seiner Sehnsucht ins Nichts ertragen zu werden, jener seltnen ekstatischen Zustände mit ihrer Erhebung über Raum, Zeit und Individuum bedarf: wie diese wiederum eine Philosophie fordern, die es lehrt, die unbeschreibliche Unlust der Zwischenzustände durch eine Vorstellung zu überwinden. Ebenso notwendig gerät ein Volk, von der unbedingten Geltung der politischen Triebe aus, in eine Bahn äußerster Verweltlichung, deren großartigster, aber auch erschrecklichster Ausdruck das römische *imperium* ist.

Gliding back from these hortative tones into the mood which befits the contemplative man, I repeat that it can only be learnt from the Greeks what such a sudden and miraculous awakening of tragedy must signify for the essential basis of a people's life. It is the people of the tragic mysteries who fight the battles with the Persians: and again, the people who waged such wars required tragedy as a necessary healing potion. Who would have imagined that there was still such a uniformly powerful effusion of the simplest political sentiments, the most natural domestic instincts and the primitive manly delight in strife in this very people after it had been shaken to its foundations for several generations by the most violent convulsions of the Dionysian demon? If at every considerable spreading of the Dionysian commotion one always perceives that the Dionysian loosing from the shackles of the individual makes itself felt first of all in an increased encroachment on the political instincts, to the extent of indifference, yea even hostility, it is certain, on the other hand, that the state-forming Apollo is also the genius of the *principium individuationis*, and that the state and domestic sentiment cannot live without an assertion of individual personality. There is only one way from orgasm for a people—the way to Indian Buddhism, which, in order to be at all endured with its longing for nothingness, requires the rare ecstatic states with their elevation above space, time, and the individual; just as these in turn demand a philosophy which teaches how to overcome the indescribable depression of the intermediate states by means of a fancy. With the same necessity, owing to the unconditional dominance of political impulses, a people drifts into a path of extremest secularisation, the most magnificent, but also the most terrible expression of which is the Roman *imperium*.

Zwischen Indien und Rom hingestellt und zu verführerischer Wahl gedrängt, ist es den Griechen gelungen, in klassischer Reinheit eine dritte Form hinzuzuerfinden, freilich nicht zu langem eigenen Gebrauche aber eben darum für die Unsterblichkeit. Denn daß die Lieblinge der Götter früh sterben, gilt in allen Dingen, aber ebenso gewiß, daß sie mit den Göttern dann ewig leben. Man verlange doch von dem Alleredelsten nicht, daß es die haltbare Zähigkeit des Leders habe; die derbe Dauerhaftigkeit, wie sie z.B. dem römischen Nationaltriebe zu eigen war, gehört wahrscheinlich nicht zu den notwendigen Prädikaten der Vollkommenheit. Wenn wir aber fragen, mit welchem Heilmittel es den Griechen ermöglicht war, in ihrer großen Zeit, bei der außerordentlichen Stärke ihrer dionysischen und politischen Triebe, weder durch ein ekstatisches Brüten, noch durch ein verzehrendes Haschen nach Weltmacht und Weltehre sich zu erschöpfen, sondern jene herrliche Mischung zu erreichen, wie sie ein edler, zugleich befeuernder und beschaulich stimmender Wein hat, so müssen wir der ungeheuren, das ganze Volksleben erregenden, reinigenden und entladenden Gewalt der *Tragödie* eingedenk sein; deren höchsten Wert wir erst ahnen werden, wenn sie uns, wie bei den Griechen, als Inbegriff aller prophylaktischen Heilkräfte, als die zwischen den stärksten und an sich verhängnisvollsten Eigenschaften des Volkes waltende Mittlerin entgegentritt.

Die Tragödie saugt den höchsten Musikorgiasmus in sich hinein, so daß sie geradezu die Musik, bei den Griechen wie bei uns, zur Vollendung bringt, stellt dann aber den tragischen Mythus und den tragischen Helden daneben, der dann, einem mächtigen Titanen gleich, die ganze dionysische Welt auf seinen Rücken nimmt und uns davon entlastet: während sie andrerseits durch denselben tragischen Mythus, in der Person des tragischen Helden, von dem gierigen Drange nach diesem Dasein zu erlösen weiß und mit mahnender Hand an ein anderes Sein und an eine höhere Lust erinnert, zu welcher der kämpfende Held durch seinen Untergang, nicht durch seine Siege, sich ahnungsvoll vorbereitet. Die Tragödie stellt zwischen die universale Geltung ihrer Musik und den dionysisch empfänglichen Zuhörer ein erhabenes Gleichnis, den Mythus, und erweckt bei jenem den Schein, als ob die Musik nur ein höchstes Darstellungsmittel zur Belebung der plastischen Welt des Mythus sei. Dieser edlen Täuschung vertrauend darf sie jetzt ihre Glieder zum dithyrambischen Tanze bewegen und sich unbedenklich einem orgiastischen Gefühle der Freiheit hingeben, in welchem sie als

Placed between India and Rome, and constrained to a seductive choice, the Greeks succeeded in devising in classical purity still a third form of life, not indeed for long private use, but just on that account for immortality. For it holds true in all things that those whom the gods love die young, but, on the other hand, it holds equally true that they then live eternally with the gods. One must not demand of what is most noble that it should possess the durable toughness of leather; the staunch durability, which, for instance, was inherent in the national character of the Romans, does not probably belong to the indispensable predicates of perfection. But if we ask by what physic it was possible for the Greeks, in their best period, notwithstanding the extraordinary strength of their Dionysian and political impulses, neither to exhaust themselves by ecstatic brooding, nor by a consuming scramble for empire and worldly honour, but to attain the splendid mixture which we find in a noble, inflaming, and contemplatively disposing wine, we must remember the enormous power of *tragedy*, exciting, purifying, and disburdening the entire life of a people; the highest value of which we shall divine only when, as in the case of the Greeks, it appears to us as the essence of all the prophylactic healing forces, as the mediator arbitrating between the strongest and most inherently fateful characteristics of a people.

Tragedy absorbs the highest musical orgasm into itself, so that it absolutely brings music to perfection among the Greeks, as among ourselves; but it then places alongside thereof tragic myth and the tragic hero, who, like a mighty Titan, takes the entire Dionysian world on his shoulders and disburdens us thereof; while, on the other hand, it is able by means of this same tragic myth, in the person of the tragic hero, to deliver us from the intense longing for this existence, and reminds us with warning hand of another existence and a higher joy, for which the struggling hero prepares himself presentiently by his destruction, not by his victories. Tragedy sets a sublime symbol, namely the myth between the universal authority of its music and the receptive Dionysian hearer, and produces in him the illusion that music is only the most effective means for the animation of the plastic world of myth. Relying upon this noble illusion, she can now move her limbs for the dithyrambic dance, and abandon herself unhesitatingly to an orgiastic feeling of freedom,

Musik an sich, ohne jene Täuschung, nicht zu schwelgen wagen dürfte. Der Mythus schützt uns vor der Musik, wie er ihr andrerseits erst die höchste Freiheit gibt. Dafür verleiht die Musik, als Gegengeschenk, dem tragischen Mythus eine so eindringliche und überzeugende metaphysische Bedeutsamkeit, wie sie Wort und Bild, ohne jene einzige Hilfe, nie zu erreichen vermögen; und insbesondere überkommt durch sie den tragischen Zuschauer gerade jenes sichere Vorgefühl einer höchsten Lust, zu der der Weg durch Untergang und Verneinung führt, so daß er zu hören meint, als ob der innerste Abgrund der Dinge zu ihm vernehmlich spräche.

Habe ich dieser schwierigen Vorstellung mit den letzten Sätzen vielleicht nur einen vorläufigen, für wenige sofort verständlichen Ausdruck zu geben vermocht, so darf ich gerade an dieser Stelle nicht ablassen, meine Freunde zu einem nochmaligen Versuche anzureizen und sie zu bitten, an einem einzelnen Beispiele unsrer gemeinsamen Erfahrung sich für die Erkenntnis des allgemeinen Satzes vorzubereiten. Bei diesem Beispiele darf ich mich nicht auf jene beziehn, welche die Bilder der szenischen Vorgänge, die Worte und Affekte der handelnden Personen benutzen, um sich mit dieser Hilfe der Musikempfindung anzunähern; denn diese alle reden nicht Musik als Muttersprache und kommen auch, trotz jener Hilfe, nicht weiter als in die Vorhallen der Musikperzeption, ohne je deren innerste Heiligtümer berühren zu dürfen; manche von diesen, wie Gervinus, gelangen auf diesem Wege nicht einmal in die Vorhallen. Sondern nur an diejenigen habe ich mich zu wenden, die unmittelbar verwandt mit der Musik, in ihr gleichsam ihren Mutterschoß haben und mit den Dingen fast nur durch unbewußte Musikrelationen in Verbindung stehen. An diese echten Musiker richte ich die Frage, ob sie sich einen Menschen denken können, der den dritten Akt von »Tristan und Isolde« ohne alle Beihilfe von Wort und Bild, rein als ungeheuren symphonischen Satz zu perzipieren imstande wäre, ohne unter einem krampfartigen Ausspannen aller Seelenflügel zu veratmen? Ein Mensch, der wie hier das Ohr gleichsam an die Herzkammer des Weltwillens gelegt hat, der das rasende Begehren zum Dasein als donnernden Strom oder als zartesten zerstäubten Bach von hier aus in alle Adern der Welt sich ergießen fühlt, er sollte nicht jählings zerbrechen? Er sollte es ertragen, in der elenden gläsernen Hülle des menschlichen Individuums, den Widerklang zahlloser Lust- und Weherufe aus dem »weiten Raum der

in which she could not venture to indulge as music itself, without this illusion. The myth protects us from the music, while, on the other hand, it alone gives the highest freedom thereto. By way of return for this service, music imparts to tragic myth such an impressive and convincing metaphysical significance as could never be attained by word and image, without this unique aid; and the tragic spectator in particular experiences thereby the sure presentiment of supreme joy to which the path through destruction and negation leads; so that he thinks he hears, as it were, the innermost abyss of things speaking audibly to him.

If in these last propositions I have succeeded in giving perhaps only a preliminary expression, intelligible to few at first, to this difficult representation, I must not here desist from stimulating my friends to a further attempt, or cease from beseeching them to prepare themselves, by a detached example of our common experience, for the perception of the universal proposition. In this example I must not appeal to those who make use of the pictures of the scenic processes, the words and the emotions of the performers, in order to approximate thereby to musical perception; for none of these speak music as their mother-tongue, and, in spite of the aids in question, do not get farther than the precincts of musical perception, without ever being allowed to touch its innermost shrines; some of them, like Gervinus, do not even reach the precincts by this path. I have only to address myself to those who, being immediately allied to music, have it as it were for their mother's lap, and are connected with things almost exclusively by unconscious musical relations. I ask the question of these genuine musicians: whether they can imagine a man capable of hearing the third act of *Tristan und Isolde* without any aid of word or scenery, purely as a vast symphonic period, without expiring by a spasmodic distention of all the wings of the soul? A man who has thus, so to speak, put his ear to the heart-chamber of the cosmic will, who feels the furious desire for existence issuing therefrom as a thundering stream or most gently dispersed brook, into all the veins of the world, would he not collapse all at once? Could he endure, in the wretched fragile tenement of the human individual, to hear the re-echo of countless cries of joy and sorrow from the "vast void of cosmic night," without flying

Weltennacht« zu vernehmen, ohne bei diesem Hirtenreigen der Metaphysik sich seiner Urheimat unaufhaltsam zuzuflüchten. Wenn aber doch ein solches Werk als Ganzes perzipiert werden kann, ohne Verneinung der Individualexistenz, wenn eine solche Schöpfung geschaffen werden konnte, ohne ihren Schöpfer zu zerschmettern – woher nehmen wir die Lösung eines solchen Widerspruches?

Hier drängt sich zwischen unsre höchste Musikerregung und jene Musik der tragische Mythus und der tragische Held, im Grunde nur als Gleichnis der alleruniversalsten Tatsachen, von denen allein die Musik auf direktem Wege reden kann. Als Gleichnis würde nun aber der Mythus, wenn wir als rein dionysische Wesen empfänden, gänzlich wirkungslos und unbeachtet neben uns stehen bleiben und uns keinen Augenblick abwendig davon machen, unser Ohr dem Widerklang der *universalia ante rem* zu bieten. Hier bricht jedoch die *apollinische* Kraft, auf Wiederherstellung des fast zersprengten Individuums gerichtet, mit dem Heilbalsam einer wonnevollen Täuschung hervor: plötzlich glauben wir nur noch Tristan zu sehen, wie er bewegungslos und dumpf sich fragt: »die alte Weise; was weckt sie mich?« Und was uns früher wie ein hohles Seufzen aus dem Mittelpunkte des Seins anmutete, das will uns jetzt nur sagen, wie »öd und leer das Meer«. Und wo wir atemlos zu erlöschen wähnten, im krampfartigen Sichausrecken aller Gefühle, und nur ein weniges uns mit dieser Existenz zusammenknüpfte, hören und sehen wir jetzt nur den zum Tode verwundeten und doch nicht sterbenden Helden, mit seinem verzweiflungsvollen Rufe: »Sehnen! Sehnen! Im Sterben mich zu sehnen, vor Sehnsucht nicht zu sterben!« Und wenn früher der Jubel des Horns nach solchem Übermaß und solcher Überzahl verzehrender Qualen fast wie der Qualen höchste uns das Herz zerschnitt, so steht jetzt zwischen uns und diesem »Jubel an sich« der jauchzende Kurwenal, dem Schiffe, das Isolden trägt, zugewandt. So gewaltig auch das Mitleiden in uns hineingreift, in einem gewissen Sinne rettet uns doch das Mitleiden vor dem Urleiden der Welt, wie das Gleichnisbild des Mythus uns vor dem unmittelbaren Anschauen der höchsten Weltidee, wie der Gedanke und das Wort uns vor dem ungedämmten Ergusse des unbewußten Willens rettet. Durch jene herrliche apollinische Täuschung dünkt es uns, als ob uns selbst das Tonreich wie eine plastische Welt gegenüberträte, als ob auch in ihr nur Tristans und Isoldens Schicksal, wie in einem allerzartesten und ausdrucksfähigsten Stoffe, geformt und bildnerisch ausgeprägt worden sei.

irresistibly towards his primitive home at the sound of this pastoral dance-song of metaphysics? But if, nevertheless, such a work can be heard as a whole, without a renunciation of individual existence, if such a creation could be created without demolishing its creator—where are we to get the solution of this contradiction?

Here there interpose between our highest musical excitement and the music in question the tragic myth and the tragic hero—in reality only as symbols of the most universal facts, of which music alone can speak directly. If, however, we felt as purely Dionysian beings, myth as a symbol would stand by us absolutely ineffective and unnoticed, and would never for a moment prevent us from giving ear to the re-echo of the *universalia ante rem*. Here, however, the *Apollonian* power, with a view to the restoration of the well-nigh shattered individual, bursts forth with the healing balm of a blissful illusion: all of a sudden we imagine we see only Tristan, motionless, with hushed voice saying to himself: “the old tune, why does it wake me?” And what formerly interested us like a hollow sigh from the heart of being, seems now only to tell us how “waste and void is the sea.” And when, breathless, we thought to expire by a convulsive distention of all our feelings, and only a slender tie bound us to our present existence, we now hear and see only the hero wounded to death and still not dying, with his despairing cry: “Longing! Longing! In dying still longing! for longing not dying!” And if formerly, after such a surplus and superabundance of consuming agonies, the jubilation of the born rent our hearts almost like the very acme of agony, the rejoicing Kurwenal now stands between us and the “jubilation as such,” with face turned toward the ship which carries Isolde. However powerfully fellow-suffering encroaches upon us, it nevertheless delivers us in a manner from the primordial suffering of the world, just as the symbol-image of the myth delivers us from the immediate perception of the highest cosmic idea, just as the thought and word deliver us from the unchecked effusion of the unconscious will. The glorious Apollonian illusion makes it appear as if the very realm of tones presented itself to us as a plastic cosmos, as if even the fate of Tristan and Isolde had been merely formed and moulded therein as out of some most delicate and impressible material.

So entreißt uns das Apollinische der dionysischen Allgemeinheit und entzückt uns für die Individuen; an diese fesselt es unsre Mitleidserregung, durch diese befriedigt es den nach großen und erhabenen Formen lechzenden Schönheitssinn; es führt an uns Lebensbilder vorbei und reizt uns zu gedankenhaftem Erfassen des in ihnen enthaltenen Lebenskernes. Mit der ungeheuren Wucht des Bildes, des Begriffs, der ethischen Lehre, der sympathischen Erregung reißt das Apollinische den Menschen aus seiner orgiastischen Selbstvernichtung empor und täuscht ihn über die Allgemeinheit des dionysischen Vorganges hinweg zu dem Wahne, daß er ein einzelnes Weltbild, z.B. Tristan und Isolde, sehe und es *durch die Musik*, nur noch besser und innerlicher *sehen* solle. Was vermag nicht der heilkundige Zauber des Apollo, wenn er selbst in uns die Täuschung aufregen kann, als ob wirklich das Dionysische, im Dienste des Apollinischen, dessen Wirkungen zu steigern vermöchte, ja als ob die Musik sogar wesentlich Darstellungskunst für einen apollinischen Inhalt sei?

Thus does the Apollonian wrest us from Dionysian universality and fill us with rapture for individuals; to these it rivets our sympathetic emotion, through these it satisfies the sense of beauty which longs for great and sublime forms; it brings before us biographical portraits, and incites us to a thoughtful apprehension of the essence of life contained therein. With the immense potency of the image, the concept, the ethical teaching and the sympathetic emotion—the Apollonian influence uplifts man from his orgiastic self-annihilation, and beguiles him concerning the universality of the Dionysian process into the belief that he is seeing a detached picture of the world, for instance, Tristan and Isolde, and that, *through music*, he will be enabled to *see* it still more clearly and intrinsically. What can the healing magic of Apollo not accomplish when it can even excite in us the illusion that the Dionysian is actually in the service of the Apollonian, the effects of which it is capable of enhancing; yea, that music is essentially the representative art for an Apollonian substance?

Bei jener prästabilierten Harmonie, die zwischen dem vollendeten Drama und seiner Musik waltet, erreicht das Drama einen höchsten, für das Wortdrama sonst unzugänglichen Grad von Schaubarkeit. Wie alle lebendigen Gestalten der Szene in den selbständig bewegten Melodienlinien sich zur Deutlichkeit der geschwungenen Linie vor uns vereinfachen, ertönt uns das Nebeneinander dieser Linien in dem mit dem bewegten Vorgange auf zarteste Weise sympathisierenden Harmonienwechsel: durch welchen uns die Relationen der Dinge in sinnlich wahrnehmbarer, keinesfalls abstrakter Weise, unmittelbar vernehmbar werden, wie wir gleichfalls durch ihn erkennen, daß erst in diesen Relationen das Wesen eines Charakters und einer Melodienlinie sich rein offenbare. Und während uns so die Musik zwingt, mehr und innerlicher als sonst zu sehen und den Vorgang der Szene wie ein zartes Gespinst vor uns auszubreiten, ist für unser vergeistigtes, ins Innere blickende Auge die Welt der Bühne ebenso unendlich erweitert als von innen heraus erleuchtet. Was vermöchte der Wortdichter Analoges zu bieten, der mit einem viel vollkommneren Mechanismus, auf indirektem Wege, vom Wort und vom Begriff aus, jene innerliche Erweiterung der schaubaren Bühnenwelt und ihre innere Erleuchtung zu erreichen sich abmüht? Nimmt nun zwar auch die musikalische Tragödie das Wort hinzu, so kann sie doch zugleich den Untergrund und die Geburtsstätte des Wortes

With the pre-established harmony which obtains between perfect drama and its music, the drama attains the highest degree of conspicuousness, such as is usually unattainable in mere spoken drama. As all the animated figures of the scene in the independently evolved lines of melody simplify themselves before us to the distinctness of the catenary curve, the coexistence of these lines is also audible in the harmonic change which sympathises in a most delicate manner with the evolved process: through which change the relations of things become immediately perceptible to us in a sensible and not at all abstract manner, as we likewise perceive thereby that it is only in these relations that the essence of a character and of a line of melody manifests itself clearly. And while music thus compels us to see more extensively and more intrinsically than usual, and makes us spread out the curtain of the scene before ourselves like some delicate texture, the world of the stage is as infinitely expanded for our spiritualised, introspective eye as it is illumined outwardly from within. How can the word-poet furnish anything analogous, who strives to attain this internal expansion and illumination of the visible stage-world by a much more imperfect mechanism and an indirect path, proceeding as he does from word and concept? Albeit musical tragedy likewise avails itself of the word, it is at the same time able to

danebenstellen und uns das Werden des Wortes, von innen heraus, verdeutlichen.

Aber von diesem geschilderten Vorgang wäre doch ebenso bestimmt zu sagen, daß er nur ein herrlicher Schein, nämlich jene vorhin erwähnte appolinische *Täuschung* sei, durch deren Wirkung wir von dem dionysischen Andrange und Übermaße entlastet werden sollen. Im Grunde ist ja das Verhältnis der Musik zum Drama gerade das umgekehrte: die Musik ist die eigentliche Idee der Welt, das Drama nur ein Abglanz dieser Idee, ein vereinzeltes Schattenbild derselben. Jene Identität zwischen der Melodienlinie und der lebendigen Gestalt, zwischen der Harmonie und den Charakterrelationen jener Gestalt ist in einem entgegengesetzten Sinne wahr, als es uns, beim Anschaun der musikalischen Tragödie, dünken möchte. Wir mögen die Gestalt uns auf das sichtbarste bewegen, beleben und von innen heraus beleuchten, sie bleibt immer nur die Erscheinung, von der es keine Brücke gibt, die in die wahre Realität, ins Herz der Welt führte. Aus diesem Herzen heraus aber redet die Musik; und zahllose Erscheinungen jener Art dürften an der gleichen Musik vorüberziehn, sie würden nie das Wesen derselben erschöpfen, sondern immer nur ihre veräußerlichten Abbilder sein. Mit dem populären und gänzlich falschen Gegensatz von Seele und Körper ist freilich für das schwierige Verhältnis von Musik und Drama nichts zu erklären und alles zu verwirren; aber die unphilosophische Rohheit jenes Gegensatzes scheint gerade bei unseren Ästhetikern, wer weiß aus welchen Gründen, zu einem gern bekannten Glaubensartikel geworden zu sein, während sie über einen Gegensatz der Erscheinung und des Dinges an sich nichts gelernt haben oder, aus ebenfalls unbekannten Gründen, nichts lernen mochten.

Sollte es sich bei unserer Analysis ergeben haben, daß das Apollinische in der Tragödie durch seine Täuschung völlig den Sieg über das dionysische Urelement der Musik davongetragen und sich diese zu ihren Absichten, nämlich zu einer höchsten Verdeutlichung des Dramas, nutzbar gemacht habe, so wäre freilich eine sehr wichtige Einschränkung hinzuzufügen: in dem allerwesentlichsten Punkte ist jene apollinische Täuschung durchbrochen und vernichtet. Das Drama, das in so innerlich erleuchteter Deutlichkeit aller Bewegungen und Gestalten, mit Hilfe der Musik, sich vor uns ausbreitet, als ob wir das Gewebe am Webstuhl im Auf- und Niederzucken entstehen sehen – erreicht als Ganzes eine Wirkung, die *jenseits aller apollinischen*

place alongside thereof its basis and source, and can make the unfolding of the word, from within outwards, obvious to us.

Of the process just set forth, however, it could still be said as decidedly that it is only a glorious appearance, namely the afore-mentioned Apollonian *illusion,* through the influence of which we are to be delivered from the Dionysian obtrusion and excess. In point of fact, the relation of music to drama is precisely the reverse; music is the adequate idea of the world, drama is but the reflex of this idea, a detached umbrage thereof. The identity between the line of melody and the lining form, between the harmony and the character-relations of this form, is true in a sense antithetical to what one would suppose on the contemplation of musical tragedy. We may agitate and enliven the form in the most conspicuous manner, and enlighten it from within, but it still continues merely phenomenon, from which there is no bridge to lead us into the true reality, into the heart of the world. Music, however, speaks out of this heart; and though countless phenomena of the kind might be passing manifestations of this music, they could never exhaust its essence, but would always be merely its externalised copies. Of course, as regards the intricate relation of music and drama, nothing can be explained, while all may be confused by the popular and thoroughly false antithesis of soul and body; but the unphilosophical crudeness of this antithesis seems to have become—who knows for what reasons—a readily accepted Article of Faith with our æstheticians, while they have learned nothing concerning an antithesis of phenomenon and thing-in-itself, or perhaps, for reasons equally unknown, have not cared to learn anything thereof.

Should it have been established by our analysis that the Apollonian element in tragedy has by means of its illusion gained a complete victory over the Dionysian primordial element of music, and has made music itself subservient to its end, namely, the highest and clearest elucidation of the drama, it would certainly be necessary to add the very important restriction: that at the most essential point this Apollonian illusion is dissolved and annihilated. The drama, which, by the aid of music, spreads out before us with such inwardly illumined distinctness in all its movements and figures, that we imagine we see the texture

Kunstwirkungen liegt. In der Gesamtwirkung der Tragödie erlangt das Dionysische wieder das Übergewicht; sie schließt mit einem Klange, der niemals von dem Reiche der apollinischen Kunst her tönen könnte. Und damit erweist sich die apollinische Täuschung als das, was sie ist, als die während der Dauer der Tragödie anhaltende Umschleierung der eigentlichen dionysischen Wirkung: die doch so mächtig ist, am Schluß das apollinische Drama selbst in eine Sphäre zu drängen, wo es mit dionysischer Weisheit zu reden beginnt und wo es sich selbst und seine apollinische Sichtbarkeit verneint. So wäre wirklich das schwierige Verhältnis des Apollinischen und des Dionysischen in der Tragödie durch einen Bruderbund beider Gottheiten zu symbolisieren: Dionysus redet die Sprache des Apollo, Apollo aber schließlich die Sprache Dionysus: womit das höchste Ziel der Tragödie und der Kunst überhaupt erreicht ist.

unfolding on the loom as the shuttle flies to and fro—attains as a whole an effect which *transcends all Apollonian artistic effects*. In the collective effect of tragedy, the Dionysian gets the upper hand once more; tragedy ends with a sound which could never emanate from the realm of Apollonian art. And the Apollonian illusion is thereby found to be what it is—the assiduous veiling during the performance of tragedy of the intrinsically Dionysian effect: which, however, is so powerful, that it finally forces the Apollonian drama itself into a sphere where it begins to talk with Dionysian wisdom, and even denies itself and its Apollonian conspicuousness. Thus then the intricate relation of the Apollonian and the Dionysian in tragedy must really be symbolised by a fraternal union of the two deities: Dionysus speaks the language of Apollo; Apollo, however, finally speaks the language of Dionysus; and so the highest goal of tragedy and of art in general is attained.

22

Mag der aufmerksame Freund sich die Wirkung einer wahren musikalischen Tragödie rein und unvermischt, nach seinen Erfahrungen, vergegenwärtigen. Ich denke das Phänomen dieser Wirkung nach beiden Seiten hin so beschrieben zu haben, daß er sich seine eignen Erfahrungen jetzt zu deuten wissen wird. Er wird sich nämlich erinnern, wie er, im Hinblick auf den vor ihm sich bewegenden Mythus, zu einer Art von Allwissenheit sich gesteigert fühlte, als ob jetzt die Sehkraft seiner Augen nicht nur eine Flächenkraft sei, sondern ins Innere zu dringen vermöge, und als ob er die Wallungen des Willens, den Kampf der Motive, den anschwellenden Strom der Leidenschaften, jetzt, mit Hilfe der Musik, gleichsam sinnlich sichtbar, wie eine Fülle lebendig bewegter Linien und Figuren vor sich sehe und damit bis in die zartesten Geheimnisse unbewußter Regungen hinabtauchen könne. Während er so einer höchsten Steigerung seiner auf Sichtbarkeit und Verklärung gerichteten Triebe bewußt wird, fühlt er doch ebenso bestimmt, daß diese lange Reihe apollinischer Kunstwirkungen doch *nicht* jenes beglückte Verharren in willenlosem Anschauen erzeugt, das der Plastiker und der epische Dichter, also die eigentlich apollinischen Künstler, durch ihre Kunstwerke bei ihm hervorbringen: das heißt die in jenem Anschauen erreichte Rechtfertigung der Welt der *individuatio*, als welche die Spitze und der

Let the attentive friend picture to himself purely and simply, according to his experiences, the effect of a true musical tragedy. I think I have so portrayed the phenomenon of this effect in both its phases that he will now be able to interpret his own experiences. For he will recollect that with regard to the myth which passed before him he felt himself exalted to a kind of omniscience, as if his visual faculty were no longer merely a surface faculty, but capable of penetrating into the interior, and as if he now saw before him, with the aid of music, the ebullitions of the will, the conflict of motives, and the swelling stream of the passions, almost sensibly visible, like a plenitude of actively moving lines and figures, and could thereby dip into the most tender secrets of unconscious emotions. While he thus becomes conscious of the highest exaltation of his instincts for conspicuousness and transfiguration, he nevertheless feels with equal definitiveness that this long series of Apollonian artistic effects still does *not* generate the blissful continuance in will-less contemplation which the plasticist and the epic poet, that is to say, the strictly Apollonian artists, produce in him by their artistic productions: to wit, the justification of the world of the *individuatio* attained in this contemplation—which is the object and essence of

Inbegriff der apollinischen Kunst ist. Er schaut die verklärte Welt der Bühne und verneint sie doch. Er sieht den tragischen Helden vor sich in epischer Deutlichkeit und Schönheit und erfreut sich doch an seiner Vernichtung. Er begreift bis ins Innerste den Vorgang der Szene und flüchtet sich gern ins Unbegreifliche. Er fühlt die Handlungen des Helden als gerechtfertigt und ist doch noch mehr erhoben, wenn diese Handlungen den Urheber vernichten. Er schaudert vor den Leiden, die den Heldentreffen werden, und ahnt doch bei ihnen eine höhere, viel übermächtigere Lust. Er schaut mehr und tiefer als je und wünscht sich doch erblindet. Woher werden wir diese wunderbare Selbstentzweiung, dies Umbrechen der apollinischen Spitze, abzuleiten haben, wenn nicht aus dem *dionysischen* Zauber, der, zum Schein die apollinischen Regungen aufs höchste reizend, doch noch diesen Überschwang der apollinischen Kraft in seinen Dienst zu zwingen vermag. *Der tragische Mythus* ist nur zu verstehen als eine Verbildlichung dionysischer Weisheit durch apollinische Kunstmittel; er führt die Welt der Erscheinung an die Grenzen, wo sie sich selbst verneint und wieder in den Schoß der wahren und einzigen Realitäten zurückzuflüchten sucht; wo sie dann, mit Isolden, ihren metaphysischen Schwanengesang also anzustimmen scheint:

In des Wonnemeeres
wogendem Schwall,
in der Duft-Wellen
tönendem Schall,
in des Weltatems
wehendem All –
ertrinken – versinken –
unbewußt – höchste Lust!

So vergegenwärtigen wir uns, an den Erfahrungen des wahrhaft ästhetischen Zuhörers, den tragischen Künstler selbst, wie er, gleich einer üppigen Gottheit der *individuatio*, seine Gestalten schafft, in welchem Sinne sein Werk kaum als »Nachahmung der Natur« zu begreifen wäre, – wie dann aber sein ungeheurer dionysischer Trieb diese ganze Welt der Erscheinungen verschlingt, um hinter ihr und durch ihre Vernichtung eine höchste künstlerische Urfreude im Schoße des Ur-Einen ahnen zu lassen. Freilich wissen von dieser Rückkehr zur Urheimat, von dem Bruderbunde der beiden Kunstgottheiten in der Tragödie und von der sowohl apollinischen als dionysischen Erregung des Zuhörers unsere Ästhetiker nichts zu berichten, während sie nicht müde werden, den Kampf des Helden mit dem Schicksal, den Sieg der sittlichen Weltordnung oder

Apollonian art. He beholds the transfigured world of the stage and nevertheless denies it. He sees before him the tragic hero in epic clearness and beauty, and nevertheless delights in his annihilation. He comprehends the incidents of the scene in all their details, and yet loves to flee into the incomprehensible. He feels the actions of the hero to be justified, and is nevertheless still more elated when these actions annihilate their originator. He shudders at the sufferings which will befall the hero, and yet anticipates therein a higher and much more overpowering joy. He sees more extensively and profoundly than ever, and yet wishes to be blind. Whence must we derive this curious internal dissension, this collapse of the Apollonian apex, if not from the *Dionysian* spell, which, though apparently stimulating the Apollonian emotions to their highest pitch, can nevertheless force this superabundance of Apollonian power into its service? *Tragic myth* is to be understood only as a symbolisation of Dionysian wisdom by means of the expedients of Apollonian art: the mythus conducts the world of phenomena to its boundaries, where it denies itself, and seeks to flee back again into the bosom of the true and only reality; where it then, like Isolde, seems to strike up its metaphysical swan-song:—

In the heaving roll
of the sea of bliss,
in the echoing sound
of the fragrant waves,
in the whole wave
of the world's breath—
drowning—sinking—
unconscious—highest joy!

We thus realise to ourselves in the experiences of the truly æsthetic hearer the tragic artist himself when he proceeds like a luxuriously fertile divinity of individuation to create his figures (in which sense his work can hardly be understood as an "imitation of nature")—and when, on the other hand, his vast Dionysian impulse then absorbs the entire world of phenomena, in order to anticipate beyond it, and through its annihilation, the highest artistic primal joy, in the bosom of the Primordial Unity. Of course, our æsthetes have nothing to say about this return in fraternal union of the two art-deities to the original home, nor of either the Apollonian or Dionysian excitement of the hearer, while they are indefatigable in characterising

eine durch die Tragödie bewirkte Entladung von Affekten als das eigentlich Tragische zu charakterisieren: welche Unverdrossenheit mich auf den Gedanken bringt, sie möchten überhaupt keine ästhetisch erregbaren Menschen sein und beim Anhören der Tragödie vielleicht nur als moralische Wesen in Betracht kommen. Noch nie, seit Aristoteles, ist eine Erklärung der tragischen Wirkung gegeben worden, aus der auf künstlerische Zustände, auf eine ästhetische Tätigkeit der Zuhörer geschlossen werden dürfte. Bald soll Mitleid und Furchtsamkeit durch die ernsten Vorgänge zu einer erleichternden Entladung gedrängt werden, bald sollen wir uns bei dem Sieg guter und edler Prinzipien, bei der Aufopferung des Helden im Sinne einer sittlichen Weltbetrachtung erhoben und begeistert fühlen; und so gewiß ich glaube, daß für zahlreiche Menschen gerade das, und nur das, die Wirkung der Tragödie ist, so deutlich ergibt sich daraus, daß diese alle, samt ihren interpretierenden Ästhetikern, von der Tragödie als einer höchsten *Kunst* nichts erfahren haben. Jene pathologische Entladung, die Katharsis des Aristoteles, von der die Philologen nicht recht wissen, ob sie unter die medizinischen oder die moralischen Phänomene zu rechnen sei, erinnert an eine merkwürdige Ahnung Goethes. »Ohne ein lebhaftes pathologisches Interesse«, sagt er, »ist es auch mir niemals gelungen, irgendeine tragische Situation zu bearbeiten, und ich habe sie daher lieber vermieden als aufgesucht. Sollte es wohl auch einer von den Vorzügen der Alten gewesen sein, daß das höchste Pathetische auch nur ästhetisches Spiel bei ihnen gewesen wäre, da bei uns die Naturwahrheit mitwirken muß, um ein solches Werk hervorzubringen?« Diese so tiefsinnige letzte Frage dürfen wir jetzt, nach unseren herrlichen Erfahrungen, bejahen, nachdem wir gerade an der musikalischen Tragödie mit Staunen erlebt haben, wie wirklich das höchste Pathetische doch nur ein ästhetisches Spiel sein kann: weshalb wir glauben dürfen, daß erst jetzt das Urphänomen des Tragischen mit einigem Erfolg zu beschreiben ist. Wer jetzt noch nur von jenen stellvertretenden Wirkungen aus außerästhetischen Sphären zu erzählen hat und über den pathologisch-moralischen Prozeß sich nicht hinausgehoben fühlt, mag nur an seiner ästhetischen Natur verzweifeln: wogegen wir ihm die Interpretation Shakespeares nach der Manier des Gervinus und das fleißige Aufspüren der »poetischen Gerechtigkeit« als unschuldigen Ersatz anempfehlen.

the struggle of the hero with fate, the triumph of the moral order of the world, or the disburdenment of the emotions through tragedy, as the properly Tragic: an indefatigableness which makes me think that they are perhaps not æsthetically excitable men at all, but only to be regarded as moral beings when hearing tragedy. Never since Aristotle has an explanation of the tragic effect been proposed, by which an æsthetic activity of the hearer could be inferred from artistic circumstances. At one time fear and pity are supposed to be forced to an alleviating discharge through the serious procedure, at another time we are expected to feel elevated and inspired at the triumph of good and noble principles, at the sacrifice of the hero in the interest of a moral conception of things; and however certainly I believe that for countless men precisely this, and only this, is the effect of tragedy, it as obviously follows therefrom that all these, together with their interpreting æsthetes, have had no experience of tragedy as the highest *art*. The pathological discharge, the catharsis of Aristotle, which philologists are at a loss whether to include under medicinal or moral phenomena, recalls a remarkable anticipation of Goethe. "Without a lively pathological interest," he says, "I too have never yet succeeded in elaborating a tragic situation of any kind, and hence I have rather avoided than sought it. Can it perhaps have been still another of the merits of the ancients that the deepest pathos was with them merely æsthetic play, whereas with us the truth of nature must co-operate in order to produce such a work?" We can now answer in the affirmative this latter profound question after our glorious experiences, in which we have found to our astonishment in the case of musical tragedy itself, that the deepest pathos can in reality be merely æsthetic play: and therefore we are justified in believing that now for the first time the proto-phenomenon of the tragic can be portrayed with some degree of success. He who now will still persist in talking only of those vicarious effects proceeding from ultra-æsthetic spheres, and does not feel himself raised above the pathologically-moral process, may be left to despair of his æsthetic nature: for which we recommend to him, by way of innocent equivalent, the interpretation of Shakespeare after the fashion of Gervinus, and the diligent search for poetic justice.

So ist mit der Wiedergeburt der Tragödie auch der *ästhetische Zuhörer* wieder geboren, an dessen Stelle bisher in den Theaterräumen ein seltsames *Quidproquo*, mit halb moralischen und halb gelehrten Ansprüchen, zu sitzen pflegte, der »Kritiker«. In seiner bisherigen Sphäre war alles künstlich und nur mit einem Scheine des Lebens übertüncht. Der darstellende Künstler wußte in der Tat nicht mehr, was er mit einem solchen, kritisch sich gebärdenden Zuhörer zu beginnen habe und spähte daher, samt dem ihn inspirierenden Dramatiker oder Opernkomponisten, unruhig nach den letzten Resten des Lebens in diesem anspruchsvoll öden und zum Genießen unfähigen Wesen. Aus derartigen »Kritikern« bestand aber bisher das Publikum; der Student, der Schulknabe, ja selbst das harmloseste weibliche Geschöpf war wider sein Wissen bereits durch Erziehung und Journale zu einer gleichen Perzeption eines Kunstwerks vorbereitet. Die edleren Naturen unter den Künstlern rechneten bei einem solchen Publikum auf die Erregung moralisch-religiöser Kräfte, und der Anruf der »sittlichen Weltordnung« trat vikarierend ein, wo eigentlich ein gewaltiger Kunstzauber den echten Zuhörer entzücken sollte. Oder es wurde vom Dramatiker eine großartigere, mindestens aufregende Tendenz der politischen und sozialen Gegenwart so deutlich vorgetragen, daß der Zuhörer seine kritische Erschöpfung vergessen und sich ähnlichen Affekten überlassen konnte, wie in patriotischen oder kriegerischen Momenten, oder vor der Rednerbühne des Parlaments, oder bei der Verurteilung des Verbrechens und des Lasters: welche Entfremdung der eigentlichen Kunstabsichten hier und da geradezu zu einem Kultus der Tendenz führen mußte. Doch hier trat ein, was bei allen erkünstelten Künsten von jeher eingetreten ist, eine reißend schnelle Depravation jener Tendenzen, so daß zum Beispiel die Tendenz, das Theater als Veranstaltung zur moralischen Volksbildung zu verwenden, die zu Schillers Zeit ernsthaft genommen wurde, bereits unter die unglaubwürdigen Antiquitäten einer überwundenen Bildung gerechnet wird. Während der Kritiker in Theater und Konzert, der Journalist in der Schule, die Presse in der Gesellschaft zur Herrschaft gekommen war, entartete die Kunst zu einem Unterhaltungsobjekt der niedrigsten Art, und die ästhetische Kritik wurde als das Bindemittel einer eitlen, zerstreuten, selbstsüchtigen und überdies ärmlich-unoriginalen Geselligkeit benutzt, deren Sinn jene Schopenhauerische Parabel von den Stachelschweinen zu verstehen gibt; so daß zu keiner Zeit so viel über Kunst geschwatzt und so wenig von

Thus with the re-birth of tragedy the *æsthetic hearer* is also born anew, in whose place in the theatre a curious *quid pro quo* was wont to sit with half-moral and half-learned pretensions—the "critic." In his sphere hitherto everything has been artificial and merely glossed over with a semblance of life. The performing artist was in fact at a loss what to do with such a critically comporting hearer, and hence he, as well as the dramatist or operatic composer who inspired him, searched anxiously for the last remains of life in a being so pretentiously barren and incapable of enjoyment. Such "critics," however, have hitherto constituted the public; the student, the school-boy, yea, even the most harmless womanly creature, were already unwittingly prepared by education and by journals for a similar perception of works of art. The nobler natures among the artists counted upon exciting the moral-religious forces in such a public, and the appeal to a moral order of the world operated vicariously, when in reality some powerful artistic spell should have enraptured the true hearer. Or again, some imposing or at all events exciting tendency of the contemporary political and social world was presented by the dramatist with such vividness that the hearer could forget his critical exhaustion and abandon himself to similar emotions, as, in patriotic or warlike moments, before the tribune of parliament, or at the condemnation of crime and vice:—an estrangement of the true aims of art which could not but lead directly now and then to a cult of tendency. But here there took place what has always taken place in the case of factitious arts, an extraordinary rapid depravation of these tendencies, so that for instance the tendency to employ the theatre as a means for the moral education of the people, which in Schiller's time was taken seriously, is already reckoned among the incredible antiquities of a surmounted culture. While the critic got the upper hand in the theatre and concert-hall, the journalist in the school, and the press in society, art degenerated into a topic of conversation of the most trivial kind, and æsthetic criticism was used as the cement of a vain, distracted, selfish and moreover piteously unoriginal sociality, the significance of which is suggested by the Schopenhauerian parable of the porcupines, so that there has never been so much gossip about art and so little esteem for it. But is it still possible to have intercourse with a man capable of conversing on Beethoven or Shakespeare? Let each answer this question

der Kunst gehalten worden ist. Kann man aber mit einem Menschen noch verkehren, der imstande ist, sich über Beethoven und Shakespeare zu unterhalten? Mag jeder nach seinem Gefühl diese Frage beantworten: er wird mit der Antwort jedenfalls beweisen, was er sich unter »Bildung« vorstellt, vorausgesetzt, daß er die Frage überhaupt zu beantworten sucht und nicht vor Überraschung bereits verstummt ist.

Dagegen dürfte mancher edler und zarter von der Natur Befähigte, ob er gleich in der geschilderten Weise allmählich zum kritischen Barbaren geworden war, von einer ebenso unerwarteten als gänzlich unverständlichen Wirkung zu erzählen haben, die etwa eine glücklich gelungene Lohengrinaufführung auf ihn ausübte: nur daß ihm vielleicht jede Hand fehlte, die ihn mahnend und deutend anfaßte, so daß auch jene unbegreiflich verschiedenartige und durchaus unvergleichliche Empfindung, die ihn damals erschütterte, vereinzelt blieb und wie ein rätselhaftes Gestirn nach kurzem Leuchten erlosch. Damals hatte er geahnt, was der ästhetische Zuhörer ist.

according to his sentiments: he will at any rate show by his answer his conception of "culture," provided he tries at least to answer the question, and has not already grown mute with astonishment.

On the other hand, many a one more nobly and delicately endowed by nature, though he may have gradually become a critical barbarian in the manner described, could tell of the unexpected as well as totally unintelligible effect which a successful performance of *Lohengrin,* for example, exerted on him: except that perhaps every warning and interpreting hand was lacking to guide him; so that the incomprehensibly heterogeneous and altogether incomparable sensation which then affected him also remained isolated and became extinct, like a mysterious star after a brief brilliancy. He then divined what the æsthetic hearer is.

23

Wer recht genau sich selber prüfen will, wie sehr er dem wahren ästhetischen Zuhörer verwandt ist oder zur Gemeinschaft der sokratisch-kritischen Menschen gehört, der mag sich nur aufrichtig nach der Empfindung fragen, mit der er das auf der Bühne dargestellte *Wunder* empfängt: ob er etwa dabei seinen historischen, auf strenge psychologische Kausalität gerichteten Sinn beleidigt fühlt, ob er mit einer wohlwollenden Konzession gleichsam das Wunder als ein der Kindheit verständliches, ihm entfremdetes Phänomen zuläßt, oder ob er irgend etwas anderes dabei erleidet. Daran nämlich wird er messen können, wieweit er überhaupt befähigt ist, den *Mythus,* das zusammengezogene Weltbild, zu verstehen, der, als Abbreviatur der Erscheinung, das Wunder nicht entbehren kann. Das Wahrscheinliche ist aber, daß fast jeder, bei strenger Prüfung, sich so durch den kritisch-historischen Geist unserer Bildung zersetzt fühlt, um nur etwa auf gelehrtem Wege, durch vermittelnde Abstraktionen, sich die einstmalige Existenz des Mythus glaublich zu machen. Ohne Mythus aber geht jede Kultur ihrer gesunden schöpferischen Naturkraft verlustig: erst ein mit Mythen umstellter Horizont schließt eine ganze Kulturbewegung zur Einheit ab. Alle Kräfte der

He who wishes to test himself rigorously as to how he is related to the true æsthetic hearer, or whether he belongs rather to the community of the Socrato-critical man, has only to enquire sincerely concerning the sentiment with which he accepts the *wonder* represented on the stage: whether he feels his historical sense, which insists on strict psychological causality, insulted by it, whether with benevolent concession he as it were admits the wonder as a phenomenon intelligible to childhood, but relinquished by him, or whether he experiences anything else thereby. For he will thus be enabled to determine how far he is on the whole capable of understanding *myth,* that is to say, the concentrated picture of the world, which, as abbreviature of phenomena, cannot dispense with wonder. It is probable, however, that nearly every one, upon close examination, feels so disintegrated by the critico-historical spirit of our culture, that he can only perhaps make the former existence of myth credible to himself by learned means through intermediary abstractions. Without myth, however, every culture loses its healthy, creative natural power: it is only a horizon encompassed with myths which rounds off to

Phantasie und des apollinischen Traumes werden erst durch den Mythus aus ihrem wahllosen Herumschweifen gerettet. Die Bilder des Mythus müssen die unbemerkt allgegenwärtigen dämonischen Wächter sein, unter deren Hut die junge Seele heranwächst, an deren Zeichen der Mann sich sein Leben und seine Kämpfe deutet: und selbst der Staat kennt keine mächtigeren ungeschriebnen Gesetze als das mythische Fundament, das seinen Zusammenhang mit der Religion, sein Herauswachsen aus mythischen Vorstellungen verbürgt.

Man stelle jetzt daneben den abstrakten, ohne Mythen geleiteten Menschen, die abstrakte Erziehung, die abstrakte Sitte, das abstrakte Recht, den abstrakten Staat: man vergegenwärtige sich das regellose, von keinem heimischen Mythus gezügelte Schweifen der künstlerischen Phantasie: man denke sich eine Kultur, die keinen festen und heiligen Ursitz hat, sondern alle Möglichkeiten zu erschöpfen und von allen Kulturen sich kümmerlich zu nähren verurteilt ist – das ist die Gegenwart, als das Resultat jenes auf Vernichtung des Mythus gerichteten Sokratismus. Und nun steht der mythenlose Mensch, ewig hungernd, unter allen Vergangenheiten und sucht grabend und wühlend nach Wurzeln, sei es daß er auch in den entlegensten Altertümern nach ihnen graben müßte. Worauf weist das ungeheure historische Bedürfnis der unbefriedigten modernen Kultur, das Umsichsammeln zahlloser anderer Kulturen, das verzehrende Erkennenwollen, wenn nicht auf den Verlust des Mythus, auf den Verlust der mythischen Heimat, des mythischen Mutterschoßes? Man frage sich, ob das fieberhafte und so unheimliche Sichregen dieser Kultur etwas anderes ist als das gierige Zugreifen und Nach-Nahrung-Haschen des Hungernden – und wer möchte einer solchen Kultur noch etwas geben wollen, die durch alles, was sie verschlingt, nicht zu sättigen ist, und bei deren Berührung sich die kräftigste, heilsamste Nahrung in »Historie und Kritik« zu verwandeln pflegt?

Man müßte auch an unserem deutschen Wesen schmerzlich verzweifeln, wenn es bereits in gleicher Weise mit seiner Kultur unlösbar verstrickt, ja eins geworden wäre, wie wir das an dem zivilisierten Frankreich zu unserem Entsetzen beobachten können; und das, was lange Zeit der große Vorzug Frankreichs und die Ursache seines ungeheuren Übergewichts war, eben jenes Einssein von Volk und Kultur, dürfte uns, bei diesem Anblick, nötigen, darin das Glück zu preisen, daß diese unsere so fragwürdige Kultur bis

unity a social movement. It is only by myth that all the powers of the imagination and of the Apollonian dream are freed from their random rovings. The mythical figures have to be the invisibly omnipresent genii, under the care of which the young soul grows to maturity, by the signs of which the man gives a meaning to his life and struggles: and the state itself knows no more powerful unwritten law than the mythical foundation which vouches for its connection with religion and its growth from mythical ideas.

Let us now place alongside thereof the abstract man proceeding independently of myth, the abstract education, the abstract usage, the abstract right, the abstract state: let us picture to ourselves the lawless roving of the artistic imagination, not bridled by any native myth: let us imagine a culture which has no fixed and sacred primitive seat, but is doomed to exhaust all its possibilities, and has to nourish itself wretchedly from the other cultures—such is the Present, as the result of Socratism, which is bent on the destruction of myth. And now the myth-less man remains eternally hungering among all the bygones, and digs and grubs for roots, though he have to dig for them even among the remotest antiquities. The stupendous historical exigency of the unsatisfied modern culture, the gathering around one of countless other cultures, the consuming desire for knowledge—what does all this point to, if not to the loss of myth, the loss of the mythical home, the mythical source? Let us ask ourselves whether the feverish and so uncanny stirring of this culture is aught but the eager seizing and snatching at food of the hungerer—and who would care to contribute anything more to a culture which cannot be appeased by all it devours, and in contact with which the most vigorous and wholesome nourishment is wont to change into "history and criticism"?

We should also have to regard our German character with despair and sorrow, if it had already become inextricably entangled in, or even identical with this culture, in a similar manner as we can observe it to our horror to be the case in civilised France; and that which for a long time was the great advantage of France and the cause of her vast preponderance, to wit, this very identity of people and culture, might compel us at the sight thereof to congratulate ourselves that this culture of ours, which is so questionable, has hitherto had nothing

jetzt mit dem edlen Kerne unseres Volkscharakters nichts gemein hat. Alle unsere Hoffnungen strecken sich vielmehr sehnsuchtsvoll nach jener Wahrnehmung aus, daß unter diesem unruhig auf und niederzuckenden Kulturleben und Bildungskrampfe eine herrliche, innerlich gesunde, uralte Kraft verborgen liegt, die freilich nur in ungeheuren Momenten sich gewaltig einmal bewegt und dann wieder einem zukünftigen Erwachen entgegenträumt. Aus diesem Abgrunde ist die deutsche Reformation hervorgewachsen: in deren Choral die Zukunftsweise der deutschen Musik zuerst erklang. So tief, mutig und seelenvoll, so überschwänglich gut und zart tönte dieser Choral Luthers, als der erste dionysische Lockruf, der aus dichtverwachsenem Gebüsch, im Nahen des Frühlings, hervordringt. Ihm antwortete in wetteiferndem Widerhall jener weihevoll übermütige Festzug dionysischer Schwärmer, denen wir die deutsche Musik danken – und denen wir *die Wiedergeburt des deutschen Mythus* danken werden!

in common with the noble kernel of the character of our people. All our hopes, on the contrary, stretch out longingly towards the perception that beneath this restlessly palpitating civilised life and educational convulsion there is concealed a glorious, intrinsically healthy, primeval power, which, to be sure, stirs vigorously only at intervals in stupendous moments, and then dreams on again in view of a future awakening. It is from this abyss that the German Reformation came forth: in the choral-hymn of which the future melody of German music first resounded. So deep, courageous, and soul-breathing, so exuberantly good and tender did this chorale of Luther sound—as the first Dionysian-luring call which breaks forth from dense thickets at the approach of spring. To it responded with emulative echo the solemnly wanton procession of Dionysian revellers, to whom we are indebted for German music—and to whom we shall be indebted for *the* re-birth of German myth.

Ich weiß, daß ich jetzt den teilnehmend folgenden Freund auf einen hochgelegenen Ort einsamer Betrachtungen führen muß, wo er nur wenige Gefährten haben wird, und rufe ihm ermutigend zu, daß wir uns an unseren leuchtenden Führern, den Griechen, festzuhalten haben. Von ihnen haben wir bis jetzt, zur Reinigung unserer ästhetischen Erkenntnis, jene beiden Götterbilder entlehnt, von denen jedes ein gesondertes Kunstreich für sich beherrscht, und über deren gegenseitige Berührung und Steigerung wir durch die griechische Tragödie zu einer Ahnung kamen. Durch ein merkwürdiges Auseinanderreißen beider künstlerischer Urtriebe mußte uns der Untergang der griechischen Tragödie herbeigeführt erscheinen: mit welchem Vorgange eine Degeneration und Umwandlung des griechischen Volkscharakters im Einklang war, uns zu ernstem Nachdenken auffordernd, wie notwendig und eng die Kunst und das Volk, Mythus und Sitte, Tragödie und Staat, in ihren Fundamenten verwachsen sind. Jener Untergang der Tragödie war zugleich der Untergang des Mythus. Bis dahin waren die Griechen unwillkürlich genötigt, alles Erlebte sofort an ihre Mythen anzuknüpfen, ja es nur durch diese Anknüpfung zu begreifen: wodurch auch die nächste Gegenwart ihnen sofort *sub specie aeterni* und in gewissem Sinne als zeitlos erscheinen mußte. In diesen Strom des Zeitlosen aber tauchte sich ebenso der Staat wie die Kunst, um in ihm vor der Last und der Gier des Augenblicks Ruhe zu finden. Und gerade nur so viel ist ein Volk – wie übrigens auch ein

I know that I must now lead the sympathising and attentive friend to an elevated position of lonesome contemplation, where he will have but few companions, and I call out encouragingly to him that we must hold fast to our shining guides, the Greeks. For the rectification of our æsthetic knowledge we previously borrowed from them the two divine figures, each of which sways a separate realm of art, and concerning whose mutual contact and exaltation we have acquired a notion through Greek tragedy. Through a remarkable disruption of both these primitive artistic impulses, the ruin of Greek tragedy seemed to be necessarily brought about: with which process a degeneration and a transmutation of the Greek national character was strictly in keeping, summoning us to earnest reflection as to how closely and necessarily art and the people, myth and custom, tragedy and the state, have coalesced in their bases. The ruin of tragedy was at the same time the ruin of myth. Until then the Greeks had been involuntarily compelled immediately to associate all experiences with their myths, indeed they had to comprehend them only through this association: whereby even the most immediate present necessarily appeared to them *sub specie æterni* and in a certain sense as timeless. Into this current of the timeless, however, the state as well as art plunged in order to find repose from the burden and eagerness of the moment. And a people—for the rest, also a man—is worth just as

Mensch – wert, als es auf seine Erlebnisse den Stempel des Ewigen zu drücken vermag: denn damit ist es gleichsam entweltlicht und zeigt seine unbewußte innerliche Überzeugung von der Relativität der Zeit und von der wahren, d.h. der metaphysischen Bedeutung des Lebens. Das Gegenteil davon tritt ein, wenn ein Volk anfängt, sich historisch zu begreifen und die mythischen Bollwerke um sich herum zu zertrümmern: womit gewöhnlich eine entschiedene Verweltlichung, ein Bruch mit der unbewußten Metaphysik seines früheren Daseins, in allen ethischen Konsequenzen, verbunden ist. Die griechische Kunst und vornehmlich die griechische Tragödie hielt vor allem die Vernichtung des Mythus auf: man mußte sie mit vernichten, um, losgelöst von dem heimischen Boden, ungezügelt in der Wildnis des Gedankens, der Sitte und der Tat leben zu können. Auch jetzt noch versucht jener metaphysische Trieb sich eine, wenngleich abgeschwächte Form der Verklärung zu schaffen, in dem zum Leben drängenden Sokratismus der Wissenschaft: aber auf den niederen Stufen führte derselbe Trieb nur zu einem fieberhaften Suchen, das sich allmählich in ein Pandämonium überallher zusammengehäufter Mythen und Superstitionen verlor: in dessen Mitte der Hellene dennoch ungestillten Herzens saß, bis er es verstand, mit griechischer Heiterkeit und griechischem Leichtsinn, als Graeculus, jenes Fieber zu maskieren oder in irgendeinem orientalisch dumpfen Aberglauben sich völlig zu betäuben.

Diesem Zustande haben wir uns, seit der Wiedererweckung des alexandrinisch-römischen Altertums im fünfzehnten Jahrhundert, nach einem langen schwer zu beschreibenden Zwischenakte, in der auffälligsten Weise angenähert. Auf den Höhen dieselbe überreiche Wissenslust, dasselbe ungesättigte Finderglück, diese ungeheure Verweltlichung, daneben ein heimatloses Herumschweifen, ein gieriges Sichdrängen an fremde Tische, eine leichtsinnige Vergötterung der Gegenwart oder stumpf betäubte Abkehr, alles *sub specie saeculi*, der »Jetztzeit«: welche gleichen Symptome auf einen gleichen Mangel im Herzen dieser Kultur zu raten geben, auf die Vernichtung des Mythus. Es scheint kaum möglich zu sein, mit dauerndem Erfolge einen fremden Mythus überzupflanzen, ohne den Baum durch dieses Überpflanzen heillos zu beschädigen: welcher vielleicht einmal stark und gesund genug ist, jenes fremde Element mit furchtbarem Kampfe wieder auszuscheiden, für gewöhnlich aber siech und verkümmert oder in krampfhaftem Wuchern sich

much only as its ability to impress on its experiences the seal of eternity: for it is thus, as it were, desecularised, and reveals its unconscious inner conviction of the relativity of time and of the true, that is, the metaphysical significance of life. The contrary happens when a people begins to comprehend itself historically and to demolish the mythical bulwarks around it: with which there is usually connected a marked secularisation, a breach with the unconscious metaphysics of its earlier existence, in all ethical consequences. Greek art and especially Greek tragedy delayed above all the annihilation of myth: it was necessary to annihilate these also to be able to live detached from the native soil, unbridled in the wilderness of thought, custom, and action. Even in such circumstances this metaphysical impulse still endeavours to create for itself a form of apotheosis (weakened, no doubt) in the Socratism of science urging to life: but on its lower stage this same impulse led only to a feverish search, which gradually merged into a pandemonium of myths and superstitions accumulated from all quarters: in the midst of which, nevertheless, the Hellene sat with a yearning heart till he contrived, as Græculus, to mask his fever with Greek cheerfulness and Greek levity, or to narcotise himself completely with some gloomy Oriental superstition.

We have approached this condition in the most striking manner since the reawakening of the Alexandro-Roman antiquity in the fifteenth century, after a long, not easily describable, interlude. On the heights there is the same exuberant love of knowledge, the same insatiate happiness of the discoverer, the same stupendous secularisation, and, together with these, a homeless roving about, an eager intrusion at foreign tables, a frivolous deification of the present or a dull senseless estrangement, all *sub speci sæculi,* of the present time: which same symptoms lead one to infer the same defect at the heart of this culture, the annihilation of myth. It seems hardly possible to transplant a foreign myth with permanent success, without dreadfully injuring the tree through this transplantation: which is perhaps occasionally strong enough and sound enough to eliminate the foreign element after a terrible struggle; but must ordinarily consume itself in a languishing and stunted condition or in sickly luxuriance. Our opinion of the pure and vigorous kernel of the German being is such that we

verzehren muß. Wir halten so viel von dem reinen und kräftigen Kerne des deutschen Wesens, daß wir gerade von ihm jene Ausscheidung gewaltsam eingepflanzter fremder Elemente zu erwarten wagen und es für möglich erachten, daß der deutsche Geist sich auf sich selbst zurückbesinnt. Vielleicht wird mancher meinen, jener Geist müsse seinen Kampf mit der Ausscheidung des Romanischen beginnen: wozu er eine äußerliche Vorbereitung und Ermutigung in der siegreichen Tapferkeit und blutigen Glorie des letzten Krieges erkennen dürfte, die innerliche Nötigung aber in dem Wetteifer suchen muß, der erhabenen Vorkämpfer auf dieser Bahn, Luthers ebensowohl als unserer großen Künstler und Dichter, stets wert zu sein. Aber nie möge er glauben, ähnliche Kämpfe ohne seine Hausgötter, ohne seine mythische Heimat, ohne ein »Wiederbringen« aller deutschen Dinge, kämpfen zu können! Und wenn der Deutsche zagend sich nach einem Führer umblicken sollte, der ihn wieder in die längst verlorne Heimat zurückbringe, deren Wege und Stege er kaum mehr kennt – so mag er nur dem wonnig lockenden Rufe des dionysischen Vogels lauschen, der über ihm sich wiegt und ihm den Weg dahin deuten will.

venture to expect of it, and only of it, this elimination of forcibly ingrafted foreign elements, and we deem it possible that the German spirit will reflect anew on itself. Perhaps many a one will be of opinion that this spirit must begin its struggle with the elimination of the Romanic element: for which it might recognise an external preparation and encouragement in the victorious bravery and bloody glory of the late war, but must seek the inner constraint in the emulative zeal to be for ever worthy of the sublime protagonists on this path, of Luther as well as our great artists and poets. But let him never think he can fight such battles without his household gods, without his mythical home, without a "restoration" of all German things I And if the German should look timidly around for a guide to lead him back to his long-lost home, the ways and paths of which he knows no longer—let him but listen to the delightfully luring call of the Dionysian bird, which hovers above him, and would fain point out to him the way thither.

24

Wir hatten unter den eigentümlichen Kunstwirkungen der musikalischen Tragödie eine apollinische *Täuschung* hervorzuheben, durch die wir vor dem unmittelbaren Einssein mit der dionysischen Musik gerettet werden sollen, während unsre musikalische Erregung sich auf einem apollinischen Gebiete und an einer dazwischengeschobenen sichtbaren Mittelwelt entladen kann. Dabei glaubten wir beobachtet zu haben, wie eben durch diese Entladung jene Mittelwelt des szenischen Vorgangs, überhaupt das Drama, in einem Grade von innen heraus sichtbar und verständlich wurde, der in aller sonstigen apollinischen Kunst unerreichbar ist: so daß wir hier, wo diese gleichsam durch den Geist der Musik beschwingt und emporgetragen war, die höchste Steigerung ihrer Kräfte und somit in jenem Bruderbunde des Apollo und des Dionysus die Spitze ebensowohl der apollinischen als der dionysischen Kunstabsichten anerkennen mußten.

Freilich erreichte das apollinische Lichtbild gerade bei der inneren Beleuchtung durch die Musik nicht die eigentümliche Wirkung der schwächeren Grade apollinischer Kunst; was das Epos oder der beseelte Stein vermögen, das anschauende Auge zu jenem

Among the peculiar artistic effects of musical tragedy we had to emphasise an Apollonian *illusion,* through which we are to be saved from immediate oneness with the Dionysian music, while our musical excitement is able to discharge itself on an Apollonian domain and in an interposed visible middle world. It thereby seemed to us that precisely through this discharge the middle world of theatrical procedure, the drama generally, became visible and intelligible from within in a degree unattainable in the other forms of Apollonian art: so that here, where this art was as it were winged and borne aloft by the spirit of music, we had to recognise the highest exaltation of its powers, and consequently in the fraternal union of Apollo and Dionysus the climax of the Apollonian as well as of the Dionysian artistic aims.

Of course, the Apollonian light-picture did not, precisely with this inner illumination through music, attain the peculiar effect of the weaker grades of Apollonian art. What the epos and the animated stone can do—constrain the contemplating eye to calm delight in the world of

ruhigen Entzücken an der Welt der *individuatio* zu zwingen, das wollte sich hier, trotz einer höheren Beseeltheit und Deutlichkeit, nicht erreichen lassen. Wir schauten das Drama an und drangen mit bohrendem Blick in seine innere bewegte Welt der Motive – und doch war uns, als ob nur ein Gleichnisbild an uns vorüberzöge, dessen tiefsten Sinn wir fast zu erraten glaubten und das wir, wie einen Vorhang, fortzuziehen wünschten, um hinter ihm das Urbild zu erblicken. Die hellste Deutlichkeit des Bildes genügte uns nicht: denn dieses schien ebensowohl etwas zu offenbaren als zu verhüllen; und während es mit seiner gleichnisartigen Offenbarung zum Zerreißen des Schleiers, zur Enthüllung des geheimnisvollen Hintergrundes aufzufordern schien, hielt wiederum gerade jene durchleuchtete Allsichtbarkeit das Auge gebannt und wehrte ihm, tiefer zu dringen.

the *individuatio*—could not be realised here, notwithstanding the greater animation and distinctness. We contemplated the drama and penetrated with piercing glance into its inner agitated world of motives—and yet it seemed as if only a symbolic picture passed before us, the profoundest significance of which we almost believed we had divined, and which we desired to put aside like a curtain in order to behold the original behind it. The greatest distinctness of the picture did not suffice us: for it seemed to reveal as well as veil something; and while it seemed, with its symbolic revelation, to invite the rending of the veil for the disclosure of the mysterious background, this illumined all-conspicuousness itself enthralled the eye and prevented it from penetrating more deeply

Wer dies nicht erlebt hat, zugleich schauen zu müssen und zugleich über das Schauen hinaus sich zu sehnen, wird sich schwerlich vorstellen, wie bestimmt und klar diese beiden Prozesse bei der Betrachtung des tragischen Mythus nebeneinander bestehen und nebeneinander empfunden werden: während die wahrhaft ästhetischen Zuschauer mir bestätigen werden, daß unter den eigentümlichen Wirkungen der Tragödie jenes Nebeneinander die merkwürdigste sei. Man übertrage sich nun dieses Phänomen des ästhetischen Zuschauers in einen analogen Prozeß im tragischen Künstler, und man wird die Genesis des *tragischen Mythus* verstanden haben. Er teilt mit der apollinischen Kunstsphäre die volle Lust am Schein und am Schauen und zugleich verneint er diese Lust und hat eine noch höhere Befriedigung an der Vernichtung der sichtbaren Scheinwelt. Der Inhalt des tragischen Mythus ist zunächst ein episches Ereignis mit der Verherrlichung des kämpfenden Helden: woher stammt aber jener an sich rätselhafte Zug, daß das Leiden im Schicksale des Helden, die schmerzlichsten Überwindungen, die qualvollsten Gegensätze der Motive, kurz die Exemplifikation jener Weisheit des Silen, oder, ästhetisch ausgedrückt, das Häßliche und Disharmonische, in so zahllosen Formen, mit solcher Vorliebe immer von neuem dargestellt wird und gerade in dem üppigsten und jugendlichsten Alter eines Volkes, wenn nicht gerade an diesem allen eine höhere Lust perzipiert wird?

He who has not experienced this—to have to view, and at the same time to have a longing beyond the viewing—will hardly be able to conceive how clearly and definitely these two processes coexist in the contemplation of tragic myth and are felt to be conjoined; while the truly æsthetic spectators will confirm my assertion that among the peculiar effects of tragedy this conjunction is the most noteworthy. Now let this phenomenon of the æsthetic spectator be transferred to an analogous process in the tragic artist, and the genesis of *tragic myth* will have been understood. It shares with the Apollonian sphere of art the full delight in appearance and contemplation, and at the same time it denies this delight and finds a still higher satisfaction in the annihilation of the visible world of appearance. The substance of tragic myth is first of all an epic event involving the glorification of the fighting hero: but whence originates the essentially enigmatical trait, that the suffering in the fate of the hero, the most painful victories, the most agonising contrasts of motives, in short, the exemplification of the wisdom of Silenus, or, æsthetically expressed, the Ugly and Discordant, is always represented anew in such countless forms with such predilection, and precisely in the most youthful and exuberant age of a people, unless there is really a higher delight experienced in all this?

Denn daß es im Leben wirklich so tragisch zugeht, würde am wenigsten die Entstehung einer Kunstform erklären; wenn anders die Kunst nicht nur Nachahmung der Naturwirklichkeit, sondern gerade

For the fact that things actually take such a tragic course would least of all explain the origin of a form of art; provided that art is not merely an imitation of the reality of nature, but in truth a

ein metaphysisches Supplement der Naturwirklichkeit ist, zu deren Überwindung neben sie gestellt. Der tragische Mythus, sofern er überhaupt zur Kunst gehört, nimmt auch vollen Anteil an dieser metaphysischen Verklärungsabsicht der Kunst überhaupt: was verklärt er aber, wenn er die Erscheinungswelt unter dem Bilde des leidenden Helden vorführt? Die »Realität« dieser Erscheinungswelt am wenigsten, denn er sagt uns gerade: »Seht hin! Seht genau hin! Dies ist euer Leben! Dies ist der Stundenzeiger an eurer Daseinsuhr!«

metaphysical supplement to the reality of nature, placed alongside thereof for its conquest. Tragic myth, in so far as it really belongs to art, also fully participates in this transfiguring metaphysical purpose of art in general: What does it transfigure, however, when it presents the phenomenal world in the guise of the suffering hero? Least of all the "reality" of this phenomenal world, for it says to us: "Look at this! Look carefully! It is your life! It is the hour-hand of your clock of existence!"

Und dieses Leben zeigte der Mythus, um es vor uns damit zu verklären? Wenn aber nicht, worin liegt dann die ästhetische Lust, mit der wir auch jene Bilder an uns vorüberziehen lassen? Ich frage nach der ästhetischen Lust und weiß recht wohl, daß viele dieser Bilder außerdem mitunter noch eine moralische Ergötzung, etwa unter der Form des Mitleidens oder eines sittlichen Triumphes, erzeugen können. Wer die Wirkung des Tragischen aber allein aus diesen moralischen Quellen ableiten wollte, wie es freilich in der Ästhetik nur allzu lange üblich war, der mag nur nicht glauben, etwas für die Kunst damit getan zu haben: die vor allem Reinheit in ihrem Bereiche verlangen muß. Für die Erklärung des tragischen Mythus ist es gerade die erste Forderung, die ihm eigentümliche Lust in der rein ästhetischen Sphäre zu suchen, ohne in das Gebiet des Mitleids, der Furcht, des Sittlich-Erhabenen überzugreifen. Wie kann das Häßliche und das Disharmonische, der Inhalt des tragischen Mythus, eine ästhetische Lust erregen?

And myth has displayed this life, in order thereby to transfigure it to us? If not, how shall we account for the æsthetic pleasure with which we make even these representations pass before us? I am inquiring concerning the æsthetic pleasure, and am well aware that many of these representations may moreover occasionally create even a moral delectation, say under the form of pity or of a moral triumph. But he who would derive the effect of the tragic exclusively from these moral sources, as was usually the case far too long in æsthetics, let him not think that he has done anything for Art thereby; for Art must above all insist on purity in her domain. For the explanation of tragic myth the very first requirement is that the pleasure which characterises it must be sought in the purely æsthetic sphere, without encroaching on the domain of pity, fear, or the morally-sublime. How can the ugly and the discordant, the substance of tragic myth, excite an æsthetic pleasure?

Hier nun wird es nötig, uns mit einem kühnen Anlauf in eine Metaphysik der Kunst hineinzuschwingen, indem ich den früheren Satz wiederhole, daß nur als ein ästhetisches Phänomen das Dasein und die Welt gerechtfertigt erscheint: in welchem Sinne uns gerade der tragische Mythus zu überzeugen hat, daß selbst das Häßliche und Disharmonische ein künstlerisches Spiel ist, welches der Wille, in der ewigen Fülle seiner Lust, mit sich selbst spielt. Dieses schwer zu fassende Urphänomen der dionysischen Kunst wird aber auf direktem Wege einzig verständlich und unmittelbar erfaßt in der wunderbaren Bedeutung der *musikalischen Dissonanz*: wie überhaupt die Musik, neben die Welt hingestellt, allein einen Begriff davon geben kann, was unter der Rechtfertigung der Welt als eines ästhetischen Phänomens zu verstehen ist. Die Lust, die der tragische Mythus erzeugt, hat eine gleiche Heimat, wie die lustvolle Empfindung der Dissonanz in der Musik. Das

Here it is necessary to raise ourselves with a daring bound into a metaphysics of Art. I repeat, therefore, my former proposition, that it is only as an æsthetic phenomenon that existence and the world, appear justified: and in this sense it is precisely the function of tragic myth to convince us that even the Ugly and Discordant is an artistic game which the will, in the eternal fulness of its joy, plays with itself. But this not easily comprehensible proto-phenomenon of Dionysian Art becomes, in a direct way, singularly intelligible, and is immediately apprehended in the wonderful significance of *musical dissonance:* just as in general it is music alone, placed in contrast to the world, which can give us an idea as to what is meant by the justification of the world as an æsthetic phenomenon. The joy that the tragic myth excites has the same origin as the joyful sensation of

Dionysische, mit seiner selbst am Schmerz perzipierten Urlust, ist der gemeinsame Geburtsschoß der Musik und des tragischen Mythus.

Sollte sich nicht inzwischen dadurch, daß wir die Musikrelation der Dissonanz zu Hilfe nahmen, jenes schwierige Problem der tragischen Wirkung wesentlich erleichtert haben? Verstehen wir doch jetzt, was es heißen will, in der Tragödie zugleich schauen zu wollen und sich über das Schauen hinaus zu sehnen: welchen Zustand wir in betreff der künstlerisch verwendeten Dissonanz eben so zu charakterisieren hätten, daß wir hören wollen und über das Hören uns zugleich hinaussehnen. Jenes Streben ins Unendliche, der Flügelschlag der Sehnsucht, bei der höchsten Lust an der deutlich perzipierten Wirklichkeit, erinnern daran, daß wir in beiden Zuständen ein dionysisches Phänomen zu erkennen haben, das uns immer von neuem wieder das spielende Aufbauen und Zertrümmern der Individualwelt als den Ausfluß einer Urlust offenbart, in einer ähnlichen Weise, wie wenn von Heraklit dem Dunklen die weltbildende Kraft einem Kinde verglichen wird, das spielend Steine hin und her setzt und Sandhaufen aufbaut und wieder einwirft.

Um also die dionysische Befähigung eines Volkes richtig abzuschätzen, dürften wir nicht nur an die Musik des Volkes, sondern ebenso notwendig an den tragischen Mythus dieses Volkes als den zweiten Zeugen jener Befähigung zu denken haben. Es ist nun, bei dieser engsten Verwandtschaft zwischen Musik und Mythus, in gleicher Weise zu vermuten, daß mit einer Entartung und Depravation des einen eine Verkümmerung der anderen verbunden sein wird: wenn anders in der Schwächung des Mythus überhaupt eine Abschwächung des dionysischen Vermögens zum Ausdruck kommt. Über beides dürfte uns aber ein Blick auf die Entwicklung des deutschen Wesens nicht in Zweifel lassen: in der Oper wie in dem abstrakten Charakter unseres mythenlosen Daseins, in einer zur Ergötzlichkeit herabgesunkenen Kunst wie in einem vom Begriff geleiteten Leben, hatte sich uns jene gleich unkünstlerische, als am Leben zehrende Natur des sokratischen Optimismus enthüllt. Zu unserem Troste aber gab es Anzeichen dafür, daß trotzdem der deutsche Geist in herrlicher Gesundheit, Tiefe und dionysischer Kraft unzerstört, gleich einem zum Schlummer niedergesunknen Ritter, in einem unzugänglichen Abgrunde ruhe und träume: aus welchem Abgrunde zu uns das dionysische Lied emporsteigt, um uns zu verstehen zu geben, daß dieser deutsche Ritter auch jetzt noch seinen uralten

dissonance in music. The Dionysian, with its primitive joy experienced in pain itself, is the common source of music and tragic myth.

Is it not possible that by calling to our aid the musical relation of dissonance, the difficult problem of tragic effect may have meanwhile been materially facilitated? For we now understand what it means to wish to view tragedy and at the same time to have a longing beyond the viewing: a frame of mind, which, as regards the artistically employed dissonance, we should simply have to characterise by saying that we desire to hear and at the same time have a longing beyond the hearing. That striving for the infinite, the pinion-flapping of longing, accompanying the highest delight in the clearly-perceived reality, remind one that in both states we have to recognise a Dionysian phenomenon, which again and again reveals to us anew the playful up-building and demolishing of the world of individuals as the efflux of a primitive delight, in like manner as when Heraclitus the Obscure compares the world-building power to a playing child which places stones here and there and builds sandhills only to overthrow them again.

Hence, in order to form a true estimate of the Dionysian capacity of a people, it would seem that we must think not only of their music, but just as much of their tragic myth, the second witness of this capacity. Considering this most intimate relationship between music and myth, we may now in like manner suppose that a degeneration and depravation of the one involves a deterioration of the other: if it be true at all that the weakening of the myth is generally expressive of a debilitation of the Dionysian capacity. Concerning both, however, a glance at the development of the German genius should not leave us in any doubt; in the opera just as in the abstract character of our myth-less existence, in an art sunk to pastime just as in a life guided by concepts, the inartistic as well as life-consuming nature of Socratic optimism had revealed itself to us. Yet there have been indications to console us that nevertheless in some inaccessible abyss the German spirit still rests and dreams, undestroyed, in glorious health, profundity, and Dionysian strength, like a knight sunk in slumber: from which abyss the Dionysian song rises to us to let us know that this German knight even still dreams his primitive Dionysian myth in blissfully

dionysischen Mythus in selig-ernsten Visionen träumt. Glaube niemand, daß der deutsche Geist seine mythische Heimat auf ewig verloren habe, wenn er so deutlich noch die Vogelstimmen versteht, die von jener Heimat erzählen. Eines Tages wird er sich wach finden, in aller Morgenfrische eines ungeheuren Schlafes: dann wird er Drachen töten, die tückischen Zwerge vernichten und Brünnhilde erwecken – und Wotans Speer selbst wird seinen Weg nicht hemmen können!

Meine Freunde, ihr, die ihr an die dionysische Musik glaubt, ihr wißt auch, was für uns die Tragödie bedeutet. In ihr haben wir, wiedergeboren aus der Musik, den tragischen Mythus – und in ihm dürft ihr alles hoffen und das Schmerzlichste vergessen! Das Schmerzlichste aber ist für uns alle – die lange Entwürdigung, unter der der deutsche Genius, entfremdet von Haus und Heimat, im Dienst tückischer Zwerge lebte. Ihr versteht das Wort – wie ihr auch, zum Schluß, meine Hoffnungen verstehen werdet.

earnest visions. Let no one believe that the German spirit has for ever lost its mythical home when it still understands so obviously the voices of the birds which tell of that home. Some day it will find itself awake in all the morning freshness of a deep sleep: then it will slay the dragons, destroy the malignant dwarfs, and waken Brünnhilde—and Wotan's spear itself will be unable to obstruct its course!

My friends, ye who believe in Dionysian music, ye know also what tragedy means to us. There we have tragic myth, born anew from music—and in this latest birth ye can hope for everything and forget what is most afflicting. What is most afflicting to all of us, however, is—the prolonged degradation in which the German genius has lived estranged from house and home in the service of malignant dwarfs. Ye understand my allusion—as ye will also, in conclusion, understand my hopes.

25

Musik und tragischer Mythus sind in gleicher Weise Ausdruck der dionysischen Befähigung eines Volkes und voneinander untrennbar. Beide entstammen einem Kunstbereiche, das jenseits des Apollinischen liegt; beide verklären eine Region, in deren Lustakkorden die Dissonanz ebenso wie das schreckliche Weltbild reizvoll verklingt; beide spielen mit dem Stachel der Unlust, ihren überaus mächtigen Zauberkünsten vertrauend; beide rechtfertigen durch dieses Spiel die Existenz selbst der »schlechtesten Welt«. Hier zeigt sich das Dionysische, an dem Apollinischen gemessen, als die ewige und ursprüngliche Kunstgewalt, die überhaupt die ganze Welt der Erscheinung ins Dasein ruft: in deren Mitte ein neuer Verklärungsschein nötig wird, um die belebte Welt der Individuation im Leben festzuhalten. Könnten wir uns eine Menschwerdung der Dissonanz denken – und was ist sonst der Mensch? –, so würde diese Dissonanz, um leben zu können, eine herrliche Illusion brauchen, die ihr einen Schönheitsschleier über ihr eignes Wesen decke. Dies ist die wahre Kunstabsicht des Apollo: in dessen Namen wir alle jene zahllosen Illusionen des schönen Scheins zusammenfassen, die in jedem Augenblick das Dasein überhaupt lebenswert machen und zum Erleben des nächsten Augenblicks drängen.

Music and tragic myth are equally the expression of the Dionysian capacity of a people, and are inseparable from each other. Both originate in an ultra Apollonian sphere of art; both transfigure a region in the delightful accords of which all dissonance, just like the terrible picture of the world, dies charmingly away; both play with the sting of displeasure, trusting to their most potent magic; both justify thereby the existence even of the "worst world." Here the Dionysian, as compared with the Apollonian, exhibits itself as the eternal and original artistic force, which in general calls into existence the entire world of phenomena: in the midst of which a new transfiguring appearance becomes necessary, in order to keep alive the animated world of individuation. If we could conceive an incarnation of dissonance—and what is man but that?—then, to be able to live this dissonance would require a glorious illusion which would spread a veil of beauty over its peculiar nature. This is the true function of Apollo as deity of art: in whose name we comprise all the countless manifestations of the fair realm of illusion, which each moment render life in general worth living and make one impatient for the experience of the next moment.

Dabei darf von jenem Fundamente aller Existenz, von dem dionysischen Untergrunde der Welt, genau nur soviel dem menschlichen Individuum ins Bewußtsein treten, als von jener apollinischen Verklärungskraft wieder überwunden werden kann, so daß diese beiden Kunsttriebe ihre Kräfte in strenger wechselseitiger Proportion, nach dem Gesetze ewiger Gerechtigkeit, zu entfalten genötigt sind. Wo sich die dionysischen Mächte so ungestüm erheben, wie wir dies erleben, da muß auch bereits Apollo, in eine Wolke gehüllt, zu uns herniedergestiegen sein; dessen üppigste Schönheitswirkungen wohl eine nächste Generation schauen wird.

At the same time, just as much of this basis of all existence—the Dionysian substratum of the world—is allowed to enter into the consciousness of human beings, as can be surmounted again by the Apollonian transfiguring power, so that these two art-impulses are constrained to develop their powers in strictly mutual proportion, according to the law of eternal justice. When the Dionysian powers rise with such vehemence as we experience at present, there can be no doubt that, veiled in a cloud, Apollo has already descended to us; whose grandest beautifying influences a coming generation will perhaps behold.

Daß diese Wirkung aber nötig sei, dies würde jeder am sichersten, durch Intuition, nachempfinden, wenn er einmal, sei es auch im Traume, in eine althellenische Existenz sich zurückversetzt fühlte: im Wandeln unter hohen ionischen Säulengängen, aufwärtsblickend zu einem Horizont, der durch reine und edle Linien abgeschnitten ist, neben sich Wiederspiegelungen seiner verklärten Gestalt in leuchtendem Marmor, rings um sich feierlich schreitende oder zart bewegte Menschen, mit harmonisch tönenden Lauten und rhythmischer Gebärdensprache – würde er nicht, bei diesem fortwährenden Einströmen der Schönheit, zu Apollo die Hand erhebend ausrufen müssen: »Seliges Volk der Hellenen! Wie groß muß unter euch Dionysus sein, wenn der delische Gott solche Zauber für nötig hält, um euren dithyrambischen Wahnsinn zu heilen!« – Einem so Gestimmten dürfte aber ein greiser Athener, mit dem erhabenen Auge des Äschylus zu ihm aufblickend, entgegnen: »Sage aber auch dies, du wunderlicher Fremdling: wieviel mußte dies Volk leiden, um so schön werden zu können! Jetzt aber folge mir zur Tragödie und opfere mit mir im Tempel beider Gottheiten!«

That this effect is necessary, however, each one would most surely perceive by intuition, if once he found himself carried back—even in a dream—into an Old-Hellenic existence. In walking under high Ionic colonnades, looking upwards to a horizon defined by clear and noble lines, with reflections of his transfigured form by his side in shining marble, and around him solemnly marching or quietly moving men, with harmoniously sounding voices and rhythmical pantomime, would he not in the presence of this perpetual influx of beauty have to raise his hand to Apollo and exclaim: "Blessed race of Hellenes! How great Dionysus must be among you, when the Delian god deems such charms necessary to cure you of your dithyrambic madness!"—To one in this frame of mind, however, an aged Athenian, looking up to him with the sublime eye of Aeschylus, might answer: "Say also this, curious stranger: what sufferings this people must have undergone, in order to be able to become so beautiful! But now follow me to a tragic play, and sacrifice with me in the temple of both the deities!"

Friedrich Nietzsche

Ecce Homo
[German & English]
Friedrich Nietzsche

The Anti-Christ
[German & English]
Friedrich Nietzsche

Beyond Good and Evil
[German & English]
Friedrich Nietzsche

Thus Spake Zarathustra
[German & English]
Friedrich Nietzsche

*

Friedrich Nietzsche
George Brandes

Friedrich Nietzsche
and other Exponents of Individualism
Paul Carus

Prophets of Dissent:
Essays on Maeterlinck, Strindberg, Nietzsche, Tolstoy
Otto Heller

Egoists: A Book of Supermen
Henry Beyle-Stendhal, Charles Baudelaire, Gustave Flaubert, Anatole France,
Joris-Karl Huysman, Maurice Barrès, Friedrich Nietzsche, William Blake,
Henrik Ibsen, Max Stirner, Ernest Hello
James Huneker

Nietzsche and Art
Anthony M. Ludovici

The Philosophy of Friedrich Nietzsche
H. L. Mencken

& more

Made in the USA
Monee, IL
22 September 2021